TREASON
MUST BE MADE
ODIOUS

KTO STUDIES
IN
AMERICAN HISTORY

Consulting Editor: Harold M. Hyman
William P. Hobby Professor of History
Rice University

TREASON
MUST BE MADE
ODIOUS

Military Occupation and
Wartime Reconstruction
in Nashville,
Tennessee,
1862–65

Peter Maslowski

kto press

A U.S. Division of Kraus-Thomson Organization Ltd.
Millwood, New York

First printing

Printed in the United States of America

Library of Congress Cataloging in Publication Data

Maslowski, Peter, 1944–
Treason must be made odious.

(KTO studies in American history)
Bibliography: p. 153
Includes index.
1. Nashville—History—Civil War, 1861–1865.
I. Title. II. Series.
F444.N257M38   976.8′55   78-16799
ISBN 0-527-62185-4

For
Mom and Dad,
and Jed and Laurel
The Past and the
Future

CONTENTS

PREFACE

Historians of the Civil War have written about the gallant charge up Cemetery Ridge perhaps too many times. They have chronicled Grant's gory campaign through the Wilderness until the death and maiming seem a part of our own lives, and they have too often described Lincoln, tired and worried, sitting in the War Department telegraph room awaiting the latest dispatches from his temperamental generals. In fact, it now seems that everything of importance about the tactical and strategic aspects of the military history of the Civil War is already known.

There is also an abundance of scholarly work on the Reconstruction era. Roughly speaking, there are two notable characteristics in almost all Reconstruction literature. First, although there may be radical differences of interpretation among authors, most Reconstruction studies concentrate on the postwar years and emphasize political, social, and economic aspects of the period. Relatively recent books by John Hope Franklin, Kenneth M. Stampp, W. R. Brock, Lawanda and John H. Cox, and Eric L. McKitrick all fit into this category, as do earlier volumes by William A. Dunning, Claude G. Bowers, and George Fort Milton.[1] A number of state-oriented studies also emphasize postwar social, political, and economic events.[2] Secondly, those volumes which do recognize that Reconstruction was as much a part of the Civil War as Chancellorsville and Vicksburg almost invariably focus on the national level, and view the situation primarily from Washington. Charles H. McCarthy and William B. Hesseltine differ on the question of whether or not Lincoln actually had a "plan" of

Reconstruction, but both wrote from a national perspective.[3] A more recent book, written by Herman Belz, maintains the tradition of observing the Reconstruction process through political events in Washington.[4]

In all of this writing covering the years 1861–1877 our knowledge remains deficient about the role of the Union army in both wartime and postwar Reconstruction, and about Reconstruction at the local level. Only a few articles and full length monographs lend much insight into these aspects of the era. Articles by A. H. Carpenter, Ralph H. Gabriel, Frank Freidel, and Robert J. Futrell give tantalizing overviews of the operation of military government in the South during the war, but are sparse on actual details of civil-military relations.[5] Along with these major articles there are also scattered articles in state and local historical publications which deal with wartime occupation and civil-military relations. But these usually fail to view military occupation as a part of the Reconstruction process and do not emphasize the ebb and flow of events between Washington and the local level.[6]

There are three important exceptions to the above generalizations. Studies by Willie Lee Rose, Gerald M. Capers, Jr., and Harold M. Hyman do give recognition to the army's part in wartime Reconstruction and do make clear that the confusion and frustration of wartime Reconstruction were portents of what happened after the war. Rose has written with great detail, perception, and understanding about wartime Reconstruction efforts in the Sea Islands of South Carolina, and Capers' investigation of occupied New Orleans provides valuable insights into wartime Reconstruction in that city. Most importantly, Professor Hyman, during a long and distinguished career, has consistently emphasized that the fall of Fort Sumter signified the beginning of the Civil War *and* Reconstruction and that the Army's role in wartime Reconstruction required, and deserved, greater study. Any historian venturing into the field stands greatly in his debt, as I do.[7]

The present case study was undertaken as a local case history to help bridge the gap—which Rose, Capers, and Hyman have already started to fill—in our knowledge about wartime civil-military relations and Reconstruction efforts. Or, stated another way, the idea was to broaden our knowledge about the non-battlefield activities of the Union army by examining one location and army garrison in detail.

Several factors dictated the selection of Nashville as the focus of this study. Union forces captured the city early in the war, and a comparatively large army garrison occupied it throughout the conflict. Tennessee's capital, more than many other cities in the South, should have been susceptible to Reconstruction efforts. It had a diversified economy which linked it as much to the North as to the South, and though slavery was prevalent throughout Middle Tennessee, it was generally not the plantation variety and not the dominant institution that it was in areas of the Deep South. Nashville was a city of merchants, artisans, mechanics, and manufacturers, surrounded by a rich agricultural area tilled by hundreds of relatively small landowners and slaveowners. If Reconstruction failed in Nashville, a city with strong commercial ties to the North and a modest dependence upon slavery, then it could be expected to fail elsewhere. And the reasons for its failure in Nashville might well provide insights into its failure in the South as a whole.

Finally, Nashville was chosen because of the availability of good source material. Many newspapers were published in the city throughout the Civil War era, and although some existed for only a year or two, others ran for long periods. Andrew Johnson, whose personal papers were a rich fund of evidence, was military governor of Tennessee and was in Nashville during most of the war. Almost any soldier who served in the western theater passed through the Rock City at one time or another, and many repositories have excellent collections of letters, diaries, and memoirs written by soldiers stationed there for varying lengths of time. Army records in the National Archives in Washington, D. C., are voluminous. A perusal of the footnotes and bibliography will readily demonstrate the great number of other relevant sources. In short, the data necessary to give an accurate portrayal of civil society in Nashville, and the army's impact upon it, were available.

In his book on the army's role in postwar Reconstruction, James E. Sefton assumed wartime Reconstruction "was fundamentally different from that of the twelve postwar years." He maintained that the "paramount goal" of speedily concluding military operations against hostile forces overshadowed all political considerations. Only after the conclusion of hostilities, said Sefton, did Reconstruction "become the nation's main concern."[8] But the study of wartime Reconstruction in Nashville indicates Sefton's assumption about a sharp break between 1862–65 and 1865–77 is incorrect because the military was doing much more than just fighting battles. Some examples of activities the Union army in Nashville was undertaking include: employing various methods to control a hostile civilian population;

performing many necessary municipal functions after the city government proved virtually helpless; attempting to provide both short
and long term relief for freedmen; and engaging in politics by supporting a small faction of radical Unionists against all challengers.

Indeed, postwar events in Tennessee cannot be understood
without a thorough knowledge of the wartime Reconstruction effort
and the army's role in it. Wartime events shaped the whole political
struggle in postwar Tennessee, and the military played an important
part in determining those events. Furthermore, there was a basic continuity between the social programs initiated by the army during the
war and those continued by the Freedmen's Bureau during Reconstruction. In Tennessee at least, Reconstruction began in 1862, not
1865. Any study which begins in 1865 automatically omits the three
years most critical to understanding the Reconstruction process.

Thus, it is important to see Reconstruction as part of the Civil
War, not just a postwar phenomenon. Military occupation in
Nashville, New Orleans, and other areas was supposed to restore the
Union. The goal of occupation forces, symbolized in Tennessee by
Andrew Johnson, was to establish loyal state governments which
commanded broad local support for loyalty to the federal government.
Nashville provided a microcosm of the attempted process of Recon-
struction of the seceded states and particularly pointed up the difficul-
ties and frustrations encountered by those entrusted with the task.
These wartime problems, and the attempted solutions, provide insight into the ultimate fate of postwar Reconstruction.

NOTES

1. John Hope Franklin, *Reconstruction After the Civil War*; Kenneth M. Stampp,
The Era of Reconstruction, 1865–1877; W. R. Brock, *An American Crisis*; Lawanda and
John H. Cox, *Politics, Principle, and Prejudice, 1865–1866*; Eric L. McKitrick, *An-
drew Johnson and Reconstruction*; William A. Dunning, *Reconstruction, Political and
Economic, 1865–1877*; Claude G. Bowers, *The Tragic Era*; George Fort Milton, *The
Age of Hate*.

2. For example, in the case of Tennessee, see Thomas B. Alexander, *Political
Reconstruction in Tennessee*; Alrutheus Ambush Taylor, *The Negro in Tennessee, 1865–
1880*; James Welch Patton, *Unionism and Reconstruction in Tennessee, 1860–1869*.

3. Charles H. McCarthy, *Lincoln's Plan of Reconstruction*; William B. Hesseltine, *Lincoln's Plan of Reconstruction*.

4. Herman Belz, *Reconstructing the Union*.

5. A. H. Carpenter, "Military Government of Southern Territory, 1861–1865"; Ralph H. Gabriel, "American Experience with Military Government"; Frank Freidel, "General Orders 100 and Military Government"; Robert J. Futrell, "Federal Military Government in the South, 1861–1865."

6. Typical articles dealing with Tennessee cities include Stanley F. Horn, "Nashville During the Civil War"; Gilbert E. Govan and James W. Livingood, "Chattanooga Under Military Occupation, 1863–1865"; Joseph Howard Parks, "Memphis Under Military Rule, 1862 to 1865."

7. Willie Lee Rose, *Rehearsal for Reconstruction*; Gerald M. Capers, Jr., *Occupied City*. Among Harold M. Hyman's more important and relevant works are "Deceit in Dixie," *Stanton*, and *A More Perfect Union*.

8. James E. Sefton, *The United States Army and Reconstruction, 1865–1877*.

ACKNOWLEDGMENTS

Composing acknowledgments might have been the most difficult task encountered while writing this book. Only the author realizes how deeply indebted he is to the kindness and advice of others. And only he realizes how inadequate the English language is to express his heartfelt thanks to those who have provided assistance.

Professor Allan R. Millett of the Ohio State University has read the entire manuscript and made many valuable comments and criticisms. It is a substantial understatement to say that he has given unsparingly of his time and energy to me during this project. His wise counsel and friendship are among my most treasured possessions. Three other persons also read the manuscript and suggested changes which improved the final product: Professors Merton L. Dillon and Michael Les Benedict, both of the Ohio State University, and the late Dr. Jesse Burt of Nashville. My most sincere thanks go to them.

I am also indebted to the entire staff of the Tennessee State Library and Archives in Nashville, particularly the Archivist, John H. Thweatt. The cost of the paper, envelopes, and postage involved in the correspondence between the Library and myself must have added at least one more zero to that institution's budget. The staffs of the Michigan Historical Collections, the Ohio Historical Society, The University of Chicago Library, and the Library of Congress were most helpful, as was Michael P. Musick of the Navy and Old Army Branch, Military Archives Division, of the National Archives and Records Service. Thanks also go to Harriet McLoone of The Huntington Library, David W. Brown of the William R. Perkins Library, and Anne

Caiger of the University Research Library.

The Research Council of the University of Nebraska-Lincoln generously gave me two grants without which this project could not have been completed. My colleagues in the Department of History at the University of Nebraska-Lincoln have provided a most congenial working atmosphere.

Professor Harold Melvin Hyman (Consulting Editor for the KTO Studies in American History series), Mrs. Marion Sader (Editor at KTO Press), and Mary Ann Mitura (Assistant Editor at KTO) were all extremely helpful in guiding me through the final stages of the publication process.

Mrs. Lawrence M. Kenny, who typed the final draft of the manuscript, combined unparalleled efficiency with constant cheerfulness and an uncanny ability to read my scrawled writing.

While I was doing research in Nashville, Mr. and Mrs. Irvin Wells kindly took me into their home on several different occasions and treated me as a son, even though we had never met before my first research jaunt to that lovely city. The warm hospitality of these fine people made my work considerably more enjoyable.

A special word of gratitude goes to Pern, my wife, who typed rough drafts and proofread copy like a demon, but provided sympathy and understanding like a saint.

I have lovingly dedicated this book, in part, to my Mom and Dad. Whatever is good about me I owe to them; any defects are the result of my own individual initiative despite their best efforts.

Finally, during the long hours of research and writing, I was frequently kept company—unbeknown to them, of course—by Mick Jagger and the Stones. I am sure I could listen to "Gimme Shelter" and "Sympathy for the Devil" another five thousand times and still wish I was banging on a guitar rather than a typewriter.

ABBREVIATIONS
USED IN NOTES AND
BIBLIOGRAPHY

AHR	*The American Historical Review*
AJ	Andrew Johnson
AJP	Andrew Johnson Papers
AMAM, T	American Missionary Association Manuscripts, Tennessee
ETHSP	*East Tennessee Historical Society's Publications*
House Ex. Docs.	*House Executive Documents*
JSH	*The Journal of Southern History*
LC	Library of Congress, Manuscript Division, Washington, D.C.
MHC	Michigan Historical Collections, Bentley Historical Library, University of Michigan
NA	National Archives, Washington, D.C.
OHS	Ohio Historical Society, Manuscript Division, Columbus, Ohio
OR	*The War of the Rebellion: A Compilation of the Official Records of the Union and Confederate Armies*

RG   Record Group

Sen. Ex. Docs.   *Senate Executive Documents*

THM   *Tennessee Historical Magazine*

THQ   *Tennessee Historical Quarterly*

TSLA   Tennessee State Library and Archives, Nashville, Tennessee

TREASON
MUST BE MADE
ODIOUS

Chapter 1

THE BEACON LIGHT
TWINKLES OUT

By 1860 Nashville was rapidly leaving its frontier heritage behind and evolving into a distinct urban community. Situated in the heart of scenic Davidson County, the city sprawled over an area of six square miles and, along with its suburbs, contained some thirty-seven thousand inhabitants, including large German and Irish elements and a growing Jewish population. The heroic exploits of the city's founders, who braved the wilderness to plant a tiny settlement on the banks of the Cumberland, were becoming folklore and legend. The howl of the timber wolf and the war cry of the Indian had given way to operatic arias fresh from Italy and the melodious voice of Jenny Lind, "the Swedish Nightingale." And where once beautiful forests of mixed hardwoods and cedars adorned the hilltops, now stood the neat cottages of artisans and merchants and the marble mansions of the city's wealthiest families.

Evidence of progress met the eye in every direction. In 1858 one of the town's leading citizens noted that "Nashville is improving more at present than I ever knew it before, notwithstanding the complaints about hard times, and the stringency of the money market." "So vast have the changes been which have transpired in ten years," reported the 1860–61 city directory, "that those who were familiar with the city then, and have not seen it since, can scarcely recognize that it is the same place."[1]

Perhaps the most obvious symbol of the city's maturing culture was the recently completed state capitol. This magnificent edifice, built from stratified limestone with a bluish-gray tint and at a cost of over $800,000, impressed visitors and Nashvillians alike. From its cupola, both strangers and citizens looked "down upon the city of Nashville, packed between the Capitol-crowned hill and the coiling Cumberland" and "round upon the panoramic valley, dotted with villas and villages, smiling with fields, and fringed with distant, dark, forest-covered mountains. . . . " Another architectural marvel was the wire suspension bridge over the Cumberland, an imposing 700-foot long structure which rose 110 feet above the low water mark.[2]

Citizens had many other reasons to be proud of their community because in all aspects the basic thrust was toward newness and improvement. To guard against fires, the municipal government, consisting of a mayor, board of aldermen, and board of councilmen, had created a paid steam fire department and built an enormous cistern in the downtown area. Most of the streets had been named, and the houses and buildings along them bore systematic addresses. Gas lamps illuminated the city at night, a street sprinkler system kept the dust down during hot summer months, and although the streets themselves remained unpaved, pedestrians enjoyed brick sidewalks. In the spring of 1860, the first street railroad company in the city was incorporated, although nothing was done under its charter because the Civil War intervened.[3]

Few cities in the West or South in the late antebellum years could compare with the "Athens of the South" as an intellectual and educational center. At the pinnacle of the educational structure stood the University of Nashville, noted most for its medical department which had become one of the foremost in the nation. Of only slightly lesser renown was the Nashville Female Academy, established in 1817 but reaching the peak of its development during the late 1850s when the enrollment inched over the five hundred mark for the first time. Ranking below these two highly esteemed establishments were a large number of exclusive private schools, but the foundation for the whole educational complex was a free public school system. Although the idea of public education had first attracted attention in Nashville in 1821, it did not become a reality until the mid-1850s. By 1860 five public schools were bringing education and enlightenment to approximately two thousand pupils. Five daily papers, eight religious publications, a medical journal, and a temperance magazine, which were all published in the city in 1860, complemented these educational institutions.[4]

Nashville also provided a rich and varied cultural life for its inhabitants. The theater suffered a precarious existence during the 1840s but prospered in the next decade, using local talent and attracting the best traveling comedians and tragedians in the country. Eliza Logan, Charlotte Cushman, Edwin Booth, and other nationally known performers graced the stage of the handsome Adelphia Theater which had first opened its doors in the summer of 1850. In 1854 the city witnessed the first full production of an opera, Donizetti's *Lucia di Lammermoor,* presented by Signor Luigi Arditi's Italian Opera Company; other operas followed sporadically until the war. Concerts featuring famed singers, violinists, and pianists delighted large and enthusiastic audiences dressed in the most fashionable attire. Minstrels, who reflected a romantic conception of American slaves and plantation life, likewise enjoyed great popularity in Nashville.[5]

During the 1850s, Nashville became an important transportation and communication center. Broad turnpikes and newly constructed railroad lines radiated from the city in every direction, steamboats regularly plied the Cumberland, and a growing network of telegraph lines linked the city to Louisville, St. Louis, and New Orleans. Because of these transportation and communication advantages, Nashville was the state's most important commercial and agricultural center.[6]

The city's commercial activity was so vast that Nashville was a port of entry with its own collector of customs. Most forms of economic enterprise grew so dramatically during the prewar decade that by 1860 the number and variety of businesses made an impressive list. For example, in 1850 the three wholesale dry goods firms did an aggregate business of only $375,000; ten years later, the much larger number of such establishments sold goods valued at $2,225,000. The wholesale grocery trade, which extended over nearly all of Tennessee and into parts of Kentucky, Georgia, and Alabama, also underwent spectacular growth. Firms dealing in hardware, boots and shoes, hats and bonnets, liquor, ready-made clothing, furniture, iron, leather, and seeds and agricultural implements dotted the main streets, as did foundries, machine shops, and flour mills.[7]

Middle Tennessee, stretching from the Cumberland plateau to the Tennessee River and watered by the Cumberland and its tributaries, was a rich agricultural region. It was but a continuation of the fertile bluegrass region of Kentucky, and the rich soil, temperate climate, and plentiful water resulted in enormous harvests of cotton, wheat, oats, potatoes, tobacco, and corn. In 1860 alone, Davidson County farmers and planters raised 1,114,901 bushels of corn and equally impressive amounts of other products. Livestock also flourished in the area. Tens of thousands of mules, horses, sheep, swine, and cattle grew strong and fat on the lush pasturage and abundant silage. Nashville merchants, of course, acted as middlemen for much of this produce, taking their fair profits when these foodstuffs passed from producers to consumers.[8]

I

Despite all this improvement, prosperity, and growth, Nashville in the winter of 1860–61 was an unhappy, troubled city. As in so many other communities, North and South, agitation over the momentous sectional questions of the day disrupted political life. During much of the antebellum era, prominent men in Nashville called themselves Whigs or Democrats, but despite these party labels the city's elite exhibited a remarkable cohesiveness. Leading Whigs and Democrats did not noticeably differ from each other in educational level, economic interest, occupation, birthplace, ethnocultural background, or religion. Instead, family and friendships largely determined party affiliation, and even these ties cut across party lines. Nashville had remained far more politically harmonious than many deeply divided Northern and Eastern communities.[9]

In the late 1850s, as the secession issue became more urgent, this essential unity disintegrated. As early as 1856, talk of disunion and civil war dampened the enthusiasm of Nashville's Fourth of July celebration, but it was not until four years later that the bitter struggle between Unionists and secessionists began in earnest and introduced unprecedented dissension into the city's political life.

The contest between those for and those against the preservation of the Union was reflected in a series of elections beginning with the presidential election of 1860. Tennesseans conducted this campaign along traditional party lines because in their opinion there were only two candidates: John Bell, representing Whig-Unionist sentiment, and John C. Breckinridge, representing Democratic-secessionist sentiment. The result was a Union victory as Bell swept the state. In Davidson County, which had been consistently Whiggish since 1847, his majority was a substantial one thousand votes.[10]

Despite the Unionist victory, secession was far from dead in Tennessee or its capital. Both sides engaged in a war of agitation and denunciation which kept Nashville in a continual state of tension. In late December 1861, John S. Brien, a prominent Nashville conservative Unionist, deplored "the increasing disposition upon the part of the conservative masses of the people, in this state, to embrace the idea of immediate secession by the entire South." "I sincerely fear," he wrote, "that the preservation of the Union is now beyond the reach of all the conservative elements of the country."[11]

The Democrats who controlled the state government soon provoked another election battle. When the legislature met in January 1861, it called for an election on February 9 to decide whether or not Tennessee would have a sovereign convention to consider secession. At the same time voters were to select delegates to this convention in case it gained approval. While this was clearly a vote on union or disunion, it was also simply another party fight between Bell Unionists and Breckinridge Democrats. In the election, however, a number of prominent East Tennessee Democrats joined the Whigs in support of the Union.[12]

Tennessee secessionists suffered another disappointment in the February election as voters not only soundly defeated the convention, but also elected a large majority of Union delegates. Once again, as ex-Whig Governor Neill S. Brown wrote, the "mad waves of secession found an iron embankment around" the state "which dified [*sic*] all their fury."[13] East Tennessee opposed the convention by a majority of twenty-five thousand and Middle Tennessee by a majority of about one thousand, while West Tennessee voted for the convention by a majority of thirteen thousand. In Nashville the majority against the convention was only two hundred forty-six, but Union delegates achieved majorities of well over two thousand. Many Nashvillians obviously believed it might be wise to hold a convention to consider the situation but that such a convention should be thoroughly dominated by men committed to the Union.[14]

II

As the crisis developed, Andrew Johnson, Democratic senator from East Tennessee, emerged as the dominant personality. He took a firm stand against secession in several widely circulated speeches which had a great impact on Tennessee and the Nashville community. While Breckinridge Democrats detested Johnson's stand and showed their displeasure by burning him in effigy in the streets of Nashville,[15] Tennessee Unionists considered Johnson a hero and showered him with lavish praise. Among those who supported Johnson were many Unionists who played important roles during the federal occupation of the city. H.G. Scovel, a prominent real estate dealer who served in the municipal government during the war, termed the senator's speeches "the great efforts of the age" and thanked Almighty God for having raised Johnson to such an exalted position where he could do so much for the Union and the Constitution. William Shane, city recorder in occupied Nashville, seconded Scovel's sentiments, as did Horace H. Harrison and John Trimble, both of whom served as war-time U.S. district attorneys in Middle Tennessee.[16]

Many men previously opposed to Johnson on political grounds now became his admirers. "You have taught men to love you and to call you blessed," wrote one of Johnson's closest Nashville confidants, "who have passed their lives in political hostility and opposition to you."[17] One such convert was John Hugh Smith, ex-mayor of Nashville, who again assumed the post during the war.[18] Another was Henry S. French, a wealthy Rock City merchant, and a third was Alexander B. Shankland, who had once been introduced to Johnson but had hated him so much at the time that he made no effort at conversation.[19]

Johnson was important during the crisis not only because of his strong stand against secession but also because he was the Lincoln administration's patronage broker for Tennessee. Since Bell's Unionist supporters had won two major victories over the secessionists and constituted the Union party per se in Tennessee, they had valid expectations of having patronage liberally bestowed upon them rather than the Democrats. In fact, in order to survive and flourish, Bell's political organization needed patronage; considering Johnson's pro-Union stand, Tennessee Unionists could be very hopeful about receiving it.[20]

Thus, throughout February and March of 1861, Unionists seemed in firm control in Middle Tennessee. On the national level, the situation appeared equally favorable because secession had been quarantined to seven states of the lower South as a tier of border slave states, including Tennessee, had rejected secession and remained in the Union. To Johnson, and to many others throughout the nation, it seemed altogether possible that these states might serve as a bridge over which the seceded states would return to the Union.[21]

But, for several reasons, the Unionist position in the Volunteer State soon deteriorated. First of all, secessionist Democrats still did not admit defeat, and "the Precipitators" did all they could to keep public passions inflamed. As one Nashville Unionist wrote Johnson shortly after the February election, the "machinations and efforts of the disaffected among us are by no means terminated: *of this we are confident*. And they have the boldness to proclaim openly that Tennessee *will* of choice—or of necessity—join in the Southern Confederacy."[22]

Second, by early April, Unionists clearly perceived that Johnson was "misusing" the patronage. Instead of dispensing it to Bell men without exception, he was attempting to build a personal following which would sustain and perhaps improve his own political fortunes.[23] In Nashville there were three important and hotly contested positions to be filled: attorney general for the Middle Division of Tennessee; U.S. marshal for the Middle Division of Tennessee; and postmaster in Nashville. The first position went to Herman Cox, "a firm *Union man*," and the second went to another staunch Unionist, Edwin R. Glascock. But the third and most important position went to William D. McNish, a longtime clerk in the Post Office and a Democrat. The postmastership was crucial because it controlled appointments to a great many lesser post office jobs throughout Middle Tennessee. The fact that some of the city's most rabid secessionists, including McNish, composed the "Post Office Clique" made this appointment particularly distasteful to Unionists.[24]

The loss of control over federal patronage eroded the morale of the Unionist organization. Tennessee loyalists had been denied one of the main incentives for continuing their struggle to save the Union, and by the time of the Fort Sumter attack, many of them were ready to abandon the Union if given a plausible pretext. Lincoln's call for troops provided the excuse. Unhappy Unionists used opposition to "coercion" to defend their action and give it at least the appearance of consistency.[25]

This suggests a third reason for the eventual collapse of Tennessee Unionism: its nebulous and tenuous character. The fact that it could be bought by political patronage tells something of its nature, but the explanation goes much deeper. Southern Unionism was quite unlike Northern Unionism. While the Northern variety unconditionally opposed secession, the same thing could not be said for its Southern counterpart. Most Nashville Unionists were for the Union only as long as it could be maintained *honorably*—only if the North respected "Southern rights," made some concessions to Southern demands, and abstained from violence and coercion. John S. Brien, though an avowed Unionist, insisted "that the rights of the South have been violated by the North" and that "these wrongs ought to be redressed." If they were not, "then the South would be justified, before the world and in the conscience of its people—in availing itself of the only remedy left, for the violated rights and oppression of minorities—*revolution*."[26] Ex-Governor Brown warned Johnson that if violence occurred, a large number of Union men "would be carried off in a storm," and another of the senator's Nashville correspondents hoped that "the incoming Administration may be enabled to avoid a collision—for I should fear a *revulsion* in the present good Union Sentiment of Tennessee."[27]

Continued secessionist agitation, the loss of lucrative patronage by Unionists, and the conditional quality of Tennessee Unionism combined to weaken loyalists in the next secessionist crisis in Tennessee which came when Confederate batteries fired upon Fort Sumter and Lincoln called upon the states for troops. The pro-Unionist *Republican Banner* reported that the news of Sumter's bombardment was "received regretfully by the conservative Union men of the community, while the announcement was greeted by leading Disunionists with exultation."[28]

III

Although they deplored both the Sumter incident and Lincoln's request for troops, at first a few Nashville Unionists grimly tried to hold the line. Some stood firmly for peace, advocated a policy of neutrality, and counseled moderation. On April 16 the *Banner* cautioned against unnecessary excitement and urged that the border states stand firm "as long as there is a plank of the old ship of State between us and the angry waves of destruction, and until the last beacon light of hope twinkles out in the distance."[29]

But the last beacon light of hope quickly flickered out. On April 17 the *Banner* sadly reported that "Excitement and passion is [*sic*] making rapid inroads into our ranks." The same day a young Nashville businessman, Henry Clay Yeatman, wrote his wife that "Nashville has been in a high state of excitement for three days past culminating yesterday in a revolutionary flood that has overwhelmed all those feeble lovers of the Union who act from impulse rather than Judgement [*sic*]." Yeatman considered himself "a Union man but not a submissionist" and was determined not to "be carried away by sensational dispatches." But he was also resolved to "resist in whatever way most effectual northern aggression when it shall be made plain to me that Lincoln intends to invade southern soil."[30]

The combination of increased determination on the part of the North and war enthusiasm in Nashville soon convinced almost all Unionists in the city that the Union was a lost cause and Tennessee should join the Confederacy. On April 23 even Bell, who for so long had stood for sectional harmony, the Union, and the Constitution, capitulated. The next day the *Banner* fell into line, declaring that the "time for discussion has indeed passed. All are united and enthusiastic in a deep and firm resolve to go forward."[31]

The avidly pro-southern Democratic governor of Tennessee, Isham G. Harris, immediately took advantage of the new situation by calling an extra session of the legislature on April 25. This body quickly adopted resolutions authorizing the governor to enter into a military league with the Confederate States and passed an ordinance of secession which it submitted to the people for ratification on June 8. The vote on the ordinance revealed a dramatic reversal in sentiment in the state since the events of mid-April. The Middle and Western divisions of the state voted overwhelmingly for disunion, while only East Tennessee held fast. There the exertions of Unionists such as Johnson, T. A. R. Nelson, Horace Maynard, and Oliver P. Temple delivered an eighteen-thousand-vote majority against secession. In Davidson County a more than five-thousand-vote majority favored separation and, as if to give special emphasis to the state's action, Nashville's City Council began an earnest, but unsuccessful, campaign to have the Rock City made the capital of the confederacy.[32]

As soon as Governor Harris knew the election results, he issued a proclamation announcing Tennessee's withdrawal from the Union. Shortly afterward, Jefferson Davis officially declared that Tennessee had joined the Confederacy.

IV

In some respects Tennessee *actually* left the Union before it *officially* did so since the defense of sacred southern soil could not await formal resolutions. A great deal of military preparation on the state and local level preceded the June vote for secession. The state legislature levied a special war tax, and in early May, Governor Harris established a military league with the Confederacy and began raising and equipping the Provisional Army of Tennessee, which became the nucleus of the Army of Tennessee.[33]

Nashville, meanwhile, was agog with fifing, drumming, confusion, and swirling dust stirred up by the tramp of men learning how to march. One woman recalled that after Fort Sumter, "every one commenced planning and trying to do something to aid the South."[34] A group of women devoted their energies to making flags, volunteer militia companies organized, and the city council appropriated $100,000 to arm and protect the city. Machine shops, foundries, and ordnance works sprang up in the city and produced tons of material and equipment, while other military supplies poured in from throughout the state and the South. Soon Nashville became "the great storehouse and arsenal of the western Confederacy."[35]

As martial ardor increased, the plight of the few remaining Nashville loyalists became proportionally worse. Secessionists logically did not want citizens of doubtful loyalty in their midst and so put intense pressure on Unionists to conform—or face the consequences. In late April, self-constituted committees or individuals on their own responsibility began requesting some Northern-born citizens to leave the city. Mayor Richard B. Cheatham officially deplored such vigilante actions, and he urged that all complaints and suspicions against Northern-born persons be lodged with him for investigation and appropriate action. A Committee of Vigilance and Safety was organized to work with the police and the mayor in ferreting out disloyalty to the Confederacy.[36]

Although Nashville's press denied that Unionists suffered persecution,[37] these denials were simply not true. Unionists lived in a state of fear, "all alarmed and afraid to say anything on the street."[38] By late summer, the position of Unionists was untenable. In early August, the Confederate Congress passed an Act of Banishment which said that every male citizen over fourteen years of age, but adhering to the United States government, had to depart within forty days. Any who remained would be treated as alien enemies, subject to arrest, confinement, and deportation. Two weeks later, the Congress passed a Sequestration Act which outlined the policy for confiscating the property of alien enemies.[39] Nashville authorities soon began enforcing these acts. For instance, they hauled H. G. Scovel before the Confederate Court as an alien enemy. Although the court decided he was not an alien enemy, it did require a bond of $10,000 with two good securities for his future good conduct.[40]

Nashville Unionists faced persecution not only from their own neighbors and the Confederate Congress, but also from the Confederate military stationed in the city. On August 22 the post commander issued an order forbidding anyone without a passport to leave

Nashville or any place in the adjoining counties, for the purpose of going out of the Confederate States. Passports could be obtained only from a secessionist-dominated special committee which demanded proof from Confederate, state, or local authorities that the applicant was "worthy of respect," however that might be interpreted.[41]

Hounded, closely watched, and persecuted, it is not surprising that only a tiny handful of Unionists endured the harrassment and remained in the city. Many Unionists simply gave up the fight and went with the Confederacy. As one Unionist recalled after the war, it was "not strange that many men loyal in heart when placed in circumstances of peculiar danger and temptation where the federal government could not protect them yielded and gave aid and comfort to the rebellion. Perhaps very few native Tennesseans who were not in the federal army did not succumb to the pressure of the rebellion and float in treason for a longer or shorter period."[42] Rather than support the South, other Unionists fled to safety beyond the Ohio River, leaving all their property behind and arriving penniless and jobless in the North. Probably few of these exiles imagined that their banishment would last less than six months.[43]

The explanation for Nashville's swift conversion from a pro-Union city in March to a Confederate stronghold by June lies in the conditional nature of Southern Unionism. Most Nashville loyalists, who were against coercion to save the Union, would not organize to fight. Secessionists, however, willingly organized for battle and prepared to use force, if necessary, to take Tennessee out of the Union. A secessionist editor undoubtedly spoke for many leading disunionists when he wrote, in early April, that he was ready to pledge himself to the Confederacy and "raise the standard of rebellion against Lincoln's Government" in Nashville.[44] As early as February, the Rock City Guards, a pro-Southern volunteer militia company, began initiating many new members, and after mid-April, other secessionist militia companies organized for "home protection" and took to the streets with a bold display of Confederate colors.[45]

During all this vigorous secessionist military activity, Nashville Unionists remained lethargic. Before Sumter they had little reason to organize militarily since they appeared to be in complete command of the situation; after Sumter they were unwilling to organize for a cause in which they no longer had complete faith. Even if some Unionists had wanted to organize pro-Union forces, it is doubtful that the pro-Confederate Rock City Guards—already trained and armed—would have permitted them to do so.

V

Despite Nashville's military and political significance, it was poorly defended. Since Governor Harris believed Kentucky's neutrality protected the state from the North, he focused defensive efforts on the Mississippi River and neglected the inland rivers and Nashville. When Albert Sidney Johnston took command in the West, he established the center of his line in Bowling Green, Kentucky, some seventy miles north of Nashville. Although the importance of the inland river forts behind him should have been obvious to even the most untrained observer, they remained in weak condition.[46]

When Forts Henry and Donelson surrendered to Union forces under General Ulysses S. Grant, Johnston hastily retreated to Nashville under the erroneous impression that a strong defensive line was under construction between that city and Clarksville. Only when he arrived in the Rock City did he realize that there were no defenses there, due in part to Governor Harris' neglect but also because of the apathy of Nashville residents. Leading citizens refused to lend their slaves for work on planned fortifications and were so busy getting rich on military contracts that they had little time to worry about the lack of fortifications.[47]

After the fall of Fort Donelson, rumor spread in Nashville that "the army would make a stand, and every one who could shoulder a musket must help defend Nashville to the last ditch."[48] But when the Army of Tennessee reached the city in mid-February, it was obviously in rapid retreat, much to the dismay of both soldiers in the ranks and Nashville civilians. In their anger and bitterness at giving up the city without a fight, soldiers "committed all excesses possible" as they wrecked gardens, fences, and beautiful homes.[49]

With the army in full retreat, Nashvillians panicked. "During all Sunday [February 16] from about 10 a.m. when the news of the fall of Fort Donelson reached here, the wildest excitement prevailed in the city," and the next day was one "of panic and terrified confusion." Many Southern sympathizers, including the governor and legislature, fled the city at once, leaving behind an orgy of looting and plundering. John B. Lindsley, chancellor of the University of Nashville and an eminent scholar, witnessed the "irregular and disgraceful as well as demoralizing pillage and scramble" for goods which became so bad that Nathan Bedford Forrest's cavalrymen had to disperse the crowd.[50] One of the city's few remaining Unionists regretted the disgraceful exhibitions by soldiers and civilians alike; "but Still," he said, "they are Somewhat refreshing to a poor *Subjugated downtrodden lover of the Union.*"[51]

Advance patrols of the federal army arrived in the suburbs of Nashville on Sunday, February 23. On Monday, Mayor Cheatham and a small delegation of prominent citizens surrendered the city to Major General Don Carlos Buell, and federal troops formally occupied the town during the next few days.[52] As troops arrived aboard gunboats, a soldier described the situation: "the bluff above the landing was black with people, but not a sound was heard from those thousands watching with awe the steadily approaching army . . . ; the townsfolk were dumb with apprehension; hospital flags everywhere; not a Confederate nor an American flag in sight . . . . We meant business, and were prepared to act on the instant, and the people knew it."[53]

One of the first citizens to greet the federals was the diehard Unionist, William Driver, a short, broad-shouldered, gray-haired man who had moved to Nashville after retiring from the sea. In 1831, on sailing for the South Pacific, he had been presented with a large American flag which he christened "old Glory," a term which has symbolized the United States flag ever since. Now, more than thirty years later, Driver extracted that same flag from his bedquilt where he and his wife had carefully preserved it during the Confederate rule of Nashville. "This is the flag," said Driver to the Union officer in command, that "I hope to see hoisted on that flagstaff in place of the d——d Confederate flag set there by that d——d rebel governor, Isham G. Harris." With tears in his eyes the old sailor gave the flag to the officer, who then raised it over the city.[54]

NOTES

1. Herschel Gower and Jack Allen, eds., *Pen and Sword*, p. 487; *Nashville City and Business Directory for 1860–61*, p. 25.

2. *Nashville Directory for 1860–61*, pp. 32–38, 56. The quote is in W. W. Clayton, *History of Davidson County, Tennessee, with Illustrations and Biographical Sketches of Its Prominent Men and Pioneers*, p. 209.

3. Joseph Tant MacPherson, Jr., "Nashville's German Element 1850–1870," p. 15; *Republican Banner*, 2 October 1861; Fedora S. Frank, *Five Families and Eight Young Men (Nashville and Her Jewry, 1850–1861)*, p. 84; [John Wooldridge], *History of Nashville, Tenn. . . . ,* pp. 148–149, 336.

4. Allen Kelton, "The University of Nashville, 1850–75," chapters 1–4; *Nashville Directory for 1860–61*, pp. 26–28; Leland Hume, *Early History of the*

Nashville Public Schools, pp. 10–11; [Wooldridge], *History of Nashville*, pp. 438–44; Alfred Leland Crabb, "The Twilight of the Nashville Gods," pp. 293–94.

5. The best account of Nashville's cultural life is F. Gavin Davenport, *Cultural Life in Nashville, 1825–1860*, especially chapters 5 and 6.

6. Clayton, *Davidson County*, pp. 213–17; Macpherson, "Nashville's German Element," pp. 12–14.

7. *Nashville Directory for 1860–61*, pp. 58–61.

8. *Ibid.*, p. 84; Frank L. and Harriet C. Owsley, "The Economic Structure of Rural Tennessee, 1850–1860," pp. 167–70. For examples of production on some individual Davidson County farms see Chase C. Mooney, *Slavery in Tennessee*, pp. 198–99.

9. Burton W. Folsom, II, "The Politics of Elites," pp. 359–78.

10. Mary Emily Robertson Campbell, *The Attitudes of Tennesseans Toward the Union, 1847–1861*, pp. 131, 286.

11. John S. Brien to R. M. Corwin, 31 December 1860, Buell-Brien Papers, TSLA.

12. John Randoph Neal, *Disunion and Restoration in Tennessee*, p. 14; Robert Love Partin, *The Secession Movement in Tennessee*, p. 5; William B. Hesseltine, *Lincoln's Plan of Reconstruction*, p. 50.

13. Neill S. Brown to AJ, 17 February 1861, AJP, Presidential Papers Microfilm.

14. *Republican Banner*, 10, 22 February 1861.

15. William H. Morrow to AJ, 22 February 1861, AJP; J. M. Hammer to Thomas A. R. Nelson, 25 January 1861, Thomas A. R. Nelson Papers, McClung Collection, Lawson McGhee Library.

16. H. G. Scovel to AJ, 12 February 1861; William Shane to AJ, 7 February 1861; Horace H. Harrison to AJ, 20 March 1861; John Trimble to AJ, 25 February 1861. All in AJP.

17. Return J. Meigs to AJ, 7 February 1861, AJP. Also see John Rains to AJ, 20 February 1861, AJP.

18. Thomas F. Murphey to AJ, 18 February 1861, AJP.

19. H. S. French to AJ, 18 February 1861, and Alexander B. Shankland to AJ, 12 February 1861, both in AJP.

20. J. Milton Henry, "The Revolution in Tennessee, February, 1861 to June, 1861," develops this thesis. For an example of Johnson's influence in determining patronage appointments, see Leroy P. Graf and Ralph W. Haskins, eds., *The Papers of Andrew Johnson*, 4: pp. 431–32.

21. Graf and Haskins, eds., *Papers of Andrew Johnson*, 4: pp. 160, 163.

22. A. W. Putnam to AJ, 14 February 1861, AJP. Also see the *Nashville Union and American*, 10 February 1861, and Jeptha Fowlkes to AJ, 23 March 1861, AJP.

23. Henry, "Revolution in Tennessee," p. 110; Leroy P. Graf, "Andrew Johnson and the Coming of the War," p. 220; James L. Baumgardner, "Lincoln, Johnson, and the Patronage," pp. 57–59.

24. A. J. Putnam to AJ, 20 March 1861; J. B. Clements to AJ, 1 March 1861; W. R. Hurley to AJ, 25 March 1861. All in AJP. Also see John Lellyett to Thomas A. R. Nelson, 27 March 1861, Nelson Papers. Cox was one of those men who had been politically antagonistic to Johnson, but now fully agreed with the senator's pro-Union stand. See Cox to AJ, 21 December 1860, AJP.

25. Henry, "Revolution in Tennessee," pp. 113–17.

26. John S. Brien to R. M. Corwin, 31 December 1861, Buell-Brien Papers.

27. Neill S. Brown to AJ, 17 February 1861, and A. W. Putnam to AJ, 14 February 1861, both in AJP. See also *Republican Banner*, 22 January 1861; William Lellyett to AJ, 12 February 1861, A. W. Putnam to AJ, 18 February 1861, and Jeptha Fowlkes to AJ, 17 March 1861. All in AJP.

28. *Republican Banner*, 14 April 1861.

29. *Ibid.*, 16 April 1861. Also see *ibid.*, 18, 19 April 1861, and Stanley F. Horn, "Nashville During the Civil War," p. 4.

30. *Republican Banner*, 17 April 1861; Henry Clay Yeatman to his wife, 17 April 1861, Yeatman-Polk Collection, TSLA.

31. Bell's actions and feelings during the secession crisis are fully described in Joseph Howard Parks, *John Bell of Tennessee*; *Republican Banner*, 24 April 1861.

32. General Marcus J. Wright, *Tennessee in the War, 1861–1865. Lists of Military Organizations and Officers from Tennessee in both the Confederate and Union Armies. . . . ,* pp. 9–10; Charles H. McCarthy, *Lincoln's Plan of Reconstruction*, p. 8; *Republican Banner*, 27, 28 June 1861.

33. *Republican Banner*, 4 June 1861; Thomas Lawrence Connelly, *Army of the Heartland*, pp. 25–45.

34. Mrs. Irby Morgan, *How It Was*, p. 9.

35. Horn, "Nashville During the War," p. 5; Connelly, *Army of the Heartland*, pp. 4–10; also, practically every issue of the *Republican Banner* during April 1861.

36. *Republican Banner*, 25, 27 April 1861.

37. *Ibid.*, 2, 4, 9 June 1861.

38. Robert Johnson to AJ, 29 April 1861, AJP. Also see John Lellyett to AJ, 10 June 1861, AJP; John Williams to Thomas A. R. Nelson, 27 April 1861, Nelson Papers; and John B. Lindsley Diary, 8 June 1861, Lindsley Family Papers, TSLA.

39. *Republican Banner*, 20 August 1861; Frank W. Klingberg, *The Southern Claims Commission*, p. 14.

40. *Republican Banner*, 5 November 1861; *Nashville Daily Union*, 24 April 1862.

41. *Republican Banner*, 23 August, 11 September 1861.

42. William M. Connelly to Thaddeus Stevens, 9 February 1868, Thaddeus Stevens Papers, LC.

43. For Nashvillians who fled, read the AJP from December 1861 through March 1862. Similar persecution of Unionists occurred in Richmond and New Orleans; see Emory M. Thomas, *The Confederate State of Richmond*, and Gerald M. Capers, Jr., *Occupied City*.

44. John C. Burch to L. P. Walker, 6 April 1861, *OR*, 1, 52, 2, pp. 36–37.

45. *Republican Banner*, 9 February, 16, 20, 21, 25, 26 April, 1 May 1861; Horn, "Nashville During the War," pp. 6–7.

46. Connelly, *Army of the Heartland*, pp. 25–45; *Republican Banner*, 2 November 1861.

47. Connelly, *Army of the Heartland*, pp. 73–74, 133–34; Stanley J. Folmsbee, Robert E. Corlew and Enoch L. Mitchell, *Tennessee, A Short History*, pp. 330–31.

48. Morgan, *How It Was*, p. 18.

49. Lindsley Diary, 16 February 1862; Charles R. Mott, Jr., ed., "War Journal of a Confederate Officer," p. 240; Rees W. Porter to AJ, 1 March 1862, AJP; Mrs. James E. Caldwell, *A Chapter From the Life of a Little Girl of the Confederacy*, p. 10.

50. Lindsley Diary, 16, 17, 18 February 1862. Also see Connelly, *Army of the Heartland*, p. 136.

51. Rees W. Porter to AJ, 1 March 1862, AJP.

52. Clayton, *Davidson County*, p. 178; Horn, "Nashville During the War," pp. 10–11.

53. Lieut.-Col. Horace N. Fisher. "Reminiscences of the Raising of the Original 'Old Glory' Over the Capitol at Nashville, Tenn., on February 27, 1862," pp. 98–99.

54. *Ibid.*, pp. 99–100.

Chapter 2

ANDREW JOHNSON RETURNS TO TENNESSEE

The capture of Nashville made Reconstruction a practical issue on two levels. On the local level, the Reconstruction process in Nashville itself began almost as soon as the first Yankee troops marched into the city. Indeed, the effort by Union authorities to regenerate loyalty to the Union among the citizenry formed the central theme in the city's history for the next three years.

The federal conquest of Nashville, and all of the northern half of Middle Tennessee, also thrust the problem of Reconstruction into the national limelight. President Lincoln wanted to reorganize loyal state governments quickly on the assumption that the speedy return of some of the seceded states would severely weaken the rebellion and prevent radical social changes. As the president emphasized in his Annual Message to Congress in December 1861, in "considering the policy to be adopted for suppressing the insurrection, I have been anxious and careful that the inevitable conflict for this purpose shall not degenerate into a violent and remorseless revolutionary struggle." Four months later, Lincoln, noting that as long as resistance continued so would the war, said "it is impossible to foresee all the incidents, which may attend and all the ruin which may follow it. Such as may seem indispensable, or may obviously promise great efficiency towards ending the struggle, must and will come."[1]

Lincoln also wanted to act promptly in reorganizing the seceded state governments because he believed Reconstruction was an executive responsibility. Through decisive action he hoped to forestall congressional "interference" in the process. There was, of course, no Constitutional provision making Reconstruction an executive affair. Congress' claim to control it was certainly as valid as the president's, and by February 1862, some Republican congressmen were suggesting that the national legislature, not the chief executive, should be in charge of reestablishing civil governments in conquered Confederate states.

When the occupation of Nashville presented Lincoln with an opportunity to initiate Reconstruction proceedings under his personal direction, he responded immediately. Less than two weeks after Buell's troops occupied Nashville, Lincoln appointed Andrew Johnson as military governor of Tennessee.

I

It may be that Lincoln acted too hastily in appointing a military governor for Tennessee. The appointment of a powerful civil leader in the state ensured a confusion of command because a senior military commander, Buell, was already in the vicinity. With the duties and responsibilities of both officers ill-defined and overlapping, severe clashes of authority were almost inevitable.

Throughout the war, federal commanders generally found little need for Lincoln's military governors. The "fighting" generals believed that military objectives should come first: win the war and then worry about political ramifications. They no doubt thought that their military efforts would be weakened by the simultaneous pursuit of both military and political objectives because time and energy spent on political activity would detract from their primary goal of winning the war. Thus, both Buell and his successor, Major General William S. Rosecrans, sought supreme command within their geographical area of responsibility, believing that war must be left to warriors, not politicians.

At the same time, Johnson, who had little regard for Buell or Rosecrans and tried to dominate Tennessee affairs himself, believed that he needed a great deal of direct control over Tennessee to achieve his political goal of reestablishing a loyal state government. Thus, both the military governor and the commanding generals assumed that they should be able to manage Tennessee to their own ends and that their own particular sphere of responsibility was paramount. In short, the appointment of Johnson breached the military principle that "Unity of command within a particular military government is an absolute necessity."[2]

Lincoln's selection of Johnson to fill the post of military governor is also subject to criticism. Although Johnson was a virtual folk hero with many Middle Tennesseans until mid-April 1861, many who stood with him until then turned against him after Fort Sumter and joined the Confederacy. Persuading these people to return to their former allegiance demanded leadership and inspiration from someone who could empathize with their decision to go with the South. Since Johnson loathed everything about the Confederacy and constantly attacked the "odious and abominable doctrine" of secession, he was probably not the best man for the job.[3]

Furthermore, Johnson, whose main constituency had always been made up of East Tennessee Democrats, was out of his natural element. Middle and West Tennessee Democrats had gone overwhelmingly for the Confederacy, while those in Middle Tennessee who steadfastly supported the Union were primarily old-line Whigs. During the course of his long political career, deep hatred developed between Johnson and Tennessee Whigs. As he rose from city alderman in Greensville to governor of the state and eventually United States senator, Johnson remained a strict-constructionist and economy-minded Locofoco Jacksonian Democrat. His rigid adherence to limited government had been an anathema to Whigs everywhere. Now the question was, could the crisis of war erase these old political scars?

Assistant Secretary of War Thomas A. Scott summed up the problems created by the senator's return to Tennessee. Johnson's appointment as military governor, said Scott, would immediately be used by the rebels as the means of organizing their party against anything he might attempt and would also "undoubtedly prevent many men (thro' false pride) from joining the Union cause." Johnson had "in times past controlled a large share of the masses of Tennessee, but many of the influential men connected with those classes which he controlled are now numbered among his enemies." Scott suggested that ex-Whig Governor William B. Campbell, who had a large following in Middle Tennessee among pro-Union Whigs, might be a better choice.[4]

Randal McGavock, a Confederate prisoner at Fort Warren who knew of Johnson's appointment through the Boston papers, recorded in his diary that the "embittered hatred entertained by all good men throughout the State of every party" toward Johnson would impair the "restoration of that peace and quiet that seems to be so much desired by the Federal Adm."[5] So intense was the hatred of Johnson that some people feared his assassination if he traveled to Middle or West Tennessee.[6]

The arrival of the military governor was, therefore, at least partially counterproductive, heightening disloyalty rather than loyalty. Brigadier General William Nelson, commander at Murfreesboro, reported to Buell in late July 1862, that hostility to the United States government was increasing in the vicinity. This growing enmity, he wrote, "seems settled into a fierce hatred to Governor Johnson, to him personally more than officially, for in questioning many people they cannot point to an act that he has not been warranted in doing by their own showing." Yet, continued Nelson, "either in manner of doing it, or that it should be done by him, or from some undefinable course touching him, their resentment is fierce and vindictive, and this country, from being neutral at least, as you left it, is now hostile and in arms, and what makes it bad for us it is in our rear."[7] Nelson and Buell personally had no love for Johnson and were in a struggle with him for control; but Nelson's assessment was basically true.

II

There was merit, however, in sending Johnson to Tennessee. Although Johnson's strong Democratic ties weakened him in Middle Tennessee, they were an asset to Lincoln who desired to make the Union cause a bipartisan struggle. The president had already dispensed a number of military commissions to powerful Northern Democratic politicians, and even though some of these military appointees proved incompetent, they were still sound investments in national cohesion. Johnson's appointment as military governor pleased Northern Democrats, further binding them to the Union war effort.[8]

Johnson's vigorous defense of both the Union and the Lincoln administration during the secession crisis and the early stages of the war also made him an admirable choice. In mid-December 1860, he rose in the Senate and repudiated the whole doctrine of secession, the only Southern senator who did so.[9] His pro-Union speech had a profound effect in the North "because of its startling unexpectedness, its daring positions, its noble patriotism, and the breathless anxiety with which the North was listening—waiting, indeed—for a word of hope from the South."[10] Throughout 1861 Johnson repeatedly lashed out against secession, that "odious, diabolical, nefarious, hell-born and hell-bound doctrine," that "prolific mother of anarchy which is the next step to despotism."[11]

Having taken a firm position against secession, having assured himself that the Union and the Constitution were good and the Confederacy was bad, Johnson never retreated or compromised because, as he said in a speech in Cincinnati in June, "a Government without the power to enforce its laws, made in conformity with the Constitution, is no Government at all."[12] His most eloquent discourse on why there could be no compromise with the South came six weeks later during another Cincinnati oration:

Whenever virtue compromises with vice; vice makes an inroad upon virtue. If virtue compromises with vice to-day; to-morrow there must be another compromise, and the next day another, until virtue is clean gone and vice rules instead. If truth compromises with falsehood, falsehood will encroach upon truth, until falsehood becomes truth, and truth falsehood. Compromise between right and wrong to-day, and you must compromise again to-morrow, and again the next day, and so on until right is gone and wrong supplies its place. The time for compromise is gone by; now is the time to put down crime and punish vice—the time to stand on those great principles of truth which underlie the Constitution. Now is the time to act.[13]

As Johnson assailed secession and disdained all compromise with the Confederacy, he also defended Lincoln's strong exercise of executive power. In the Senate on July 27, 1861, he asserted that in "great emergencies, when the life of a nation is in peril, when its very existence is flickering, to question too nicely, to scan too critically, its acts in the very midst of that crisis, when the Government is likely to be overthrown, is to make war upon it, and to try to paralyze its energies." A violation of the Constitution for the "protection and vindication" of the government, he said, is more tolerable than one for its destruction. Even if Lincoln had stretched his powers, the "question on any measure should be, it is necessary now? If it is, it should not be withheld from the Government." Lincoln was undoubtedly grateful for the expression of these sentiments.[14]

Johnson had one other important asset in Lincoln's eyes: both men had the same perception of Southern Unionism. On July 4, 1861, Lincoln sent an address to Congress questioning "whether there is, to-day, a majority of the legally qualified voters of any State, except perhaps South Carolina, in favor of disunion." He believed Union men were in the majority in other seceded states, especially Tennessee and Virginia, and that secession had been carried by the bayonet in these two states. If a free and open election were to be held, the president felt confident the people of Virginia and Tennessee would vote against secession.[15] Johnson agreed that usurping leaders in the South—traitors and conspirators—had subverted the popular will and defied the judgment of the people. In his own state, the people "when left to themselves to carry out their own government and the honest dictates of their own consciences, will be found to be opposed to this revolution." Both Lincoln and Johnson took the position that the repressed loyal citizens of a state actually comprised the state, and that the federal government owed them protection "in the enjoyment of a republican form of government."[16]

During the summer and fall of 1861, Johnson exhibited a strong personal determination to return Tennessee to the federal fold. In the Senate on March 2, 1861, he predicted that the seceded states would be restored to the Union "by the coercion of the people; and those leaders who have taken them out will fall beneath the indignation and the accumulating force of that public opinion which will ultimately crush them." And, he added, "The gentlemen who have taken those States out are not the men to bring them back." If Governor Harris took Tennessee out of the Union, then Johnson would redeem it.[17]

Johnson especially desired the liberation of his beloved East Tennessee and acted almost as a self-appointed secretary of war for the area, working on invasion plans both at the War Department and in Kentucky. As early as 1841, he had proposed the creation of a separate state in East Tennessee and now, perhaps, he looked forward to the fulfillment of this long held vision.[18] Lincoln, too, perceived the importance of East Tennessee, partially because he wanted to nourish loyalty wherever he found it, but also because of its vital strategic location. The capture of East Tennessee would deprive the Confederacy of the use of the East Tennessee and Georgia Railroad and put a federal army on the flank of Confederate forces in Virginia. Both the president and Johnson urged Buell to invade East Tennessee but, for reasons of personality and strategy, he refused to move. No doubt much of the later enmity between Buell and Johnson stems from the former's reluctance to at least attempt an invasion of the region.[19]

When General Ulysses S. Grant's energy and determination delivered portions of Middle and West Tennessee over to federal control, Johnson and Lincoln temporarily subordinated their hopes for East Tennessee and took advantage of this unexpected but pleasing situation. There was no debate within the Lincoln administration on the propriety of sending Johnson to Tennessee because his speeches and actions from December 1860 until February 1862 indicated there could be no better choice. As one of Johnson's fellow senators recalled, Johnson "possessed the unbounded confidence of Mr. Lincoln" and was himself anxious to leave the Senate and "accept a position in which he could be more directly helpful to the loyal cause."[20]

Much in Johnson's character made him ideally suited for the military governorship. Earnest and forthright, a man of great natural capacity and tremendous energy, Johnson possessed unquestioned zeal, fidelity to the Union, and personal courage. Moreover, he performed best during turbulent times when struggling against overwhelming odds; his talents showed most brilliantly when "all the organized forces of society could in some sense, real or symbolic, be leagued against him."[21] In this sense, Tennessee was perfect for Johnson. There is something heroic in his performance as military governor. Day after trying day, Johnson maintained his headquarters in the heavily fortified state capitol, always "ready for legislation or battle, as the day might bring forth."[22] Whether preparing to repel a cavalry attack on Nashville, devising plans for the relief of East Tennessee, or providing food and shelter for the refugees and freedmen who flocked to the city, Johnson never deserted his exposed post.

Yet this was only one side of the man, and certain aspects of his personality made him ill-prepared for his new position. Perhaps reflecting a deep sense of inferiority which came from his humble origins and hard struggle in early life, Johnson often exhibited a tactless, intolerant strain, especially in his appeals to class prejudice. While glorifying the common man in the best Jacksonian tradition, he denounced the wealthy, the refined, and the cultivated elements of society. Because of his position as self-appointed spokesman for the masses, Johnson had developed few strong ties with most of the influential men in Tennessee—men whose help he might now need. Furthermore, Johnson was inordinately ambitious, his rise through the political structure constantly fueling his desire for power until (at least as his enemies charged) it became an all-consuming passion. As early as 1856, he had viewed himself as presidential timber, and the former tailor's urge to become the chief executive had grown in the years since then.[23]

Johnson's character, then, contained great potential for rallying the extensive repressed Unionism which both he and the president thought existed in Tennessee. Brave, honest, and vigorous, he might be able to energize the Unionist cause and eventually restore harmony in the state. But his personality also harbored the potential for inflaming passions further and for increasing bitterness. His class prejudices, lack of tact, and relentless ambition might well hinder his efforts to gain the broad support among all the classes and parties which would be a prerequisite for the creation of a truly popular and loyal state government.

Two things were certain. One was that Johnson went to Tennessee armed with tremendous powers. His commission as military governor permitted him to establish all necessary offices and tribunals and to suspend the writ of habeas corpus. He was to serve "during the pleasure of the President, or until the loyal inhabitants of that state shall organize a civil government in conformity with the Constitution of the United States."[24] Johnson received no specific instructions on how to maintain peace and establish a civil government, but was informed that specific instructions would be given when requested. As a supplement to his civil powers, Lincoln commissioned Johnson a brigadier general, a gesture which conferred added dignity to his office, permitted him to perform military functions, and allowed him to command military subordinates.[25] The second certainty was that although Johnson faced an enormously difficult situation in strife-ridden Tennessee, very little in the American past prepared him, or the nation, to deal with the complexities of military government.

III

Military government is a transitional phase between the open conflict of armies and the return of an established civil government to an occupied area. The fact that Johnson received a high military rank along with his civil powers illustrates that military government is a twilight condition between peace and war, and yet, in the final analysis, military government is also "the rule of force imposed on subjects by paramount military power."[26] Generally military government proceeds through three stages. During the initial stage, which occurs while fighting is still going on in a district, military government remains rudimentary and extends no further than the boundaries of the zone of active military operations. In Tennessee this phase lasted from March 1862 until the spring of 1863. The second stage, during which military government matures and becomes an established institution, begins when fighting forces have moved beyond the district. This stage in Tennessee lasted from the summer of 1863 until the early spring of 1865, with one brief interruption in the winter of 1864. The final stage commences with the termination of the war and ends when the occupying power declares civil government restored. The second and third stages overlapped in Tennessee because the final phase was compressed into the first few months of 1865 when civil government was hurriedly reestablished.[27]

When war began in 1861, almost all Americans, even civilian legalists and army careerists, were dismally ignorant about military and martial law and military government. This was to be expected because Americans had had precious little experience in such matters and had thought about them even less. It is true, as one scholar noted, "that the Revolutionary War had involved the Continental Army in civil-military interactions, especially with regard to internal security, analogous to Civil War situations,"[28] but prior to 1860, Americans had only three limited experiences with actual military government. After the Louisiana Purchase, President Jefferson established military government in the territory; and in the Floridas, the United States resorted to a temporary military government after the Spanish had been ousted. The country had its most extensive experience with military government in New Mexico and California during the Mexican War.[29]

Compounding the scanty experience with military government was the dearth of literature on wartime civil-military relations and the rules of war which would be applicable to the Civil War. A few Americans had ventured into the field, but they generally adhered to the works of the great European theorists and codifiers, Hugo Grotius and Emeric de Vattel. Since these eminent jurists dealt with foreign wars and wrote before the Napoleonic Wars had completely transformed land warfare, their writings had little relevance to a nineteenth century American civil war.[30]

It is not surprising, therefore, that neither Lincoln nor the members of his cabinet searched the past for guidelines in establishing military governments in conquered portions of the South. Had they done so, the one clear lesson they might have gleaned from the fragmentary past experience was the necessity for flexibility: military government should be tempered by the culture of the occupied area and the immediate political and strategic imperatives.

Lincoln, unaided by reference to historical precedent or legal theory, instinctively grasped the need for flexibility and created military governments on an ad hoc basis according to immediate circumstances. Events in Maryland, Missouri, and western Virginia during the first few months of the Civil War were particularly crucial in shaping Lincoln's "plan" of Reconstruction. The basic policy which emerged in these states was to establish loyal governments by military force and then simply await the reassertion of "true" loyal sentiment amidst the populace.[31]

Maryland was, in effect, the first Southern state occupied by federal forces. In elections in the fall of 1861 in that state, Union bayonets and the illegal votes of federal soldiers insured the victory of the unconditional Unionists.[32] Events in Missouri and Virginia provided the clearest precedents for the establishment of military government in Tennessee. In Missouri, only superior Unionist military power and organization kept the state in the Union. In the early summer of 1861, the Missouri Convention, which assembled under the protection of Union forces, declared the executive and legislative offices of the state vacant, proclaimed loyalty to the Union as a prerequisite for officeholding, and chose Hamilton R. Gamble (a brother-in-law of Montgomery Blair, Lincoln's postmaster general) as governor.[33]

In Virginia, a Unionist government supposedly representing the entire state went into operation in Wheeling. Officeholders in this new government had to take a Unionist oath, and only Unionists could qualify as voters. Francis H. Pierpont became "Governor of Virginia" and a "restored" state legislature began holding sessions in Wheeling. This legislature, acting for all of Virginia, gave consent to the formation of West Virginia. Irregularity characterized all of these proceedings. Since the admission of West Virginia by Congress left the Pierpont government with nothing to govern, it transferred its seat to Alexandria where it continued the legal fiction that it was *the* government of Virginia.[34]

The Lincoln administration acted upon the theory that Virginia and Missouri could be reconstructed simply by extending the authority of the Pierpont and Gamble governments over ever-widening areas. It was simply a logical extension of the experience in these two states for Andrew Johnson to go to Tennessee as military governor and rally the "repressed" Unionist sentiment there. A loyal governor (Johnson) would replace a disloyal one (Harris), just as Pierpont and Gamble "replaced" disloyal governors in their respective states.

IV

Although Lincoln created military government on an ad hoc basis without much regard for historical precedent, the experience gained in the Civil War laid a strong foundation for all future military governments established by the United States. The promulgation of General Orders No. 100 on April 24, 1863, marked the beginning of the modern law of belligerent occupation. Known widely as the Lieber Code, this remarkable document consists of basic tenets to guide military commanders in their treatment of inhabitants who are subjected to military government. The famous Hague Conventions of 1899 and 1907 drew heavily upon it, and its words and spirit still guided Americans in World War II.

The author of General Orders No. 100 was Francis Lieber, a famous German-born politician, scientist, and educator. Arrested twice by German authorities for his liberal views, he fled to England and then in 1827 came to the United States, where he soon attracted public notice by laying the foundation for the *Encyclopaedia Americana.* By 1835 his growing fame enabled him to obtain the chair of history and political economy at South Carolina College, a position he held for twenty-one years. Lieber left South Carolina in 1857 and took a position at Columbia College, where he further enhanced his reputation as a political philosopher and expanded his interests into international law.[35]

Despite his long service in the South, Lieber possessed an overwhelming nationalism and viewed the preservation of the Union as a divine mission. When war began, he advocated its vigorous prosecution and regretted that his advanced age prevented him from "draw[ing] the sword instead of wielding nothing but the pen, in this historic period."[36] Early in the conflict, he began corresponding with the nation's foremost military intellectual, General Henry W. Halleck, who was then in command of Union forces in the western theater of the war. Halleck and Lieber had dined together years before, an event which the latter had since forgotten; but Halleck remembered it well because he had embodied the substance of Lieber's dinnertime remarks in the introductory chapter of his famous treatise, *Elements of Military Art and Strategy.* Now the renewed acquaintance between the two men flourished, and it had momentous consequences for the theory of the law and usages of land warfare.[37]

As the war progressed, Lieber, dismayed by the confusing and conflicting policies adopted by different commanders as Union armies thrust into the Confederacy, became anxious to place his profound knowledge of international law and the rules of war at the disposal of the government. He literally invited himself to write policy papers for the government on the problems of black refugees and guerrilla warfare, and the results greatly pleased both Halleck and Secretary of War Edwin M. Stanton.[38]

Having established strong connections with the highest civil and military echelons in the War Department, the Columbia professor envisioned a much grander undertaking. He believed there was urgent need for a concise field manual to guide army officers on the entire subject of military government. On November 13, 1862, he wrote a long letter to Halleck suggesting that "the President ought to issue a set of rules and definitions providing for the most urgent cases, occurring under the Law and Usages of War, and on which our Articles of War are silent." For guidance in this important matter, the president, through the secretary of war, should appoint a committee of three to draw up an appropriate code.[39] The "arduous duties connected with the war" prevented Halleck from giving immediate attention to the matter, but by the late winter of 1862–63, the proposed three-man committee had been appointed, including, of course, Francis Lieber.[40]

The result of this committee's efforts, General Orders No. 100, was almost totally Lieber's work, although Halleck helped to shape the final document. The "sworded jurist" believed Lieber's first draft was "conceived in the proper spirit and [was] a great step in the right direction," but that it was too full and complete. Halleck preferred "brevity-condensation" and so "cut in pretty deeply and perhaps a little too harshly" with his comments.[41] Lieber gladly accepted the suggested revisions. He was well aware that he wrote "something between and betwixt a code and a book—it was all new ground; and I thought it might be necessary to lay and show the foundation for the new structure—*giving the reasons.*" "But," he continued, "if you and competent authorities say it is not necessary, I have no objections."[42]

Lieber's biographer has correctly pointed out that General Orders No. 100 "was less a rigid legal code than a persuasively written essay on the ethics of conducting war." In general, the code stated that war should be fought in a conventional manner between uniformed armies. Partisans and guerrillas deserved little mercy, but an occupier was to respect the rights of noncombatants as far as possible. However, the code left two large loopholes—"military necessity" and "retaliation"—which allowed commanders to employ Draconian measures against the civilian population if necessary.[43]

Although Lieber and Halleck were justly proud of their work, there is some question as to how much impact the code actually had during the Civil War. One student of General Orders No. 100 concluded that it was only after the war that the code "began to acquire authority and the extreme veneration of army officers and experts on international law." He asserted that even though most regulations issued during the remainder of the war seem to have been in harmony with the code, Union commanders and military governors attached relatively little significance to it.[44]

Such conclusions seem unwarranted. Several European legalists immediately recognized the code as a monumental step forward in establishing international laws of war.[45] Furthermore, few Union commanders acted contrary to General Orders No. 100, which may indicate they were aware of its provisions and recognized them as legitimate orders.

Halleck and Lieber made strenuous efforts to insure that the code did exert an influence on the war. Even before the government officially promulgated the document, Halleck sent a copy to Judge Advocate Joseph Holt when he requested guidance on the treatment of spies, and the general in chief had also used the code as the basis for a letter to Rosecrans urging more severe treatment of disloyal persons within the lines of his army.[46] The Lieber-Halleck correspondence demonstrates that they frequently referred to General Orders No. 100 when discussing such important topics as retaliation, spies, the trial of civilians by military tribunals, and the treatment of prisoners of war, and that they forwarded their conclusions to Lincoln, Stanton, and Grant.[47] If men in such high positions attached significance to the code, certainly their attitude must have filtered down to those of lower rank. Johnson, for example, surely knew of the code and acted accordingly, even though he never made specific mention of it as a basis for any of his actions.[48] And in the aftermath of the conflict, Lieber heard reports about the wartime value of General Orders No. 100.[49]

Johnson's initial meager instructions from the War Department indicated that no one really knew what situations he might encounter, or precisely how a military governor should act, or what his responsibilities should be. In the absence of any historical precedents, Lincoln and Stanton seemed to have believed that Johnson should have the widest possible discretion. Thus, the responses of Johnson and

Lincoln to specific circumstances molded the military government in Tennessee until the spring of 1863, but from then on they had a written code to rely on in their efforts to deal with a hostile population.

NOTES

1. Roy P. Basler, ed., *The Collected Works of Abraham Lincoln*, 5: pp. 48–49, 145–46.

2. Ralph H. Gabriel, "American Experience with Military Government," p. 438. Excellent discussions of the problem of dual command can be found in William E. Birkhimer, *Military Government and Martial Law*, pp. 71–73, and Robert J. Futrell, "Federal Military Government in the South, 1861–1865," pp. 181–91.

3. Leroy P. Graf and Ralph W. Haskins, eds., *The Papers of Andrew Johnson*, 4: p. 493.

4. Thomas A. Scott to Edwin Stanton, 4 March 1862, Edwin M. Stanton Papers, LC.

5. Herschel Gower and Jack Allen, eds., *Pen and Sword*, p. 607.

6. Jeptha Fowlkes to AJ, 29 May 1861, AJP, Presidential Papers Microfilm; Thomas A. Scott to Edwin Stanton, 4 March 1862, Stanton Papers.

7. Gen. William Nelson to Buell, 24 July 1862, *OR*, 1, 16, 1, p. 816.

8. T. Harry Williams, *Lincoln and His Generals*, pp. 10–11; Herman Belz, *Reconstructing the Union*, p. 73.

9. *Cong. Globe*, 36th Cong., 2d sess., pp. 117–19, 134–43.

10. Oliver P. Temple, *Notable Men of Tennessee From 1833 to 1875, Their Times and Their Contemporaries*, p. 461.

11. Graf and Haskins, eds., *Papers of Andrew Johnson*, 4: pp. 161, 498.

12. *Ibid.*, p. 494.

13. *Ibid.*, p. 702. Also see *Cong. Globe*, 37th Cong., 1st sess., p. 291.

14. *Cong. Globe*, 37th Cong., 1st sess., pp. 290, 294. Also see Graf and Haskins, eds., *Papers of Andrew Johnson*, 4: p. 488.

15. Basler, ed., *Works of Lincoln*, 4: p. 437.

16. Graf and Haskins, eds., *Papers of Andrew Johnson*, 4: pp. 160, 164, 488, 564; *Cong. Globe*, 37th Cong., 1st sess., pp. 292, 295–96; Basler, ed., *Works of Lincoln*, 4: pp. 427–28.

17. *Cong. Globe*, 36th Cong., 2d sess., p. 1355.

18. Robert W. Winston, *Andrew Johnson, Plebian and Patriot*, pp. 199–201; William B. Hesseltine, *Lincoln's Plan of Reconstruction*, pp. 26–27; Lloyd Paul Stryker, *Andrew Johnson: A Study in Courage*, pp. 93–95; Graf and Haskins, eds., *Papers of Andrew Johnson*, 1: pp. 61, 75.

19. Basler, ed., *Works of Lincoln*, 5: p. 91; Jesse C. Burt, "East Tennessee, Lincoln, and Sherman" is a fine discussion of Lincoln's continuing interest in East Tennessee.

20. James G. Blaine, *Twenty Years of Congress*, 1: p. 446.

21. Eric L. McKitrick, *Andrew Johnson and Reconstruction*, pp. 85–92.

22. James F. Rusling, *Men and Things I Saw in Civil War Days*, p. 21.

23. This portrait of Johnson is constructed from reading contemporary assessments of him, his major biographies, and his papers.

24. Edwin M. Stanton to AJ, 3 March 1862, AJP.

25. Stanton to H. Hamlin, president of the Senate, 3 June 1862, *OR*, 3, 2, p. 106; Stanton to Edward Stanley, military governor of North Carolina, 18, 19 May 1862, *ibid.*, 1, 9, pp. 396–97. Johnson's instructions were the same as Stanley's.

26. Birkhimer, *Military Government*, p. 39.

27. Gabriel, "Military Government," p. 418.

28. Harold Melvin Hyman, *A More Perfect Union*, p. 147.

29. American experience with military government can be studied in Gabriel, "Military Government," and David Yancey Thomas, *A History of Military Government in Newly Acquired Territory of the United States*.

30. Hyman, *More Perfect Union*, pp. 146, 157–58.

31. Hesseltine, *Lincoln's Plan*, pp. 22–29.

32. *Ibid.*, p. 23; James G. Randall and David Donald, *The Civil War and Reconstruction*, pp. 231–33; Charles B. Clark, "Politics in Maryland During the Civil War," pp. 378–99.

33. Hesseltine, *Lincoln's Plan*, p. 25; Randall and Donald, *Civil War and Reconstruction*, pp. 234–36; Edward Conrad Smith, *The Borderland in the Civil War*, pp. 221–62, 350–55.

34. Hesseltine, *Lincoln's Plan*, pp. 27–29; Randall and Donald, *Civil War and Reconstruction*, pp. 236–42; Charles H. Ambler, *Francis H. Pierpont*.

35. Frank Freidel, *Francis Lieber, Nineteenth-Century Liberal;* Allen Johnson, Dumas Malone, and Harris E. Starr, eds., *Dictionary of American Biography*, 11: pp. 236–38.

36. Lieber to Halleck, 18 March 1862, Francis Lieber Papers, The Huntington Library.

37. Lieber to Halleck, 30 January 1862, and Halleck to Lieber, 3 February 1862, both in the Lieber Papers.

38. Lieber to Halleck, 1, 9, 10 August 1862; Halleck to Lieber, 6 August 1862. All in the Lieber Papers. Freidel, *Francis Lieber*, pp. 328–30.

39. Lieber to Halleck, 13 November 1862, Lieber Papers.

40. Halleck to Lieber, 15, 23 November 1862, both in the Lieber Papers.

41. Halleck to Lieber, 23 February, 8 April 1863, both in the Lieber Papers.

42. Lieber to Halleck, 10 April 1863, Lieber Papers.

43. Freidel, *Francis Lieber*, pp. 335–36. A copy of General Orders No. 100 is in *OR* 3, 3, pp. 148–64. Birkhimer, *Military Government* and Doris Appel Graber, *The Development of the Law of Belligerent Occupation, 1863–1914*, have excellent discussions of the Lieber Code.

44. Freidel, *Francis Lieber*, p. 339; *idem*, "General Orders 100 and Military Government," pp. 553–55.

45. Lieber to Halleck, 4 October 1863 and 28 May 1866, both in the Lieber Papers.

46. Halleck to Lieber, 23 February 1863, and Lieber to Halleck, 16 March 1863, both in the Lieber Papers.

47. See, for example, the correspondence between Lieber and Halleck from 2 June 1863 through 25 December 1864, in the Lieber Papers.

48. The *Nashville Daily Union* published General Orders No. 100 in full on 23, 24 May 1863.

49. Lieber to Halleck, 16 November 1865, and 20 March 1866, both in the Lieber Papers.

Chapter 3

CONFEDERATE THREATS
AND
COMMAND DISPUTES

Andrew Johnson's primary duty in Tennessee was to rebuild a truly loyal state government, but his struggle to achieve this goal resulted only in failure during his term as military governor. Johnson's unpopularity in Middle and West Tennessee was a severe handicap, of course, but there were reasons of greater magnitude which helped frustrate his efforts to regenerate loyalty in the state. The continued presence of Confederate forces in the area allowed Southern sympathizers in Nashville to remain optimistic about their deliverance from Yankee occupiers. Furthermore, disagreements and divided councils between Johnson and the senior military commanders in Tennessee meant that no one really knew whether the military governor or the commander of the Department of the Cumberland controlled the wartime Reconstruction process in the state. By the time Johnson consolidated his authority in late 1863, the Unionist movement had split into two factions, making any major effort toward Reconstruction doubly difficult.

I

As long as Middle Tennessee remained a battleground, there was little hope of making progress toward Reconstruction in the state. The basis of military government is overpowering force, and the ability "to exercise that force and the extent to which that ability is recognized by the people of the district occupied, determine the limits of its authority."[1] This was demonstrably true in Nashville where, at least for the first year of federal occupation, most people recognized that the force supporting the military government was far from overpowering. Because it remained a possibility that Southern forces might sweep into the city at any moment, Nashvillians saw little need to concede more than token submission to Union rule.

During much of 1862, Nashville was practically under siege and at times completely isolated from the North. All through the summer and fall, the mounted troops of Nathan Bedford Forrest and John Hunt Morgan, as well as small groups of irregulars, harassed Middle Tennessee despite Union efforts to pin them down and destroy them.[2] One Union officer complained that the difficulty with Morgan was "keeping the freebooter in one spot long enough to catch him. . . ."[3] Or, as another officer admitted, he was unaware "of large besieging armies being organized against this place but nevertheless I apprehend danger from the presence of these small bands who from their extraordinary success of late are inspired with great audacity and are encouraged to conspire with their partizans [*sic*] within the city."[4]

Bragg's thrust into Kentucky during the fall compounded the problem of holding Nashville because as Buell moved north to counter the invasion, there was talk of abandoning the city. Primarily because of Johnson's insistence that the city be held, it was not abandoned, but it remained beleaguered and surrounded, with skirmishes and artillery duels commonly occurring within sight and sound of the city. After Bragg's defeat at Perryville, his forces retreated into Tennessee and concentrated at Murfreesboro, only thirty miles southeast of Nashville. By mid-December Bragg had convinced himself, through some unfathomable process of self-delusion, that the Yankees would soon retreat and he would march triumphantly into the capital. Instead, in late December, Rosecrans, who had replaced Buell, moved against Bragg's army. The resulting Battle of Stones River was a standoff, but the Confederate general realized he lacked the strength to defeat Rosecrans' larger army and therefore withdrew into East Tennessee.[5]

Bragg's retreat "inspired much confidence with Union men of the ultimate success of the Government,"[6] but the city's complete safety was still not assured and the post commander was well advised to "exercise great vigilance, and keep your eyes to both directions."[7] Rebel conscripting operations almost reached the suburbs, small Confederate cavalry units and guerilla bands moved in and out of the vicinity with ease, and in October 1863 and again in the late summer of 1864, Middle Tennessee was subjected to large raids from Major General Joseph Wheeler's cavalry.[8] These continual rebel threats spawned countless rumors among the city's inhabitants about an impending full-scale battle for Nashville and, as Johnson lamented, had "a great tendency to keep the rebellious spirit alive."[9] Thus, for two years after Stones River, dedicated Southern sympathizers within the city could understandably still anticipate redemption.

Those who doggedly refused to embrace Unionism thought they were about to be rewarded for their fidelity to the Confederacy when, in late 1864, Lieutenant General John Bell Hood led his tattered forces within sight of Nashville. It was sheer delusion, of course, to think that Hood's army could drive the federals out of the city, but to people who had lived on hopes, dreams, and hatred of their Yankee "oppressors," this final invasion of Tennessee must have seemed like solid fare.

While the expectations of Southern sympathizers soared, Unionists remained confident. In a cruel pun, the Unionist *Daily Times* commented that "one-legged Hood is no doubt *hopping* mad because he cannot capture Nashville." A Union officer in the Quartermaster's Department reassuringly wrote his friends that the "Rebs might as well butt their brains against the Rocky Mountains, as attempt to take [Nashville]."[10] And, wrote another officer, "it is rumored that Jeff. Davis has ordered Hood to go to Nashville or H###. If this rumor is correct it remains to be seen which part of the Order Hood will try to carry out but the probability is that if he attempts to carry out the first part of the Order he will carry out the last part about the same time."[11]

The Battle of Nashville, which one historian has called *the* decisive battle of the Civil War, was a disaster for Hood and the Confederacy.[12] Shortly before 1:00 p.m. on December 15, 1864, the Union columns moved forward and the fighting commenced. "The batteries on both sides sent forth an almost continuous peal of deep toned thunder—making the whole heavens to echo with the deafening voice of the dogs of war let loose—volley after volley of musketry mingled with the roar of artillery,"[13] and when the smoke cleared and the noise subsided, Hood's army was virtually annihilated. With its demise, the hopes of Nashville secessionists for deliverance finally came to an end.

During the three years of federal occupation, the lingering Confederate threat to Nashville—whether from partisans, cavalry, or field armies—impeded the creation of a loyal and legitimate civil govern-

ment. The anticipation of liberation encouraged passive resistance, if
not outright defiance, among rebel sympathizers, while the possibility that the Confederates might regain the city kept Unionists cowed.
As John G. Nicolay, the president's private secretary, reported to Salmon P. Chase from Nashville shortly after its capture, the "secession
sentiment is still strongly predominant, and manifests itself continually in taunts and insults to federal soldiers and officials. The Union
men are yet too much intimidated to speak out and act. They still fear
and the rebels still hope that our army will have reverses and that the
confederate troops will return and occupy and control not only this
city, but the State."[14]

More than a year later, Rosecrans made essentially the same point
in letters to Stanton and Halleck: it was impossible to restore law and
order to the area from which the enemy had been driven "because no
one desires to avow his sentiments for fear the rebel Cavalry or guerrillas will wreak vengeance on them." Had Union forces been able to
provide "reasonable assurances of protection" against these Confederate forces, "it would have changed entirely the military and political
aspects of Tennessee. . . ."[15] Numerous other sources confirm that
the initial reception accorded Union troops was hostile and that many
secessionists, clinging to the vision of liberation, remained "very bitter in their prejudices" against the Yankees throughout the war.[16]

II

Perhaps some of the continued defiance in Nashville could have been
overcome if Johnson had been able to work in closer harmony with
Buell and, later, with Rosecrans. If the military governor and the
commanding generals had presented a united front, many rebels in
the city might not have been so bold, nor would they have remained so
stoutly wedded to the rebellion. The Lincoln administration made a
serious error when it failed to provide Johnson and Buell with explicit
instructions on their respective responsibilities, and thereby tacitly
fostered a power struggle between them which encouraged disloyal
sentiment among the citizens of Nashville.

Dissension loomed almost immediately when, three days after
Lincoln appointed Johnson, Buell wrote to General George B.
McClellan expressing his concern "to hear that it is proposed to organize a provincial government for Tennessee. I think it would be
injudicious at this time. It may not be necessary at all."[17] From

Buell's perspective this may well have been true. No doubt he believed that his main purpose was to defeat the enemy's armed forces and that everything else should be subordinated to military necessity. Anything which detracted from the military effort would only prolong the war, and trying to establish a civil government in the midst of a war zone would surely be a distraction. Buell probably foresaw that two masters in the same house could only spell trouble—especially when both masters were proud, ambitious, and headstrong.

For Lincoln's purposes, however, the rapid restoration of civil government in the seceded states was both essential and logical. To the president, and to Johnson, it seemed wiser to allow the people in those states to begin participating in civil processes again rather than to force them into submission. Guided by their initial misconception of the nature of the rebellion, they believed that the great mass of Southerners, though temporarily misguided and overwhelmed by cunning leaders, remained loyal and that given the truth and an opportunity, most of them would readily rejoin the Union.

Within a week after his arrival in Nashville, Johnson queried Buell about the sources and extent of military aid available for use by the military governor. Buell's reply, although conciliatory on the surface, contained an omen of future discord. He assured Johnson that the troops under his command, particularly the provost marshal in Nashville, "will be instructed to comply with the requisitions which you may in my absence make upon them for the enforcement of your authority as Military Governor. . . ." But, added Buell, "it may be unnecessary to add that any requisitions which would involve the movement of troops must of course be dependent on the plan of military operations against the enemy."[18]

Thus, Buell agreed to support Johnson only when it did not interfere with military operations. But Johnson, who wanted the rebuilding of the state government to continue regardless of battlefield activity, insisted that he needed a force at *his* disposal which was not subject to the whim of another general. After receiving Buell's reply, Johnson sent a telegram to Stanton asking what military force he was to have "to execute such order or orders as in the discharge of my official duties I may deem expedient, prudent, and proper to make." Stanton replied that General Halleck had been instructed to place an adequate military force under Johnson's command. Recognizing the potential dispute between Buell and Johnson, Stanton cautioned Halleck that the officer in command of the force placed at Johnson's disposal "should be a discreet person, who would act efficiently and harmoniously with Governor Johnson."[19]

Stanton's order was ignored because active military operations had begun in Middle Tennessee. As Buell marched south to join Grant for the Shiloh campaign, he stripped the Nashville area of troops, prompting Johnson to wire the secretary of war that the city was practically defenseless. Stanton relayed Johnson's message to Halleck, who in turn questioned Buell about the defense of Nashville. The latter replied that although a large scale advance upon the capital was unlikely, a dash at the city by fifteen thousand Confederates was possible and he would guard against such a contingency.[20]

However, Buell continued to remove troops from Nashville to support General Ormsby M. Mitchel's drive through Middle Tennessee into northern Alabama, and Johnson became convinced that the commanding general was deliberately undermining his efforts as military governor by keeping an inadequate force in Nashville. A major crisis arose when Buell ordered Colonel Lewis D. Campbell's sixty-ninth Ohio Regiment away from the city because Stanton had ordered that regiment, raised in Columbus, Ohio, with Johnson's help and under his name, to report directly to the governor.[21]

Johnson wanted Campbell's men, and other troops, to remain in Nashville, and he took his case to Horace Maynard (a Tennessee representative in Congress), Lincoln, Stanton, and Halleck. He argued that the city, which was "to a very great extent in a defenseless condition," required a substantial force not only for military reasons but also for the moral influence it would exert on the public mind. As he told Stanton, the "very fact of the forces being withdrawn from this locality has inspired secession with insolence and confidence and Union men with distrust as to the power and intention of the Government to protect and defend them." Johnson also emphasized that his Reconstruction efforts suffered from "a constant struggle between staff officers, Provost Marshals and Brigadier Generals left in command which has to a very great extent paralyzed all the efforts of Union men in bringing about a healthy and sound reaction in public sentiment." In order to solve these problems, Johnson implied that he needed *direct* command over a sufficient number of troops to enforce his rule and control over other military officers in the city—if not absolute authority, then a substantial amount of influence.[22]

Buell answered the accusation that Nashville and Middle Tennessee were defenseless by proclaiming Johnson's views upon the subject "absurd" and asserting that his troop dispositions simply defended the area from a more advanced position.[23] Here, then, was a conflict between two men who were both right, their divergent views emanating from their respective duties. Johnson, charged with reestablishing civil government, required a military force to buttress his authority. Buell, whose duty was to defeat the enemy in the field, needed every available soldier and could not afford to let another officer share command over his troops.

III

In many ways, short of making Johnson the commanding general, the Lincoln administration acceded to the governor's demand for greater control over more troops. As early as June 21, 1862, Johnson was authorized by Stanton to raise two cavalry regiments for three years or the duration of the war; less than a month later, the secretary of war broadened this authorization to include "any amount of Cavalry in your state that may be required for the service"; and on August 1 Johnson gained the power "to raise any amount of cavalry and infantry that may be required for the service in your State." However, since all of these forces went into federal service, they invariably slipped out of Johnson's immediate grasp.[24]

Johnson might well have been content merely to mobilize Tennessee's manpower if the Union generals had commanded it more effectively. Especially dismaying to the governor was the failure of these generals to capture East Tennessee, a project which he deemed essential for the restoration of the state. By the spring of 1863, Johnson had determined to redeem the area himself if necessary, and he began "making arrangements to have a force raised to go there this fall."[25] On March 28 Stanton authorized him to recruit what was in essence a personal army to invade East Tennessee, and on April 15 he even gave the governor permission to enlist recruits from other states.[26] Within weeks, Johnson, ever energetic, had recruiters scouring more than half a dozen Northern states for troops for the proposed expedition.[27] When Stanton, on June 9, suddenly revoked Johnson's authority to raise troops outside Tennessee, he was understandably chagrined, but his anger undoubtedly subsided when separate Union armies under Rosecrans and Major General Ambrose E. Burnside successfully entered East Tennessee in the early fall.[28]

Johnson, who was determined and who would not be denied, managed to acquire a personal army by building upon a clause in his original instructions which promised him "an adequate military force for the special purpose of a governor's guard" under his immediate direction.[29] On May 13, 1862, Johnson had appointed Alvan C. Gillem as colonel of the First Middle Tennessee Infantry (later designated the Tenth Tennessee Infantry) which was being recruited in Nashville as the Governor's Guard. In August 1861, Gillem, a Tennessee-born West Point graduate then stationed at Fort Taylor, Florida, sent a letter to Johnson to praise his strong Unionist stand and to announce that he was "ready at any time to go to the assistance of the loyal citizens of my native State." He and the governor soon developed an extremely close friendship, and at Johnson's insistence Gillem eventually became adjutant general of Tennessee and a brigadier general of Volunteers.[30]

By the end of 1862, Gillem's regiment mustered only 519 men present for duty with about 200 more on the sick list and, although stationed in Nashville, it was in general service subject to the commanding general's orders.[31] Johnson, who realized (as he later explained it) that a Governor's Guard "under State control as it were, might be exceedingly useful in sustaining and strengthening, more directly, the Civil Authorities," considered this an insufficient force and chafed at the command arrangement.[32] Consequently, in the same order which permitted Johnson to recruit an army for East Tennessee, Stanton also reaffirmed the government's pledge to allow the governor a guard. A month later the secretary of war ordered the Tenth Tennessee detached from general service and placed under Johnson's immediate control, which was done under strong protest from Rosecrans who not only hated to lose a regiment, but was also "apprehensive that having a regiment within the garrison of Nashville not subject to the orders of the General Commanding is far more likely to beget discord and trouble than anything else."[33] Since the regiment was only on detached service, it theoretically remained under the commanding general until June 1864, when General Thomas made the transfer absolute by dropping it from the returns of the Army of the Cumberland. Shortly thereafter the Guard was supplemented by the addition of three Tennessee cavalry regiments and a battery of Tennessee light artillery, all of which, like the Tenth Tennessee, were available for duty by Johnson's orders only.[34]

While Johnson slowly gained control over a rather substantial Governor's Guard, he also utilized another source of military power which the Lincoln administration had indicated he could have. Johnson arrived in Nashville with an authorization to spend up to $10,000 "for the purpose of organizing a Home Guard of Union men in Tennessee loyal to the United States."[35] The governor first tested the idea in the summer of 1862 when he enlisted citizens into a military company, called the Nashville Union Guards, to defend the capital.[36] Then in the summer and fall of 1863, with no large Confederate field army in Middle or West Tennessee, but with Southern partisans waging a vicious guerrilla war, harassed Unionists expressed a growing willingness to organize for their own defense against rebel "ruffians," "marauding parties," and "bushwackers & thieves."[37] As one man wrote from Memphis, "very little real progress in the work of reorganization, can be made in this region, until the people, sustained by authority of law, are encouraged to defend themselves and wage a war of extermination against the murderous bands" which infested the region.[38] And, as a Union colonel stationed at Fayetteville put it, he was "satisfied that a small force of armed citizens, who are thoroughly acquainted with this County and people would be more efficient in putting down the guerrilla bands who infest this neighborhood than a large force of regular Soldiers."[39]

Any plan to enlist volunteer local companies was fraught with difficulty. Such forces would obviously be ill-disciplined and "might carry out plans to gratify malice and revenge under the assumed sanction of the United States." Disloyal persons might subvert the organizations from within. Surely the enlistment of three-year soldiers would drop off when men had the option of joining local defense groups. Weapons provided for Home Guards might end up in Confederate hands if they suffered defeat or became demoralized.[40]

Despite the potential problems, when Major General Stephen A. Hurlbut, commanding in Memphis, ordered divisional commanders in Kentucky and Tennessee to "encourage the formation of Home Guards within their limits from unquestionably loyal men," Johnson supported the program and was optimistic about its success. Under Hurlbut's order the Guards *could* "be organized under the militia laws of the State where they are located," and would "not be required to do duty beyond the limits of their organization, but will be required to put down and suppress all robbery, violence, and irregular warfare within such limits. . . . "[41] In October, Johnson reported to both Rosecrans and Thomas that he was "succeeding very well in organizing many companies to be employed in securing the country, to expel and drive beyond our lines, rebels and Guerrillas."[42]

The governor's biggest headache was not recruits but arms, both for the regular service troops he continued to enlist and his newly organized Home Guards. Initially Stanton authorized the governor to apply directly to "the Ordnance Officers and Quartermaster at Nashville for arms, ammunitions, equipments and military supplies for all the white and colored troops raised by you in Tennessee."[43] When this arrangement led to complications with respect to orders issued by General Grant, the secretary directed Johnson to make applications to the Ordnance Department in Washington. But this, too, failed to get arms and ammunition to Johnson fast enough and in sufficient quantities, so the chief of the Ordnance department returned the burden of supply to Nashville's ordnance officer.[44] Though supply problems remained, in one way or another Johnson got his Home Guards armed and into the field. They served until early April 1865, when General Thomas disbanded them and charged the civil authorities, aided by regular troops, with the suppression of guerrillas.[45]

In the meantime, buoyed by the success of the Home Guards and impressed with the continued flow of requests for permission to raise volunteer companies, Johnson had moved the whole program off its voluntary basis and made it mandatory. On September 13, 1864, he ordered the enrollment of all able-bodied men in the state—black and white—between the ages of eighteen and fifty and made them subject to military duty in the state militia.[46] Problems with the new plan arose immediately. In some counties there were too few magistrates to serve as enrolling officers; some magistrates feared for their lives because of the determined opposition to the enrollment by guerrillas and Southern partisans; and many men hid from the magistrates believing "that the enrollment is intended for the purpose of a draft or conscription."[47] In the face of these complications, by mid-January 1865, over 18,500 men were on the militia rolls, including 2,438 whites and 3,096 blacks in Davidson County.[48] Since the end of the war was imminent, the militia never faced the stern test of battle, but because of Johnson's initiative it now stood poised and organized to maintain law and order in the postwar era.

By the last winter of the war, Johnson's personal military power had grown immensely, nearly matching his extraordinary civil authority. No matter what their deficiencies, the Governor's Guard, the Home Guards, and the state militia helped sustain his efforts to reorganize the state and blunted the depredations of Southern partisans. Problems about control and about the number of troops in Nashville and throughout Tennessee remained until the end of the war,[49] but the situation never again reached the nadir it had under Buell during the first summer of occupation.

IV

Some of the subordinate officers Buell left in command in Nashville, especially Assistant Adjutant General Oliver D. Greene and Provost Marshal Stanley Matthews, created another problem for Johnson in the summer of 1862. By mid-June, Johnson thoroughly detested both men. Greene, he said, assumed more command authority than even Buell or Halleck would have, and Matthews was "in direct complicity with the secessionists of this place, and a sympathizer with the master spirits engaged in this southern Rebellion."[50] Johnson's criticism of Matthews, at least, was probably accurate since the provost marshal enjoyed immense popularity with many "influential citizens of Nashville" whom he treated with "kind consideration."[51]

When Johnson asked Halleck to remove both officers, the latter suggested to Buell that perhaps "it would be best to make some change. I leave it, however, for you to determine."[52] Halleck also told Johnson that if Buell did not afford a remedy, then he would; but upon receiving Buell's reply which dismissed Johnson's charges against Greene and Matthews as "frivolous and absurd," Halleck took no action.[53]

Greene especially seemed to enjoy giving Johnson petty annoyances and slights. For example, Greene ordered the telegraph agent in the Quartermaster's Department not to pay Johnson's telegraph account. The governor wrote Greene about the matter twice before the assistant adjutant general replied that he could not in good conscience authorize payment of the account, but that he had referred the matter to Buell. Finally, more than three weeks after Johnson broached the subject, Buell ordered the account paid.[54]

Another instance concerned certain houses which Johnson commandeered as residences for officers of his Guard despite Buell's order that all officers in command of troops should live in camp with their men. Greene wrote to a member of Buell's staff asking specifically if the order had been changed to allow Johnson to ignore it, and was told that the order allowed no exception. Twice Greene ordered Provost Marshal Lewis D. Campbell, who had replaced Matthews, to evict the officers who were living in houses without the proper authority. Campbell, a close friend of the governor's, asked Johnson what he should do. Johnson ordered Greene's order suspended; Campbell therefore refused to obey it, and in retaliation Greene had him arrested and appointed a new provost marshal.[55]

The governor, who was outraged, wrote directly to the president requesting Greene's transfer "to some post beyond the limits of this State" and asking for explicit authority to appoint personally the provost marshal for Nashville. Johnson also bitterly complained that Greene was ordering troops around "directly in opposition to my views and with great damage to the cause." "My opinion is," he continued, "that he is at this time in complicity with the traders here, and shall therefore have him arrested and sent beyond the influence of rebels and traders if he is not immediately removed."[56]

Forced to choose between his commanding general and his military governor, Lincoln came down heavily in favor of Johnson, whom he considered "a true and a valuable man—indispensable to us in Tennessee."[57] He did gently admonish Johnson: "Do you not, my good friend, perceive that what you ask is simply to put you in command in the West? I do not suppose you desire this. You only wish to control in your own localities; but this you must know may derange all other posts."[58] Despite this rebuke, the next day Stanton authorized Johnson to appoint his own provost marshal for Nashville, and told him that Greene had been ordered to leave the city at once and report in person to Buell. To cap Johnson's victory, Buell denied he had issued any order about officers living in houses.[59]

V

Before the Buell-Johnson imbroglio finally ended with Buell's removal, the men had another serious disagreement, this time over the defense of Nashville during Bragg's offensive into Kentucky. The military governor's position became clear as early as July when Forrest captured Murfreesboro and then made menacing gestures toward the Rock City. At that time Nashville's garrison was tiny, with little hope for reinforcements, yet Johnson wrote to Halleck that "in the event the attack is made we will give them as warm a reception as we know how. . . ." If forced to yield, he implied that he would leave the Confederates a nice level spot where someday they could erect a new city.[60] Nashville secessionists reported that Johnson had declared his intention to hold the city "to the last extremity, & if defeated, leave it a heap of smouldering ruins, not one stone shall remain to mark the spot where our proud Capital now stands."[61]

The reason for Johnson's determination to hold Nashville was his fear that its loss would have disastrous moral consequences on Tennessee Unionism. Furthermore, he reasoned that "numerous secret adherents" in the city would aid a Confederate attack only if the sacrifice would not be too great, and that Confederate troops would willingly assault a well-fortified position only if they were sure of inside help from the citizenry. If they made an all-out effort to defend the city, the federals could discourage Southern sympathizers and spread doubt among potential Confederate assault forces.[62] Thus, the governor, with his typical vitality, hastened the construction of fortifications, directed the placement of cannons on the hills overlooking the highways into Nashville, had the roads barricaded with wagons chained together, and began to organize the Nashville Union Guards. Soon he had ninety men enrolled, and he expected the number to increase. The organization, while engaged in traditional military activities such as dress parade and target-shooting, also arrested alleged spies and traitors, and confiscated weapons, clothes, shoes, and tents supposedly intended for Confederate use.[63]

In late August, as Bragg moved over the mountains of East Tennessee, Buell retreated to Nashville. Johnson's dismay at this retreat no doubt increased when Buell advised a further withdrawal toward Louisville.[64] Reportedly, Johnson again demanded Nashville's destruction if it had to be evacuated, but Buell maintained that he was in command and declared that the city should be left unscathed.[65] In the midst of the crisis, Johnson and the Reverend Granville Moody knelt in prayer, and when they finished, the governor exclaimed: "I'm not a Christian—no church—but I believe in God, in the Bible, all of it, Moody, but *I'll be damned if Nashville shall be given up*."[66]

Buell later insisted he "never intimated to Governor Johnson an intention or wish to leave Nashville without a garrison," and that the decision to hold the place was his own because he realized that the political importance of Nashville outweighed any purely military considerations. Colonel James B. Fry, a member of Buell's staff, supported his superior in testimony before the military commission which was instituted to investigate Buell's command. Johnson, however, insisted that the city was held only because he demanded it, and the findings of the commission agreed with him. Based on Johnson's known determination to defend the capital and Buell's refusal to appreciate the military governor's position, there is little doubt that Johnson told the truth to the commission.[67]

Accounts of "an obstinate conflict" between the men over whether or not to hold Nashville appeared in the local press several weeks later. A ranking officer stationed in the city advised Johnson that the press should be censored to prevent the enemy from knowing of such divided councils, but this would have been a futile gesture since the populace already knew that Johnson and Buell did "not get on well" and that the governor desired a new commanding general for Tennessee.[68] The inability of the two highest ranking authorities in the state to act in concert could only provide comfort to the enemy and sow anxiety in the hearts of friends. The constant bickering and divisiveness between Buell (and his subordinates) and Johnson severely obstructed the creation of a civil government in Tennessee.

VI

By late fall 1862, Andrew Johnson had staked out a wide sphere of authority in relation to the commanding general of the Department of the Cumberland. His active role in recruiting federal troops and his budding Union Guards and Governor's Guard demonstrated his growing military power. Lincoln had removed subordinate officers who proved to be a hindrance to the governor, and Nashville had been held despite severe Confederate pressure and Buell's threat to abandon it. Above all, Johnson's authority had been consistently sustained by the Lincoln administration.

The removal of Buell in October seemed to vindicate Johnson's courageous stand in Middle Tennessee. Rosecrans, Buell's successor, should have recognized that Johnson was a powerful force whose wishes demanded respect, but he seems not to have learned from Buell's experience at all. Once again Johnson had to defend his authority.

The specific area of contention between Johnson and Rosecrans was the administration of justice and the enforcement of law in Nashville, which was, of course, only symptomatic of the larger struggle for control over Middle Tennessee. Halleck sternly rebuked Rosecrans for interfering with the administration of justice in the city and suggested that the conflicts arose because Rosecrans misunderstood the relative powers and jurisdictions of each set of authorities. To prevent future misconceptions and to insure perfect harmony in Nashville, Halleck advised the commanding general to place Johnson in command of all troops stationed there.[69]

Rosecrans replied that he knew of no conflicts with the civil authorities and that he would be happy to put Johnson in command at Gallatin but "Nashville is too important a post for me to intrust to his command at this time." This letter, which almost casually belittled the importance of the military governor, bordered on being impudent and provoked a stinging communication from Halleck in which he reasserted the superiority of the civil over the military authorities in Tennessee and restated the government's wish to have Johnson in command in Nashville.[70]

Rosecrans responded apologetically, assuring Halleck that he had done all he "possibly could, consistently with military safety, to build up and sustain the civil authority wherever I have had command, especially in Tennessee. No one appreciates the sacrifice and the delicate and trying position of Governor Johnson more than I do." But he stuck to his position that Johnson should not be placed in command in Nashville, which was an enclosed garrison and major supply depot, and full of traitors, spies, speculators, and rascals. "I am, therefore, obliged to have it commanded by an able and experienced officer, and to exercise a most rigid military policy."[71]

There was much merit in Rosecrans' position. A commanding officer in the field should be able to rest easy about his rear areas and know that his primary supply depot is secure. It was especially hard to argue this point with Rosecrans who had been one of the Union's few successful generals so far. In fact, even the War Department must have realized the justice of Rosecrans' argument because the idea of putting Johnson in command of the capital was not mentioned again.

Halleck's stern warnings, however, did convince Rosecrans that he should placate the military governor. He wrote Johnson pledging his aid in every possible way and asked Johnson to communicate with him "fully and freely" about all matters of conflict and complaint. Johnson, in turn, sent two equally gracious letters to Rosecrans, and the newly inaugurated era of good feeling continued into late May 1863.[72] Then in June, Rosecrans moved into East Tennessee in pursuit of Bragg, and the sheer distance between the commanding general and Middle Tennessee helped alleviate the conflict with Johnson. As Rosecrans turned his attention to purely military matters, the administration of civil affairs fell more fully into Johnson's hands.

In the battle for authority in Middle Tennessee, Rosecrans held his own primarily because he was a winning general until the fall of 1863. But despite his prestige, he made no encroachments on Johnson's authority. The governor rigidly maintained the limits of power he had staked out against Buell and continued to have the full support of the War Department and the president. Had Buell been a more successful general, or had Rosecrans not been defeated at Chickamauga in September, Johnson's search for authority might not have been so successful. Power might have gravitated into the hands of a commanding general who continually won battles.

As it was, Andrew Johnson emerged as the predominant force in Tennessee after October 1863. No commanding general seriously threatened his authority again, partly because of the more amenable personality of Rosecrans' successor, General George H. Thomas, and partly because Johnson had made it plain to everyone that he was in Tennessee to stay. Furthermore, for more than a year after the battle of Lookout Mountain–Missionary Ridge in November, Tennessee was free from major Confederate forces, thus allowing civil, rather than military, affairs to command the spotlight.

Until Johnson's dominance was assured, however, the system of dual command seriously hindered the restoration of a loyal state government. Together with the continued presence of Confederates in Middle Tennessee, the divided councils of the military governor and the commanding generals slowed progress toward Reconstruction. Yet, in the face of these obstacles, Johnson was able to begin the work of building a loyal political organization in Tennessee.

NOTES

1. William E. Birkhimer, *Military Government and Martial Law*, pp. 45–46.

2. *Appleton's Annual Cyclopaedia and Register of Important Events* (1862), pp. 767–68; John B. Lindsley Diary, July–September 1862, Lindsley Family Papers, TSLA.

3. F. A. Mitchel, *Ormsby MacKnight Mitchel, Astronomer and General*, p. 259.

4. Maj. W. H. Sidell to Col. J. B. Fry, 23 August 1862, RG 393, Entry 867.

5. John M. Palmer, *Personal Recollections of John M. Palmer*, pp. 135, 138–39; Lindsley Diary for October and November 1862. The best account of Bragg and the Army of Tennessee is Thomas Lawrence Connelly, *Autumn of Glory*.

6. AJ to Lincoln, 11 January 1863, *OR*, 1, 20, 2, p. 317.

7. Lt. and AAAG Henry Stone to Gen. R. B. Mitchell, 25 January 1863, RG 393, Entry 908.

8. *Nashville Dispatch*, 4 April, 3 July 1863; David Millspaugh Diary, 18 April 1863, David Millspaugh Papers, MHC; Francis Everett Hall to his mother, May 1863, Francis Everett Hall Papers, MHC.

9. AJ to Thomas, 26 September 1864, AJP, Presidential Papers Microfilm. For rumors of an impending battle see Lindsley Diary, 25 March 1863; John Weissert to his mother, 10 March 1863, John Weissert Papers, MHC.

10. *Nashville Daily Times and True Union*, 5 December 1864; James F. Rusling, *Men and Things I Saw in Civil War Days*, pp. 340–41.

11. Frank A. Handy Diary, 8 December 1864, William R. Perkins Library, Manuscript Department.

12. Stanley F. Horn, *The Decisive Battle of Nashville.*

13. Handy Diary, 15 December 1864.

14. Nicolay to Chase, 5 April 1862, in "Diary and Correspondence of Salmon P. Chase," *Annual Report of the American Historical Association for the Year 1902*, 2: p. 510.

15. Rosecrans to Halleck, 26 July 1863, and Rosecrans to Stanton, 26 July 1863, both in RG 393, Entry 908.

16. The quote is in Seth Reed, *The Story of My Life*, p. 72. Also see: John Fitch, *Annals of the Army of the Cumberland*, pp. 547, 600–01; Richard W. Johnson, *Memoir of Maj.-Gen. George H. Thomas*, p. 65; *Appleton's Annual Cyclopaedia* (1862), pp. 596–97; John Beatty, *Memoirs of a Volunteer, 1861–1863*, pp. 90–91; *Nashville Dispatch*, 15 October 1863; Sir Christopher Chancellor, ed., *An Englishman in the American Civil War*, p. 138; Clifton R. Hall, *Andrew Johnson, Military Governor of Tennessee*, pp. 71–72; *Nashville Daily Times and True Union*, 22 July 1864; O. D. Greene to Rev'd Mr. Howell, 11 April 1862, RG 393, Entry 867; AAG and Chief of Staff C. Goddard to Gen. R. B. Mitchell, 8 January 1863, RG 393, Entry 908.

17. Buell to McClellan, 6 March 1862, *OR*, 1, 10, 2, p. 11.

18. Buell to AJ, 19 March 1862, *ibid.*, p. 47.

19. AJ to Stanton, 21 March 1862; Stanton to AJ, 22 March 1862; Stanton to Halleck, 22 March 1862. All in *ibid.*, pp. 56–58.

20. AJ to Stanton, 29 March 1862; Stanton to Halleck, 30 March 1862; Buell to Halleck, 30 March 1862. All in *ibid.*, pp. 76, 79.

21. AJ to Buell, 25 April 1862, and AJ to Stanton, 25 April 1862, both in AJP.

22. AJ to Maynard, 24 April 1862; AJ to Lincoln, 26 April 1862; AJ to Stanton, 11 May 1862. All in *OR*, 1, 10, 2, pp. 126, 129, 180–81; AJ to Halleck, 17 June 1862, AJP.

23. Buell to Halleck, 26 April 1862, *OR*, 1, 10, 2, p. 129.

24. Stanton to AJ, 21 June, 16 July, 1 August 1862. All in AJP.

25. AJ to Eliza [Johnson], 27 March 1863, AJP.

26. Stanton's order, 28 March 1863, and Stanton to AJ, 15 April 1863, both in AJP.

27. AJ to To Whom it may concern, 29 April, 4 May 1863, both in AJP.

28. Provost Marshal General James B. Fry to AJ, 9, 17 June 1863; AJ to Maj. Thomas M. Vincent, 10 June 1863; AJ to Maj. Ernest M. Bement, 17 June 1863. All in AJP.

29. Stanton to Hon. Edward Stanley, Military Governor of North Carolina, 20 May 1862, *OR*, 1, 9, p. 397. Johnson's instructions were identical to Stanley's; see Stanton to Hon. H. Hamlin, 3 June 1862, *ibid.*, 3, 2, p. 106.

30. AJ to Gillem, 13 May 1862, and Gillem to AJ, 16 August 1861, both in AJP; Ezra J. Warner, *Generals in Blue*, pp. 175–76.

31. RG 94, Returns From U.S. Military Posts, 1800–1916, Post Troops at Nashville, Tennessee, 20 December 1862.

32. AJ to Gen. L. H. Rousseau, 28 May 1864, AJP.

33. Stanton's order, 28 March 1863, and Stanton to Halleck, 22 April 1863, both in AJP; Rosecrans to Brig. Gen. Lorenzo Thomas, 3 May 1863, RG 393, Entry 908.

34. Gen. L. H. Rousseau to AJ, 31 May 1864; Special Field Orders No. 154, 6 June 1864; Special Orders No. 79, 14 June 1864; Special Orders No. 168, 20 June

1864. All in AJP. RG 94, Returns From U. S. Military Posts, 1800–1916, Post Troops at Nashville, Tennessee, for the Month of June 1864; Chief of Staff to Maj. Gen. L. H. Rousseau, 21 June 1864, RG 393, Entry 908.

35. Stanton to AJ, 4 March 1862, AJP.

36. *Nashville Dispatch,* 22 July, 3 August 1862; Maj. W. H. Sidell to Col. James Fry, 18 July 1862, RG 393, Entry 867.

37. Petition from citizens of Maury County to AJ, 8 July 1863; David A. Briggs and others to AJ, 9 August 1863; R. P. Shapard to AJ, 23 August 1863. All in AJP.

38. J. M. Tomey to AJ, 9 September 1863, AJP.

39. Endorsement by Col. E. M. McCook on the letter from David A. Briggs and others to AJ, 9 August 1863, AJP. Also see Rosecrans to AJ, 4 August 1863; Lt. Col. F. R. Palmer to Capt. M. P. Beston, 10 August 1863; J. P. Gillaspie to AJ, 24 August 1863; C. G. Jameson to AJ, 14 September 1863. All in AJP.

40. Lt. Col. F. R. Palmer to Capt. M. P. Beston, 10 August 1863; R. M. Edwards to AJ, 30 September 1863; AJ to Gen. S. A. Hurlbut, 3 October 1863. All in AJP.

41. General Orders No. 129, 14 September 1863; AJ to Mr. Mercer, [15 September 1863]; AJ to Hurlbut, 3 October 1863. All in AJP.

42. AJ to Rosecrans, 12 October 1863, and AJ to Thomas, 25 October 1863, both in AJP.

43. AJ to Stanton, 7 October 1863, *OR*, 1, 30, 4, p. 150; Stanton to AJ, 8 October 1863, AJP.

44. Stanton to AJ, 20 January 1864, and Chief of Ordnance George Ramsey to Capt. Townsend, 19 February 1864, both in AJP.

45. Circular by command of Maj. Gen. Thomas, 5 April 1865, RG 393, Entry 908.

46. Lt. Col. E. C. Brott to Capt. W. Nevin, 10 November 1863; John P. Walker to AJ, 15 November 1863; Lt. Col. Andrew J. Cropsey to AJ, 6 January 1864; Alvan C. Gillem to AJ, 23 May, 9 August 1864; Horace Maynard to AJ, 30 May 1864; D. F. Harrison to Col. Paterson [*sic:* Patterson], 22 June 1864; Maj. Gen. R. H. Milroy to AJ, 6 August 1864. All in AJP. For AJ's militia proclamation see *Nashville Daily Times and True Union,* 13 September 1864.

47. Maj. Gen. R. H. Milroy to AJ, 19 September, 29 October 1864; W. A. Houston to AJ, 4 October 1864; William Bickley to AJ, 12 October 1864; A. O. Williams to AJ, 17 September 1864. All in AJP.

48. Hall, *Andrew Johnson,* p. 190; *Nashville Daily Times and True Union,* 16 January 1865.

49. Gen. John F. Miller to AJ, 1 July 1864, AJP; Capt. and AAG [unsigned] to Gen. L. H. Rousseau, 24 July 1864, RG 393, Entry 908.

50. AJ to Halleck, 17 June 1862, and AJ to John Sherman, 18 June 1862, both in AJP.

51. Mrs. Harding to her husband, 16 June, 4 July 1862, Harding Family Papers, Joint University Libraries.

52. AJ to Halleck, 17 June 1862, AJP; Halleck to Buell, 22 June 1862, *OR*, 1, 16, 2, p. 47.

53. Halleck to AJ, 22 June 1862, AJP; Buell to Halleck, 22 June 1862, *OR*, 1, 16, 2, p. 48.

54. AJ to Greene, 23 June, 1 July 1862; Greene to AJ, 2, 12 July 1862. All in AJP.

55. Greene to Col. J. B. Fry, 4 June 1862, and Fry to Greene, 6 June 1862, both in *OR*, 1, 10, 2, pp. 629–31; Greene to Campbell, 5, 8, 10 July 1862. All in RG 393, Entry 867. Campbell to AJ, 8 July 1862, and AJ to Campbell, 9 July 1862, both in AJP.

56. AJ to Lincoln, 10 July 1862 (two letters), *OR*, 1, 16, 2, pp. 118–19.

57. Lincoln to Halleck, 11 July 1862, *ibid.*, p. 122.

58. Lincoln to AJ, 11 July 1862, *ibid.*

59. Stanton to AJ, 12 July 1862, and Buell to AJ, 12 July 1862, both in AJP.

60. AJ to Halleck, 13 July 1862, *OR*, 1, 16, 2, p. 142.

61. Mrs. Harding to her husband, 24 July 1862, Harding Family Papers.

62. Maj. W. H. Sidell to Col. J. B. Fry, 1 August 1862, *OR*, 1, 16, 2, pp. 242–43.

63. AJ to Buell, 11 August 1862 and Thomas H. Cox to AJ, 24 August 1862 (two letters). All in AJP. Mrs. Harding to her husband, 24 July 1862, Harding Family Papers; Maj. W. H. Sidell to Col. J. B. Fry, 18 July 1862, RG 393, Entry 867; *Nashville Daily Union,* 29 October 1862; *Nashville Dispatch*, 22 July, 3 August 1862.

64. Buell to Gen. Rousseau (for AJ), 30 August 1862, and AJ to Buell, 31 August 1862, both in *OR*, 1, 16, 2, pp. 451, 461.

65. Gaither [?] to Col. Stager, 6 September 1862, *ibid.*, p. 490.

66. Tyler Dennett, ed., *Lincoln and the Civil War in the Diaries and Letters of John Hay,* pp. 176–77.

67. Testimony of Buell, 5 May 1863; Testimony of Col. J. B. Fry, 25 April 1863; Deposition of AJ, 22 April 1863; Findings of the Buell Commission. All in *OR*, 1, 16, 1, pp. 59–60, 712, 697–98, 17.

68. Maj. W. H. Sidell to AJ, 24 October 1862, AJP; Mrs. Harding to her husband, 24 July 1862, Harding Family Papers.

69. Halleck to Rosecrans, 20 March 1863, *OR*, 3, 3, pp. 77–78.

70. Rosecrans to Halleck, 26 March 1863, and Halleck to Rosecrans, 30 March 1863, both in *OR*, 1, 23, 2, pp. 174, 191.

71. Rosecrans to Halleck, 4 April 1863, *ibid.*, p. 208.

72. Rosecrans to Stanton (for AJ), 4 April 1863; AJ to Rosecrans, 8 April, 1 June 1863. All in *ibid.*, pp. 207, 220, 380–81.

Chapter 4

PURIFYING
THE TAINTED
ATMOSPHERE

The quest for loyalty in Nashville generally proceeded along two lines. The negative or punitive side to federal occupation consisted of the repression of the disloyal and strong attempts at general control of the population. The positive side of federal occupation encompassed political action designed to induce a renewed allegiance to the United States government among the populace. This chapter will discuss efforts at repression and population control.

Johnson's critics then and now have maintained that he inaugurated a reign of terror in Nashville, that he unsparingly exercised the "right of pulling down and setting up."[1] Certainly Johnson moved quickly to quash the influence of secessionists in the city, because he believed the great mass of Tennesseans, loyal at heart, had simply been misled by conniving leaders. Once these leaders were silenced, then the fundamental loyalty of the masses could reassert itself and bring Tennessee back into the Union. Therefore, he immediately suppressed prominent known secessionists in Nashville, including the city administration, the clergy, the press, and other leading Confederate sympathizers.

I

On May 25 Johnson requested Mayor Cheatham, members of the city council, the city police, and other city officials to take an oath supporting the Constitution of the United States. They refused on the grounds that city officials had never before taken any oath other than the simple oath of office to discharge their respective duties faithfully. Furthermore, they had never taken an oath inimical to their allegiance to the U.S. government or the state government.[2] Such shows of bravado on their part were foolish because, as William Birkhimer, an authority on military government, has pointed out, "Nothing could be more disastrous to the interests of inhabitants of occupied territory than for them to be made to believe that the invader is there by sufferance, and has no rights which they are bound to respect."[3]

Citizens in occupied territory who assume such lofty ground court disaster, and two days after the mayor's refusal to take the oath, disaster struck. Johnson deposed and arrested Cheatham, ousted the rest of the city administration, and filled their positions by appointment.[4] The mayor showed his true moral fiber by languishing in jail six weeks before turning his back on the Confederacy and pledging to support the U.S. government.[5] Cheatham's conversion was exactly what Johnson wanted since he hoped to break the back of the rebellion in Middle Tennessee by a show of force.

Johnson also moved against other prominent secessionists in Davidson County and the surrounding area. For example, orders went out to the provost marshal to arrest William G. Harding, Washington Barrow, John Overton, and Joseph Guild, all of whom had been important in leading Tennessee out of the Union. Harding, Barrow, and Guild were apprehended and sent to Fort Mackinaw in Michigan, but Overton escaped.[6] In June the captives were reportedly in good spirits, enjoying the beautiful scenery and climate of Michigan. Mrs. Harding was only too happy and proud to hear from her husband and "be assured of your health, & determination to bear your captivity as a patriotic, *honest* man *only* can endure it."[7] But by mid-fall, the men eagerly sought release, and in order to return home, Harding, for instance, gave his parole of honor, paid a $20,000 bond, and agreed to report directly to Johnson.[8]

The clergy had to conform or suffer the consequences. Those ministers and churches which were loyal, such as Catholics and Episcopalians, remained undisturbed, and some disloyal clergymen, such as Methodist minister John B. McFerrin, left the city before the federals arrived.[9] But other clergymen of Southern sympathies stayed in the city and, with audacity bordering on stupidity, refused to alter their church services to fit in with the federal occupation. By the middle of June, Johnson had had enough of their disloyal sermonizing, and he especially deplored the effect these "assumed Ministers of

Christ" had on the women of Nashville.[10] So the governor requested six ministers to take an oath of allegiance, and when they refused, he ordered their arrest and confinement in the state prison.[11]

By late July, when it became obvious the ministers still would not take the oath, Johnson wrote to the governors of Ohio and Indiana asking them to take several "rabid secession preachers" and put them in some camp or prison "where they cannot exert an evil influence on others and at the same time receive only such treatment as traitors deserve."[12] Four of the six eventually ended up in Camp Chase in Ohio, one was sent south of the federal lines, and the sixth, who was seriously ill, remained in Nashville under house arrest. When those bound for the Northern prison left Nashville, one of them boldly told those who gathered to see them off, "Don't forget your God, Jeff Davis and the Southern Confederacy."[13] But after a few months in Camp Chase, this haughtiness disappeared, and when Johnson offered the men stringent paroles, they all readily accepted.[14]

Both the North and the South widely practiced news censorship and suppression during the Civil War. Although most members of the Nashville press looked to their own safety and hastily abandoned their offices before the federals arrived, several secessionist editors remained in the city. Two of them, James T. Bell of the *Nashville Gazette* and Ira P. Jones of the *Republican Banner,* were arrested for treasonable and seditious language and conduct.[15] With the disloyal press out of the way, Johnson built up a core of loyal papers under staunch Unionists. He imported S. C. Mercer, "a talented writer and sound on all the great national questions of the day," from Kentucky. As Mercer himself admitted, he edited the news "under the auspices of Governor Johnson" and gave "zealous support to the Union cause and the war policy of the administration."[16] Benjamin C. Truman, Johnson's longtime friend who acted as "a sort of private Secretary" to the governor, also edited a Nashville paper which always "stood up squarely" for the governor.[17]

Although cleansed of outright disloyalty, Nashville's papers, which reached the enemy "regularly and promptly," constantly troubled military authorities because they contained "too much Army news . . . for the interests of our cause."[18] Officers urged caution and restraint when editors wrote about Union military activity, though no "restrictions whatever are placed upon your publishing the movements of the enemy and your Correspondents are at perfect liberty to unburden their minds by giving all such information as they may be able to secure."[19] But despite repeated admonitions, articles continued to appear throughout the war which detailed Union troop dispositions, strengths, and movements.

Even worse were the journals and papers from other cities which circulated in Nashville and which were often offensive to Union sensibilities. One, the New York *Freeman's Journal,* contained many articles favorable to the South and was, as a Nashville Unionist wrote, "full of *treason, abuse, faultfinding, and lying.*"[20] A Unionist editor asked if the Nashville papers would "be permitted to publish such articles? Certainly not, and they should not."[21] On July 27, 1863, the Union post commandant ordered sales of the *Journal* to be discontinued as well as the confiscation of all copies already in the city. Individual issues of the paper still managed to find their way into the capital but, by and large, Nashvillians read only what Johnson and the military authorities wanted them to read.[22]

Johnson's immediate and vigorous reprisals against leading Southern sympathizers had a mixed effect on Nashville's populace. It intensified anti-Union sentiment in general and increased the hatred of "King Johnson"[23] in particular. The arrests made on Johnson's orders were "a matter of public notoriety." The sight of *"old gray haired* men" packed into overcrowded jail cells, where they were denied all the amenities of life, enraged many Nashvillians.[24] Even men favorable to the Union believed some of the arrests were injudicious and did grave harm to the Union cause. It now dawned on many people who had perhaps hoped to remain neutral that in a civil war neutrality is an untenable position; they realized that "an abyss fathomless in depth now yawns between the North and South," and that they had to make a choice—and many chose the South. Hence, the seemingly vindictive policy of the conquerors, as one wavering Unionist said, "has sent thousands of men rendered desperate by their situation to fight to the last gasp in the Southern army."[25]

Johnson's policy also evoked a deep sense of insecurity and uncertainty among pro-Southerners and actually began to encourage treason to the Confederacy. Secessionist sympathizers longed for "quiet & seclusion." "It is a happy thing these days," wrote one woman, "to be obscure, & a man [']s safety *now*, depends on his insignificance. . . . "[26] But for most prominent people there was no place to hide, and the choice between imprisonment (or exile) and taking the oath had to be made. Some men, to be with friends and family and to protect their property from confiscation under the Confiscation Acts of August 1861 and July 1862, chose the oath and thereby gave public testimony against the South, exposing badly torn seams in the fabric of Southern unity.[27] Thus, very early in the war, Johnson learned that an oath was a valuable weapon which could be used to undermine Southern solidarity.

Reflecting on the first ten months of federal occupation, Lindsley recorded his impressions in his diary. "So ends this year of horrors of war," he wrote, "forever memorable in the Annals of the world, as stamping indelibly upon the northern factions the mark of Cain. Unable to conquer, they endeavor to exterminate a people." This was, of course, an extreme overstatement of Union policy. Yet, Nashvillians were justifiably frightened by Johnson's decision to hold the city at any cost and to break the grip of secessionist sentiment in Middle Tennessee. The governor's "unyielding hostility, to every true man, & his determination to crush them if possible," inevitably tended to foster despair among Southern sympathizers.[28]

II

Along with the explicit repression of well-known Confederate sympathizers, federal authorities in Nashville employed general population control measures. A young Nashvillian recalled that "every precaution was thrown around the place to prevent any communications between the citizens and the southern army."[29] One precaution was a system of passes and permits regulating movement in and around the city. In late January 1863, the post commander in Nashville ordered that "no Passes will be given to go outside the Picket lines of this city *except* to persons of known and undoubted loyalty."[30]

The pass system was not foolproof. Negligence and lack of vigilance often characterized the picket line, which at times became practically nonexistent because of the shortage of troops. On one occasion, the weakness of the line prompted the provost marshal to complain that "Any unauthorized person can now pass the Pickets by avoiding the main roads."[31] Persons who obtained passes for their private use could lend or sell them to others; although military authorities had no way of knowing the loyalty of those who bought or borrowed passes, the presumption was that they were disloyal.[32] Another problem was to keep disloyal persons, hiding behind a mask of loyalty, from obtaining passes. Despite the presence of their father and brothers in the Confederate ranks, two Nashville belles, Susan and Mary Elliott, acquired passes through the influence of their Yankee uncle, Lieutenant Colonel G. T. Elliott. The pass said they should not return to the city without express permission from headquarters; when they tried to do so, authorities arrested them and discovered that they carried a number of contraband letters to people in Nashville.[33] No doubt others got through without being caught, but despite such abuses, the pass system helped keep Nashville's population under the military's watchful eye.

Control of the mail and manipulation of postal service patronage were other tactics adopted to prevent Nashvillians from aiding and comforting the enemy. The capital's importance as a political-military center demanded censorship of the mail in order to deny the enemy access to the city's inner workings. At the same time, Union authorities hoped a careful distribution of post office patronage would aid in building a loyal foundation in Middle Tennessee.

The occupation of Nashville disrupted postal service in Middle Tennessee, but Johnson soon considered reopening post offices within Union lines. A resumption of postal service would foster the federal cause because he would see to it "that good Union and reliable men only are put in offices which can be opened with advantage to the Government." The feeling was that circulation of "proper" intelligence would surely benefit the Union effort. Hence, wherever federal military forces could protect them, mail facilities, staffed almost entirely by ex-Union soldiers and loyal refugees, reopened.[34]

Meanwhile, during the first eighteen months of federal occupation, the army censored the mail but sent inoffensive letters through the lines. Citizens soon learned that they could not write fully and freely about home conditions. Letters from loved ones are generally a strong morale booster, but when Harding received letters from his wife and friends saying that what they wanted to write would prevent their letters from going through, it must have sown seeds of anxiety and distress. What *did* they really want to write? How *bad* were conditions at home? One can only speculate, but probably letters like these weakened the willingness of men to remain imprisoned "martyrs" and hastened their decisions to accept stringent conditions for release.[35]

Federal authorities tightened postal restrictions considerably in August 1863, when the post commander ordered that letters received by the army for transmittal through the lines into enemy country would no longer be forwarded, but would instead be sent to the Dead Letter Office in Washington. With thousands of letters being mailed daily in Nashville, some information leaks were inevitable.[36] But postal censorship and control by Unionists deprived the rebels of valuable information, facilitated the dissemination of loyalist papers and propaganda, and lowered morale among those in the Confederate ranks who had friends and families in Middle Tennessee.

Johnson's militia proclamation of September 1864 not only demonstrated his increased personal military power, but also served as a method of population control because it forced men to choose sides openly. Major General Robert H. Milroy, writing to Johnson in October, indicated how the militia proclamation could be employed as a weapon against disloyalty. He sent muster rolls to the county clerks in about a dozen Middle Tennessee counties and informed the clerks that where vacancies existed in the magistrates' offices, they should "select the leading & most active secessionists" to fill the positions. If an appointee refused to act, Milroy would arrest him and send him in irons to the governor, "to be sent out of the state in accordance with the last clause of your proclamation of the 13th. . . . " Milroy ordered "that when any one failed or refused to attend at the place of enrollment in his Dist[rict] at the time notified that his name should be reported to me & I would have important, pressing business with him soon."[37]

Southern sympathizers, particularly those with friends and relatives in Confederate service, understandably detested the militia proclamation. It was "unjust and Tyranical [*sic*]," said one West Tennessean, to give citizens "the choice of either Joining these Militia Companies (under the Specious plea of defending their Homes and fire sides) or of being Banished from the Homes of their childhood," and it was unreasonable to require them "to perform Military duty unwillingly against their own Kindred. . . ."[38] Many guerrillas forcefully resisted the proclamation, but many friends of the Confederacy reportedly went South rather than cooperate with Johnson's government in any way.[39] Thus, the enrollment proclamation helped cleanse Tennessee of disloyalty. By driving away some of those of doubtful loyalty, Unionism became that much purer, and the actual enrollment enabled the military to keep closer tabs on those who remained.

The proclamation, though it seemed harsh for those who had tried to stay neutral, was in accord with the Lieber Code which allowed enemy subjects to be forced into the service of the victorious government after there had been a "fair and complete conquest of the hostile country or district," if the victor intended to keep the district permanently.[40]

Another method of population control was to increase the range of people who had to take the oath of allegiance. The Lieber Code, in three different sections, gives a commanding general the right to force the citizenry in hostile areas to take oaths of allegiance, and any other pledge the general "may consider necessary for the safety or security of his army. . . ."[41] In Tennessee, Governor Johnson and the high army command had instigated oath-taking procedures before the publication of the code, but as the war progressed, they expanded their application to include everyone of known Southern sentiment, not just prominent individuals.

In the summer of 1862, Johnson ordered that all persons arrested for using treasonable and seditious language, who refused to take the oath of allegiance and give a $1,000 bond for their future good behavior, should be sent south of the federal lines. If they returned, they would be treated as spies.[42] There was, however, little chance to enforce this order because Union forces devoted almost all their energies to saving the city from the forces of Morgan and Forrest. Furthermore, Buell believed in more gentle treatment of the civilian populace. But by late November, the capital was temporarily secure and Rosecrans had replaced Buell.

Toward the end of November, Rosecrans and Johnson developed a plan requiring bonds and sureties for good behavior after a person agreed to take the oath of allegiance or a noncombatant parole. Whichever he took, he had to give bond, with approved surety, to assure his adherence to the oath or parole. Having done this, the citizen received a guarantee of protection by the military authorities. Anyone failing to take the oath or parole faced banishment beyond the federal lines.[43]

Initially the plan applied to every citizen without regard to past political associations, thereby, in a sense, wiping out the past. All would resume their allegiance and start anew, thus erasing the "odious" distinctions which kept passions inflamed. But loyal men did not want to be classed with persons with rebel sentiments and therefore demanded preferential treatment. Consequently, Rosecrans limited the plan to the pro-rebel element of the population. On December 30, 1862, he ordered all citizens of Davidson County who had aided the rebellion by word or deed to come forward within two weeks to "make bond and oath, according to the forms provided and heretofore published by military authority." Those who did not would be "summarily dealt with, by fine, imprisonment, or exclusion from these lines."[44]

Few people responded to the plan, probably hoping that this measure, like the one Johnson proposed in the summer, would not be enforced and would therefore be forgotten. But it was not forgotten, and in March 1863, Rosecrans promulgated a general order on the subject, explaining that there were within the federal lines "many helpless and suffering families whose natural protectors and supporters are in arms against us." It was not the duty of federal authorities to feed, clothe, and protect these people. He therefore ordered everyone whose "natural protectors" were in the rebel service, or "whose sympathies and connections are such that they cannot give the assurance that they will conduct themselves as peaceable citizens," to prepare themselves to be sent South within ten days. People who took the noncombatant parole or the oath of allegiance and gave the requisite bond could remain at home.[45]

Again there was little response, but this time—to the consternation of Southern sympathizers—the order was backed up by military force. In mid-April, the military arrested between seventy-five and one hundred people of "well-known rebellious views and decided hostility to the Government."[46] On the heels of these arrests, General Robert B. Mitchell, temporarily in command in Nashville, published a strongly worded order. Sympathizers with the rebellion, he said, apparently consider their political sentiments more important than the "obligations imposed upon them by their residence and protection within the Federal lines." Consequently, all whites who had not previously taken the oath or parole, or who were not known Unionists, had to subscribe to the oath or parole and file bonds with sufficient securities within ten days. Those who did not would be sent South.[47]

The newspapers now reported a great rush to comply with Mitchell's order. Within a week, he had to triple the number of clerks detailed for taking oaths and paroles, and by the end of May, nearly ten thousand men and women had taken one or the other. In the next two months, more than a thousand more subscribed to the oath or parole, about four hundred and fifty of whom were residents of Davidson County. The bond provided ranged from $1,000 to $5,000, but the typical amount was $1,000 or $1,500.[48]

While thousands rushed to fulfill the requirements of Rosecrans' plan, others in the vicinity, whose support of the South overshadowed all else, accepted banishment.[49] A few who refused to take either the oath or parole were exiled north of the Ohio River, but most were sent South where they joined the ever-increasing number of homeless refugees in the ever-contracting territorial extent of the Confederacy and where, as Johnson realized, they would become an ever-growing burden on the Confederate government.[50] For those who sincerely believed in the Southern cause, banishment was the honorable option;

but it was also the most difficult one. To leave all that was dear and valuable behind and enter into an uncertain way of life was a courageous step, particularly in light of the alternative which federal authorities offered. By merely accepting the obligation of temporary allegiance and remaining peacefully at home, Middle Tennesseans could gain the advantage of military protection for themselves and their property.[51]

Because of the attractive alternative to banishment, no doubt many Nashvillians swore an oath without really believing in it. John B. Lindsley's wife, for example, thought that "many took it as a form." Probably very few Union officials deluded themselves into thinking that taking the oath necessarily indicated renewed, heartfelt loyalty to the Union. True, some individuals, such as Mrs. Lindsley, did feel bound by what they swore.[52] But even if most people swore the oath dishonorably, the cumulative impact of thousands of people taking the oath could only raise doubts about the survival of the Confederacy. Each individual who pledged allegiance to the United States at least indirectly questioned the ability of the Confederacy to protect him and his property.

One of the editors of the *New York Times*, a native Tennessean who had just toured the state, summed up this feeling when he wrote that the "reasoning of the citizens of Tennessee on their situation and their duties at the present hour is eminently sound and satisfactory. They say that they did join issue with the North in war, and by so doing agreed to abide by the decision of arms. They did the best they could, but the fight has gone against them. They find the Confederate authority extinguished, and the Government of the United States over them; and whether willingly or not, they must submit, accept that Government, and obey its laws."[53]

III

Johnson and Rosecrans agreed on the policy of submission or banishment, but they quarreled bitterly over other methods of population control. Their disagreement over the use of an Army Police to root out disloyalty was so sharp that at times it hampered the quest for loyalty.[54]

When Rosecrans came to Nashville to replace Buell as commanding general of the Army of the Cumberland, he created a force of secret military police commanded by William Truesdail, who had already gained much police and secret service experience while serving under Brigadier General John Pope and then Rosecrans in the Army of the Mississippi. In the eyes of Truesdail and his policemen, Nashville was "swarming with traitors, smugglers, and spies. . . . The city, in fact, was one vast 'Southern Aid Society,' whose sole aim was to plot secret treason and furnish information to the rebel leaders." The Army Police believed it was their duty to "purify this tainted atmosphere," and unquestionably they helped control smuggling, recover stolen government property, and expose disloyalty.[55]

However, Army Police methods were often so unscrupulous that they offended most citizens, loyal and disloyal alike. For example, a small number of brokers in Nashville speculated in Confederate money, a relatively harmless activity which federal authorities made no effort to curtail. In mid-January 1863, without any published orders or even private notification that the traffic was illegitimate, the Army Police arrested the brokers. The staunchly loyal *Daily Union* had "no doubt that the traffic is mischievous, corrupting, and disloyal in its tendencies and ought to be interdicted; but the summary proceedings of the police seem to us altogether oppressive and unnecessary." The proper way to bring speculation in Confederate money under control, the paper said, was a published order prohibiting its circulation.[56]

There was more than a hint of suspicion that the Army Police used their position to engage in cotton speculation and illegal seizures and confiscations. There is also evidence that they tried to control the press through bribery.[57] Even an apologist for the police admitted that "errors and wrongs may have been committed by its officials; many arrests may have been made without good reason therefor, and many goods seized that ought to have been untouched; true, many bad men may have wormed themselves into its service. . . ."[58]

Johnson was one of the most avid critics of the police, and especially of Truesdail. "Since I have been discharging the duties of Executive of the State," wrote Johnson, "I have refused and rejected the application for the release of fifty convicts confined in the cells of our State prison, who are better and more worthy men, than he is."[59] The governor believed Truesdail's police had badly damaged the Union cause in Nashville. Their summary method of handling "the persons and property of citizens, have not only excited a feeling of indignation among the more conservative portion of the community, but have greatly impaired the confidence of the loyal men. . . ." To these classes of citizens, Johnson pointed out, "we look for active support."

Furthermore, the Army Police were extraneous since ample machinery existed in Nashville for the proper execution of the laws—United States attorneys, courts, and marshals, a municipal government and police force, and a post commander and provost marshal. The use of a secret military police simply undermined the authority of these institutions.[60]

Truesdail maintained he had done no wrong and could not understand the opposition to him. "What on Earth Have I done," he wrote to Rosecrans, "other than my duty, and to Have been an active Cooperator with your Command in Support of the Cause of my Country. Watchful energy & laborious discharge of duty Seams [sic] to be my only Crime." True, he said, "I may have ered [sic]. Man is Prone to eror [sic]. If so my Superior Officers neglected to point out my erors [sic] to me . . . but they did often Say that is Right, that is Right, & called on me to do a thousand things of Service to the Army & the Country."[61]

Rosecrans refused to remove the police or even bring them under control, saying that complaints against them generally came "from smugglers and unscrupulous Jews, who have been detected in contraband trade, and their property confiscated."[62] In the spring of 1863, Rosecrans appointed a special inspector, Captain Temple Clark, to investigate the Army Police. Clark, who had once worked for Rosecrans but now served on Johnson's staff, reported that the police were highly advantageous to the government and found no evidence of misbehavior.[63] The validity of Clark's report is hard to assess, but in light of all the allegations of illegal police activities it seems reasonable to conclude it was a whitewash. However, it is probably equally true that the critics of the police overstated their argument, too.

In any event, the police remained in Nashville until Rosecrans' removal in October 1863. In the interim, Unionism suffered. The editor of the *Daily Union* spoke for many loyalists when he wrote that "we thank God devoutly in behalf of oppressed loyalty" for the abolition of the Army Police.[64]

Johnson and Rosecrans also disagreed about the use of military commissions, which were one of the foremost methods of military control over civilian populations in the South. Wherever Union armies advanced, military commissions went with them to hear cases involving both civilians and the military, including violations of the laws of war and all civilian breaches of military orders and regulations. When the local courts were not open the commissions would try cases of civil crimes and offenses normally heard by the local courts. Although military commissions met in Nashville throughout the war, during the first year and half of federal occupation, they created as many problems as they solved.[65]

Governor Johnson wanted civil courts to begin functioning in Tennessee as soon as possible as an important step toward the reestablishment of a legitimate civil government. By May 1, 1862, circuit, chancery, and magistrates' courts held daily sessions in Nashville, and the next year Johnson made arrangements for the reopening of the Criminal Court of Davidson County.[66]

Thus, when Rosecrans arrived in Nashville, two separate court systems were organized and operating. Friction soon developed between the military tribunals and the civil courts. One of the first altercations occurred in November 1862, over a trivial case which involved the violation of a municipal law. Brigadier General James F. Negley, then in command of the Union forces in Nashville, ordered the provost marshal to direct the city recorder to annul all proceedings in the case because army headquarters had already disposed of it. City Recorder Shane refused to comply, asserting that the provost marshal and recorder did not have concurrent jurisdiction in cases involving municipal law. He declared emphatically that the Recorder's Court was the sole tribunal for the trial of offenses against the city. This clear conflict between civil and military authority in Nashville soon grew worse. When cases arose which were apparently cognizable under either civil or military law, there was a scramble for jurisdiction.[67]

The War Department finally intervened in the legal conflicts in Middle Tennessee. On March 20, 1863, General in Chief Halleck sent Rosecrans detailed instructions to guide him in his relations with the civil authorities of Tennessee which came down heavily on the side of the civil courts. The military forces of the United States, said Halleck, "will not interfere with the authority and jurisdiction of the loyal officers of the State government, except in case of urgent and pressing necessity." All civil and criminal cases cognizable under the laws of Tennessee and the United States were to be tried in the reestablished state and federal courts.[68]

Despite these specific orders, legal conflicts continued while Rosecrans remained in command. Only after his removal did the military give proper recognition to the civil courts of Middle Tennessee. In early 1864, the officer in command in Nashville ordered that "Hereafter the Military Authorities of this District will refrain from taking action in, or in any manner interfering with matters which properly and exclusively belong to, and should be adjusted by the civil tribunals of the country."[69] By the fall of that year, Major General Thomas was anxious for civil courts to begin full operation in the state so that he could dissolve certain commissions then in session and turn their work over to civil authorities.[70]

The conflicts between the civil and military courts—though finally settled in favor of civil authority—had inflicted much damage on the Union cause in Nashville. The struggle for jurisdiction between Rosecrans and Johnson had engendered hostility between the two officials which prevented them from concentrating on purging the city of disloyalty.

IV

Federal officials also employed retaliation as a means of control. "The law of war," says the Lieber Code, "can no more wholly dispense with retaliation than can the law of nations, of which it is a branch." Retaliation, though, should never be used as a measure of "mere revenge, but only as a means of protective retribution and moreover cautiously and unavoidably."[71] Here again Johnson's actions meshed with the code but actually preceded its publication. Ten weeks after becoming military governor, Johnson issued a proclamation designed to stop guerrilla outrages against Union citizens. Every time "marauding bands" mistreated a Unionist, "five or more rebels from the most prominent in the immediate neighborhood shall be arrested, imprisoned, and otherwise dealt with as the nature of the case may require." If partisans destroyed Unionist property, "full and ample remuneration" would be made from the property of rebels in the vicinity who "have sympathized with, and given aid, comfort, information or encouragement to the parties committing such depredations."[72] Later in the war, regular army officers issued similar orders.[73] Unionist citizens frequently requested and received indemnification under the provisions of these orders.[74]

Another aspect of Johnson's use of retaliation was the taking of hostages to exchange for Union captives held by Confederates. On June 5, 1862, Johnson reported to Lincoln that seventy East Tennesseans imprisoned in Mobile, Alabama, were being "treated with more cruelty than wild beasts of the forest." Steps had been taken to "arrest seventy vile secessionists" in the Nashville area to offer in exchange for the East Tennesseans. Would Lincoln approve?[75] When the president gave full consent to his "proceeding of reprisal against the seces-sionists," Johnson asked Halleck to arrange an exchange of prison-ers.[76] The military governor, as well as other officers, used this re-taliatory tactic throughout the war, and in at least some instances it was effective.[77]

Johnson also levied special assessments and contributions on the civilian populace, another practice sanctioned by the Lincoln ad-ministration.[78] The Lieber Code is vague on the topic of special exac-tions but, as usual, Andrew Johnson was decisive.[79] A contemporary observer reported that he "levied at his will heavy assessments of money on the wealthy secessionists of Middle Tennessee."[80] In late August 1862, the governor sent a letter to a number of citizens de-manding that they contribute money to relieve destitute families in Nashville. The money was to be paid within five days to James Whit-worth, the judge of the County Court. Among those asked to contri-bute were some of the wealthiest Southern sympathizers in the area, such as Mark R. Cockrill and Byrd Douglas, who could well afford to pay assessments.[81]

Since most people ignored the five day limit set by Johnson, in mid-December he levied new assessments. When some people again refused to pay, the Nashville post commander ordered the First Mid-dle Tennessee Infantry to enforce Johnson's edict and, if a person balked, to seize his available property. As with the taking of oaths and paroles, the open application of force induced a quick response from recalcitrant citizens who rapidly began paying their assessments.[82]

Some have claimed that these exactions, "imposed under the plea of charity for the needy," were the first step in Johnson's policy of "punishment, disgrace, and impoverishment" of the rich.[83] This judgment is unwarranted because the need for the levies was real. Thousands of poor people huddled in Nashville under appalling cir-cumstances, literally facing death from starvation and exposure dur-ing the winter. If anything, there should have been more levies for larger amounts, more promptly and forcefully collected, to alleviate their distress, but several factors prevented this. One was certainly the unsettled condition of Middle Tennessee in the early stages of the occupation.

But a more important factor was the special protection given to property by Buell. When Mayor Cheatham surrendered the city, Buell assured him that the liberty and property of all citizens would be sacredly respected, and Buell kept his promise. The general and his fellow regular army officers were, as Nashvillians soon came to appreciate, "the most conservative men, we have among us. . . ."[84] One man, who spoke glowingly of "the just appreciation of and observance of the private rights and property of the people upon the part of the whole army," believed Buell's policy would "win the admiration of both the friends and former enemys [*sic*] of the Union" and would lead to a pro-Union revolution in public sentiment.[85] Buell's excessive leniency, of course, did not noticeably hasten progress toward re-union; instead, rebels throughout Middle Tennessee generally remained defiant.

Initially Buell's overly gentle treatment of secessionists harmonized with the Lincoln administration's conservative war aim merely to suppress the insurrection and restore the old Union. But by midsummer 1862, Buell's "excess of prudence"[86] was increasingly out of step with developments both in Washington and in Middle Tennessee as Unionist sentiment shifted from a policy of reconciliation to one of punishment. In Tennessee some men quickly concluded that Buell's policy of special protection and favoritism toward Confederate sympathizers was bankrupt.

Reuben D. Mussey, who was to play an important role in recruiting black troops in Nashville, believed that the commanding general was either a traitor or an imbecile, and demanded a halt to his "rosewater policy." "We have stood guards over Rebel property long enough," he said. "Gen. Buell has endeavored to make his Corps a mere Police for the better protection of Rebels."[87] Johnson reached a similar conclusion by August, but it was only after Rosecrans replaced Buell and Middle Tennessee was temporarily secure from Confederate attack that the governor's fiat could be enforced.

Confiscation, similar to assessments in its effect, is a form of coercion which impairs the enemy's ability to resist while it increases the means at the disposal of the appropriating government for conducting the war. The execution of the Congressional Confiscation Acts originally did not fall within the province of the military, but a presidential order empowered military commissions to seize and use any real or personal property "which may be necessary or convenient for their several commands, as supplies, or for other military purposes. . . ."[88]

Union authorities in Nashville frequently employed confiscation under the direction of United States District Marshal E. R. Glascock who sold many of the confiscated goods at public auction, with the proceeds going to the United States Treasury. The military also used some confiscable property instead of selling it. For instance, the army took possession of two gun factories in the city and converted them into military hospitals, and the confiscated Methodist Publishing House became a government printing house.[89]

V

During the occupation of Nashville, authorities attempted many other expedients to control the civilian population and make disloyalty unpleasant. However, the main efforts were: a system of passes and permits; censorship of the mails; enrollment of men into the state militia; the taking of oaths or noncombatant paroles; a secret detective force; military commissions; retaliation and special assessments; and confiscation. Combined with the initial suppression of leading secessionists, these tactics made life uncomfortable, at best, for those who adhered to the Confederacy. While Unionists suffered some inconvenience from these measures, their discomfort was minor compared to the plight of beleaguered rebels. To avoid the pressure, some Southern sympathizers accepted banishment; a few no doubt converted to Unionism; but most bent to federal authority in public while remaining sullen and unhappy captives praying for deliverance.

A man could be forced to take an oath of allegiance, but this did not mean he believed in it. As one man whose sons were in Confederate service put it, "I can tie my hands, my feet, or my tongue by the oath I have taken, but I cannot prevent my *heart from going out towards my boys.*"[90] The dilemma of federal efforts to rebuild loyalty in Nashville was that a man's demeanor could be controlled by threat of punishment, but this did not necessarily change his true feelings. "You may paint a crow white or red," said one Unionist, "but that won't prevent him from stealing your corn."[91] Somehow positive alternatives to disloyalty had to be offered. Repression alone would not rekindle genuine loyalty.

NOTES

1. Oliver P. Temple, *Notable Men of Tennessee From 1833 to 1875, Their Times and Their Contemporaries,* p. 406. Also see Herschel Gower and Jack Allen, eds., *Pen and Sword,* p. 627; Stanley F. Horn, "Nashville During the Civil War," p. 12; Alfred Leland Crabb, *Nashville: Personality of a City,* pp. 64–65.

2. City Recorder Hays to AJ, 27 March 1862, AJP, Presidential Papers Microfilm.

3. William E. Birkhimer, *Military Government and Martial Law,* p. 3.

4. AJ to Stanley Matthews, 29 March 1862, AJP; Thomas B. Alexander, *Political Reconstruction in Tennessee,* p. 15.

5. Cheatham to AJ, 12 May 1862, AJP.

6. AJ to Stanley Matthews, 31 March, 1, 2, 16 April 1862. All in AJP.

7. Mrs. Harding to her husband, 16 June 1862, Harding Family Papers, Joint University Libraries. Also see Gower and Allen, eds., *Pen and Sword,* pp. 646–47.

8. Harding's parole is in AJP, 25 September 1862.

9. Gower and Allen, eds., *Pen and Sword,* pp. 645, 647; *Christ Church Nashville, 1829–1929;* O. P. Fitzgerald, *John B. McFerrin,* pp. 269–70.

10. AJ to Gen. [Jeremiah T.] Boyle, 4 August 1862, AJP.

11. *Nashville Dispatch,* 1 July 1862.

12. AJ to Governor O. P. Morton, 24 July 1862, and AJ to Governor David Tod, 24 July, 20 August 1862. All in AJP.

13. Agreement signed by John P. Ford, 16 August 1862, and AJ to Gen. Boyle, 4 August 1862, both in AJP; Rufus B. Spain, "R.B.C. Howell," pp. 335–37.

14. The paroles of the four ministers are in the AJP for October 1862.

15. James G. Randall, *Constitutional Problems Under Lincoln,* p. 492; J. Cutler Andrews, *The South Reports the Civil War;* W. W. Clayton, *History of Davidson County, Tennessee, with Illustrations and Biographical Sketches of Its Prominent Men and Pioneers,* p. 241; *Nashville Daily Union,* 16 April 1862.

16. James S. Wallace to AJ, 5 April 1862, and S. C. Mercer to Stanton, 3 December 1863, both in AJP. Also see the *Nashville Daily Union,* 15 April 1865.

17. W. D. Bickham to Rosecrans, 1 November 1863, William S. Rosecrans Papers, University Research Library; Benjamin C. Truman to AJ, 12 November 1863, AJP.

18. Provost Marshal Horner to the Editors of the "Times," "Union," "Press," "Dispatch," and "Gazette," 19 April 1864, RG 393, Entry 1655.

19. AAG [unsigned] to the Editor of the Press, 18 February 1865, RG 393, Entry 908.

20. Letter signed by "A Tennessean" in the *Nashville Daily Press and Times,* 21 July 1863.

21. *Nashville Daily Press and Times,* 24 July 1863. Also see *ibid.,* 29, 30 May, 2 June, 15 July 1863.

22. *Ibid.,* 28 July 1863; *Nashville Daily Union,* 2 August 1863. Union authorities also controlled the press in Memphis; see Joseph Howard Parks, "Memphis Under Military Rule, 1862 to 1865," pp. 33–34.

23. Sister M. Southall to My Dear Brother, 20 June 1862, Harding Family Papers.

24. Mrs. Harding to her husband, 13 July 1862, Harding Family Papers. Also see Mrs. Harding to her husband, 11, 15 May 1862, both in the Harding Family Papers.

25. Randal M. Ewing to Dear Kinsman and Friend, 18 May 1862, Harding-Jackson Papers, TSLA. Also see Mrs. Harding to her husband, 4 July 1862, Harding Family Papers.

26. Mrs. Harding to her husband, 16 June 1862, Harding Family Papers. Also see Mrs. Harding to her husband, 24 June 1862, Harding Family Papers.

27. Mrs. Harding to her husband, 8 June 1862; [?] to My Dear Brother, 14 August 1862; M. Southall to Dear Brother, 30 July 1862. All in the Harding Family Papers. Mrs. M. C. Bass to Generals Harding and Barrow, 24 June 1862, Harding-Jackson Papers.

28. Lindsley Diary, 31 December 1862, Lindsley Family Papers, TSLA; Mrs. Harding to her husband, 31 May 1862, Harding Family Papers.

29. Narrative of John P. W. Brown, John Preston Watts Brown Collection, TSLA.

30. *Nashville Daily Union,* 23 January 1863.

31. Provost Marshal Horner to Capt. Nevin, 17 June 1864, RG 393, Entry 1655. Also see Maj. and AAG William Michael to Brig. Gen. J. D. Morgan, 27 May 1863, RG 393, Entry 908.

32. Lt. and Acting Provost Marshal General Bracken to Capt. Hunter Brooke, 20 January 1865, RG 393, Entry 901; *Nashville Daily Union,* 27 January 1863.

33. J. E. Windrow, "Collins D. Elliott and the Nashville Female Academy," pp. 97–98.

34. AJ to First Assistant Postmaster General, 24 April 1862, and A. V. S. Lindsley to AJ, 7 July 1864, both in AJP; *Nashville Daily Times and True Union,* 29 March 1864.

35. Maj. W. H. Sidell to Col. J. B. Fry, 11 August 1862, RG 393, Entry 867; Henry Clay Yeatman to his wife, 9 December 1862, Yeatman-Polk Collection, TSLA; Mrs. Harding to her husband, 16 June 1862, Harding Family Papers; Mrs. M. C. Bass to Generals Harding and Barrow, 24 June 1862, Harding-Jackson Papers.

36. *Nashville Daily Press and Times,* 14 August 1863; *Nashville Daily Times and True Union,* 29 March 1864.

37. Maj. Gen. R. H. Milroy to AJ, 29 October 1864, AJP.

38. J. R. Lisenburry to AJ, 25 August 1864 [the endorsement on this letter has it dated 25 September 1864, which I believe to be the correct date], AJP.

39. *Nashville Daily Times and True Union,* 21 September 1864.

40. *OR,* 3, 3, p. 152.

41. *Ibid.,* pp. 151, 161, 164. In fact, oath-taking was a nationwide phenomenon during the Civil War; see Harold Melvin Hyman, *Era of the Oath.*

42. *Appleton's Annual Cyclopaedia and Register of Important Events* (1862), p. 766.

43. *Nashville Daily Union,* 29 November 1862; *Nashville Dispatch,* 29 November, 4 December 1862; Rosecrans to AJ, 4 December 1862, *OR,* 2, 5, p. 24.

44. *Nashville Dispatch,* 29 November, 4, 5, December 1862; Hyman, *Era of the Oath,* pp. 39–40; *Nashville Daily Union,* 11 January 1863.

45. *OR,* 2, 5, p. 339. Memphians were equally reluctant to take loyalty oaths; see Ernest Walter Hooper, "Memphis, Tennessee," pp. 56–59.

46. *Nashville Daily Union,* 15 April 1863; *Nashville Dispatch,* 18 April 1863.

47. *Nashville Daily Union,* 22 April 1863.

48. *Ibid.,* 25, 26, 30 April 1863; *Nashville Dispatch,* 30 April 1863; RG 393, Entry 1657.

49. *Nashville Daily Press and Times,* 25, 27 May 1863.

50. AJ to Thomas, 29 July 1864, AJP.

51. Birkhimer, *Military Government,* pp. 1–3. Banishment was a common punishment for recalcitrants during the Civil War; see Robert J. Futrell, "Federal Military Government in the South, 1861–1865," p. 189. The unhappy plight of refugees in the South is detailed in Mary Elizabeth Massey, *Refugee Life in the Confederacy.*

52. Sir Christopher Chancellor, ed., *An Englishman in the American Civil War*, p. 136.

53. *New York Times*, 18 September 1863.

54. Rosecrans' biographer says the operations of the Army Police proved to be the "most trying common problem" between Rosecrans and Johnson; see William M. Lamers, *The Edge of Glory*, p. 256.

55. John Fitch, *Annals of the Army of the Cumberland*, pp. 346–49, 373–74; Stanley F. Horn, "Dr. John Rolfe Hudson and the Confederate Underground in Nashville."

56. *Nashville Daily Union*, 17 January 1863. For another use of unscrupulous methods by the Army Police, see Fitch, *Annals*, pp. 472–83, and Horn, "Dr. John Rolfe Hudson."

57. Rosecrans to AJ, 4 April 1863, and Benjamin C. Truman to AJ, 12 November 1863, both in AJP; *Nashville Daily Union*, 30, 31 October, 3 November 1863; Clifton R. Hall, *Andrew Johnson, Military Governor of Tennessee*, pp. 78–79.

58. Fitch, *Annals*, p. 351.

59. AJ to Richard Smith, 2 November 1863, AJP.

60. AJ to Rosecrans, 14 January 1863, AJP.

61. Truesdail to Rosecrans, 1 November 1863, Rosecrans Papers.

62. Rosecrans to AJ, 17 January 1863, AJP.

63. Fitch, *Annals*, pp. 353–56.

64. *Nashville Daily Union*, 31 October 1863.

65. Futrell, "Federal Military Government," p. 186; A. H. Carpenter, "Military Government of Southern Territory, 1861–1865," pp. 483–84.

66. *Nashville Daily Union*, 1 May 1862, 24 January 1863.

67. Provost Marshal A. C. Gillem to City Recorder John [*sic*: William] Shane, 7 November 1862, and Shane to Gillem, 7 November 1862 (and Gillem's endorsement on this letter). All in AJP.

68. Halleck to Rosecrans, 20 March 1863, *OR*, 3, 3, pp. 77–78; Hall, *Andrew Johnson*, pp. 45–46.

69. *Nashville Daily Union*, 9 January 1864.

70. Thomas to AJ, 23 September 1864, AJP. The ascendancy of the civil courts is demonstrated by the case of William C. Taylor; see the *Nashville Daily Times and True Union*, 13, 14 April 1864.

71. *OR*, 3, 3, p. 151.

72. *Nashville Dispatch*, 11 May 1862.

73. General Orders No. 60 issued by Gen. Grant, 3 July 1862, in John Y. Simon, ed., *Papers of Ulysses S. Grant*, 5: p. 190; General Orders No. 27, issued by Gen. Rousseau, 13 June 1864, in the *Nashville Daily Times and True Union*, 23 June 1864.

74. Sinclair & Moss to AJ, 14 July 1863; F. M. Carter to AJ, 16 July 1863; D. W. Knight to AJ, 6 October 1863. All in AJP. AAG L. Howland to Lt. Col. Abram E. Garrett, 12 October 1864, and Howland to Lt. G. A. Gowin, 13 October 1864, both in RG 393, Entry 861.

75. AJ to Lincoln, 5 June 1862, *OR*, 2, 3, p. 643.

76. Stanton to AJ, 7 June 1862, *ibid.*, p. 659; AJ to Halleck, 9 June 1862, AJP.

77. *Nashville Daily Union*, 19, 24 February, 3 March 1863. For another officer in Middle Tennessee who resorted to taking hostages, see Lt. and AAAG Henry Stone to Col. A. C. Harding, 25 February 1863, RG 393, Entry 908.

78. Stanton to AJ, 2 April 1863, AJP.

79. *OR*, 3, 3, p. 152; Doris Appel Graber, *The Development of the Law of Belligerent Occupation, 1863–1914*, p. 222.

80. Temple, *Notable Men of Tennessee*, p. 406.

81. *Nashville Dispatch*, 21 August 1862.

82. *Nashville Daily Union*, 14 December 1862, 11 January, 27 February, 1, 3 March 1863.

83. Temple, *Notable Men of Tennessee*, pp. 406–7.

84. *Appleton's Annual Cyclopaedia* (1862), p. 596; Mrs. Harding to her husband, 27 July [1862], Harding Family Papers.

85. John S. Smith to John J. Crittenden, 28 February 1862, Buell-Brien Papers, TSLA.

86. Whitelaw Reid, *Ohio In the War*, 1: p. 723.

87. R. D. Mussey to Joseph H. Barrett, 30 September, 16 October 1862, R. Delevan Mussey Papers, Lincoln Miscellaneous Manuscript Collection, The University of Chicago Library; R. D. Mussey to William H. Smith, 6 July 1862, William Henry Smith Papers, OHS. A similarly lenient policy prevailed initially both in Memphis and in the Norfolk-Portsmouth, Virginia, area during the early months of occupation; see Ernest Walter Hooper, "Memphis, Tennessee," and Spencer Wilson, "Experiment in Reunion."

88. Birkhimer, *Military Government*, p. 131; Futrell, "Federal Military Government," pp. 187–88.

89. The Nashville press teems with notices about confiscations and sales. For the gun factories see the *Nashville Daily Press and Times*, 15 May 1863 (a list of army hospitals), and the *Nashville Daily Union*, 27 May 1862; for the Publishing House see *House Ex. Docs.*, 39th Cong., 1st sess., no. 1, pt. 1, 600. There is some hint that confiscation was used for private gain. For example, the house of Sterling R. Cockrill, valued at $30,000, sold for $5,600 to Joseph S. Fowler, who was comptroller of the state; see the *Nashville Daily Times and True Union*, 31 August, 2 September 1864.

90. Quoted in Clayton, *Davidson County*, p. 433.

91. Quoted in Hall, *Andrew Johnson*, p. 163. For another statement expressing similar sentiments, see R. B. C. Howell to AJ, 16 August 1862, AJP.

Chapter 5

"LENIENCY IS CONSTRUED INTO TIMIDITY"

When Andrew Johnson arrived in Nashville on March 12, 1862, he was committed to a policy of moderation and conciliation. He believed that once he removed the leaders of the rebellion, most Tennesseans, essentially loyal at heart, would see the error of their ways and gladly return to their old allegiance. However, within six months Johnson realized his mild policy had failed completely because the Nashville citizenry construed leniency and moderation as weakness rather than kindness.

In the fall of 1862, with his initial policy having been a failure, Johnson took an increasingly hard line against those who still adhered to the rebellion. This dramatic about-face created severe strains in the Unionist coalition because many Unionists disagreed with the new stern stand against treason and continued to favor a policy of forbearance and clemency toward their erring neighbors. The Emancipation Proclamation, although it did not specifically apply to Tennessee, exacerbated beyond repair the growing split in the Unionist ranks. The Johnson faction supported the president's policy and advocated abolition in Tennessee, but the other faction opposed emancipation —or at least the manner in which it was accomplished. Thus, by the summer of 1863, there were actually two Union parties in the state.

By the end of his term as military governor, Johnson had restored a loyal state government in Tennessee. But this was done in a highly irregular manner, and the small faction which controlled the government did not represent the majority of the people of Tennessee. For propaganda purposes, the new Tennessee government could be viewed as the crowning achievement of Johnson's heroic stand in Tennessee; but in reality it represented an inglorious defeat of his efforts. When the war ended, a faint shadow of loyalty flickered across the state, but there was not much substance to it. Loyalty in any broad sense had not been regenerated. Unionism had prevailed on the battlefield, but not in civil society.

I

Philosophically, there were two ways to consider the citizens of the occupied regions of the South. One viewpoint, perhaps best expressed by General William T. Sherman, was that "when one nation is at war with another, all the people of the one are enemies of the other: then the rules are plain and easy of understanding." The general, who had little regard for the Union men of the South, believed the United States government ought to "proceed on the proper rule that all in the South *are* enemies of all in the North. . . ." Secretary of the Navy Gideon Welles neatly summarized the competing philosophy. "Instead of halting on the borders, building intrenchments, and repelling indiscriminately and treating as Rebels—enemies—all, Union as well as disunion, men in the insurrectionary regions," he wrote, "we should I thought penetrate their territory, nourish and protect the Union sentiment, and strengthen a national feeling counter to Secession."[1]

Johnson, who accepted the latter philosophy, addressed the people of Tennessee shortly after his arrival in Nashville. Since the executive and the legislature had fled, and the judiciary was in abeyance, he said, the state government had disappeared. "The great ship of state . . . has been suddenly abandoned by its officers and mutinous crew, and left to float at the mercy of the winds. . . . " In this lamentable crisis, the national government had appointed him military governor to "preserve the public property of the State, to give the protection of law actively enforced to her citizens, and, as speedily as may be, to restore her Government to the same condition as before the existing rebellion." He invited all Tennesseans to join in restoring the state, but in the interim he would appoint men to abandoned positions in the state and county governments "until their places can be filled by the action of the people."

He closed the address with a concise statement of the policy he intended to follow:

To the people themselves, the protection of the Government is extended. All their rights will be duly respected, and their wrongs redressed when made known. . . . The erring and misguided will be welcomed on their return. And while it may become necessary, in vindicating the violated majesty of the law, and in reasserting its imperial sway, to punish intelligent and conscious treason in high places, no mere retaliatory or vindictive policy will be adopted. To those, especially, who in a private, unofficial capacity have assumed an attitude of hostility to the Government, a full and complete amnesty for all past acts and declarations is offered, upon the one condition of their again yielding themselves peaceful citizens to the just supremacy of the laws.[2]

Two months later, Johnson and ex-Governor Campbell publicly restated this policy at a mass meeting of Union sympathizers in Nashville. Campbell, the chairman of the meeting, delivered the keynote address which obviously expressed the views of the governor as well as his own. "We invite all to help us in restoring the supremacy of law over Tennessee, and reinstating her in all the privileges and immunities of the Union," said Campbell. Property rights would be respected and all "deluded fellow citizens" would be cordially welcomed back and protected. "The Government intends no sweeping confiscation, no wild turning loose of slaves, against the revolted States." "We bear no malice toward any one," concluded Campbell, "but deep sympathy for the deluded. . . . The Federal Government will pursue a kind, liberal, and benevolent policy toward the people of the South, to bring them to the Union."[3]

Johnson's policy consisted of three parts: the repression of conscious disloyalty; a warm welcome for all who willingly renounced their past errors; and the initiation of political action, first through appointments but then with properly elected officials. Those who had steadfastly adhered to the Union, as well as those returning to their allegiance, would compose the political base of support.

The handling of Tennessee prisoners of war illustrated Johnson's readiness to welcome back deluded Tennesseans. Throughout March and April, letters from Tennessee soldiers confined in Northern military prisons who desired to take the oath of allegiance and be pardoned poured into the capital. Johnson considered these soldiers perfect examples of "misguided fellow citizens" who now saw the error of rebellion.

In late March, Johnson appointed Connally F. Trigg, a prominent Middle Tennessee judge, as his personal agent for the purpose of visiting Camp Chase in Columbus, Ohio, to investigate the prisoner problem. Trigg reported that a large number of Tennessee prisoners in Camp Chase would gladly take the oath and become loyal citizens but, he warned, others merely wanted to be paroled, "to have their *liberty and go home* but with the privilege of remaining *harmless rebels*, until exchanged. . . . " Trigg believed these men should remain in prison where their harmlessness could be assured, and suggested action only in cases where the prisoners were "loyally disposed and willing to attest it by the sanction of their oaths." Between five and six hundred communications from Tennessee prisoners, many of them signed by more than one person, quickly poured in to Trigg. "I would guess," he wrote to Johnson, "that the larger proportion of them are anxious to be released upon their *parole of honor*" rather than "take the *oath* and become *loyal* Citizens." This was not a good omen since it indicated most of the prisoners were not yet ready to return to total allegiance.[4]

In mid-April Johnson wrote Stanton declaring that the release of those Tennessee prisoners of war who "express a strong desire to renew their allegiance to the Government and become true and loyal citizens" might be beneficial to the Union cause. The reappearance of these men among their friends and relatives would "exert a great moral influence in favor of the perpetuity of the Union." Johnson expressed similar sentiments to Lincoln and bluntly told the president that he wanted sole control over the question of releasing Tennessee prisoners.[5]

Although Lincoln initially withheld the power of executive clemency from the military governor, Stanton told Johnson that when the right time came, the exercise of clemency would be left to his discretion. The time came in early August when the War Department granted Johnson authority over the release and exchange of Tennessee prisoners.[6] Johnson appointed Campbell to visit Northern prisons and determine which Tennessee prisoners should be released and on what terms. "All prisoners not officers," said the governor, "who are willing to take the oath of allegiance and give bonds will be released upon parole to report to the Governor of Tennessee, and all who refuse to do so will be retained in prison or exchanged."[7]

While trying to add to Unionist support with repentant Tennessee prisoners of war, Johnson also organized a Union party in the state through the appointment of other high state officials, all of them strong Unionists. Edward H. East, a Whig member of the General Assembly in 1859 and 1860 and an active campaigner for John Bell in the presidential election of 1860, became the secretary of state. The new comptroller was Joseph S. Fowler, an outspoken Unionist who fled Tennessee during the brief Confederate rule. He left all he had behind, but he wrote to Johnson at the time, "I suppose we may soon return." Meantime he intended "to make an application for a situation in the government" because "those who have stood firmly for the government when it cost so much to do it, should be preferred to those who basely deserted it." Fowler now had his reward. Attorney General Horace Maynard and Edmund Cooper, Johnson's private secretary, were similarly deserving of positions in the embryonic Union government.[8]

Johnson's first Reconstruction effort, which came barely two months after his arrival in Nashville, involved the vitally important issue of reopening the courts. Johnson called for an election for judge of the ninth circuit (which included Nashville) to be held on May 22. The Unionist candidate for the judgeship was Manson M. Brien, a fifty-year-old native Tennessean and "a thorough straightout loyalist."[9] Brien, an antebellum Whig lawyer who joined the Republican party during the war, remained one of the stalwarts of Johnson's wing of the Union party throughout the conflict. Opposing Brien was Turner S. Foster, a "fierce and intolerable Rebel" who had been secretary of the Confederate Passport Office in Nashville.[10]

After Foster won the election by two hundred votes, what followed approached the ludicrous. Johnson gave Foster his commission, had him arrested for disloyalty, and then appointed Brien to fill the vacated judgeship. Foster, a delicate man afflicted with inflammatory rheumatism, was shipped off to Camp Chase but was soon released on a parole of honor. A special condition of his parole was that he secure the release and exchange of Edmund Cooper, who had been captured by Confederates before he could assume his duties as Johnson's private secretary. Foster journeyed to Richmond, effected the exchange, and so was permitted to remain at his home under parole, during the remainder of the war.[11]

The governor had acted far too hastily in calling this election. He had seriously misjudged the spirit of the Nashville populace, a mistake for which there was no excuse. Randal McGavock, still lodged in Fort Warren, hundreds of miles from Nashville, had accurately predicted that Johnson would not be able to hold a successful election in Tennessee.[12] If McGavock could sense this, certainly Johnson should have been able to. With all his other problems, Johnson had now exposed the weakness of Unionist sentiment in Middle Tennessee.

There was also to be an election test of Union sentiment in West Tennessee during 1862, but it ended as badly as the May election in Middle Tennessee. Chances are Johnson was not eager to hold another election in the state, but Lincoln pushed him into it. The president wrote to Johnson on the matter of elections as early as July, indicating his desire for a favorable Unionist vote of some kind in Tennessee. Such an election, he said, "would be worth more to us than a battle gained." Johnson, however, did nothing to organize another test of Unionist strength.[13]

In the fall of 1862, Lincoln, desperately wanting at least one of the Southern states reconstructed, again pressured his military governor. The successful return of any state would be a vindication of the president's policy of placing Reconstruction in the hands of military governors, and would also bear favorably upon the Preliminary Emancipation Proclamation of September 22. On October 21, Lincoln addressed a letter to "Ulysses S. Grant, Andrew Johnson, and Others" asking them to conduct elections in Tennessee for "members to the Congress of the United States particularly, and perhaps a legislature, State officers, and a United States' Senator." He urged them to "follow law, and forms of law as far as convenient; but at all events get the expression of the largest number of people possible." However, Grant and Johnson should insure the election of good Union men.[14] Because Johnson could not very well ignore the wishes of the president again, he called for an election of representatives to the thirty-seventh Congress from the Union-controlled Ninth and Tenth Districts of West Tennessee. No proper election ever took place. A raid by Forrest disrupted all plans, which was perhaps just as well since West Tennessee had displayed very little Union sentiment.[15]

II

On the last day of July in 1862, Major W. H. Sidell of the Fifteenth U.S. Infantry who was also the acting assistant adjutant general in the District of the Ohio, had a protracted conversation with Military Governor Johnson. The major then reported to Buell's chief of staff that Johnson's ideas about the treatment of rebels had changed because of what he had recently observed. He now believed they "must be made to feel the burden of their own deeds and to bear everything which the necessities of the situation require should be imposed on them." Several days later, Johnson wrote to General Jeremiah T. Boyle, the commander in Louisville. "I concur with you most fully," he said, "in regard to expelling and putting to the Sword all traitors who continue to occupy a hostile attitude to the Govt. . . . *Treason must be made odious, traitors punished* and *impoverished.*" Two weeks later, Johnson dispatched a similar note to General Thomas. "Leniency," he wrote, "is construed into timidity, compromising to concession, which inspires them with a confidence & keeps alive the fell spirit of Rebellion."[16]

Johnson's initially lenient and kind attitude toward his fellow Tennesseans had been an accurate reflection of both his own beliefs about the nature of Tennessee Unionism, and of the limited national war aim of sectional reconciliation and restoration of the old Union. As battlefield casualties mounted and the Lincoln administration girded for a long war by mobilizing the industrial and emotional resources of the North, Union war aims, exemplified by the Second Confiscation Act and the Preliminary Emancipation Proclamation, shifted from mere *restoration* to the *reconstruction* of Southern society.

The sterner attitude adopted by Johnson in the late summer and early fall of 1862 mirrored this shift, but it also reflected his own perception of where Tennessee really stood. During the spring and summer, he had repressed Nashville's leading secessionists, tried to win the hearts of the people by welcoming back Tennessee prisoners of war, and taken the first hesitant steps toward reestablishing normal political operations in the state. Yet, despite his best and most sincere efforts, the city's citizenry remained committed to the Confederacy.

The change in the military governor's policy had momentous consequences for the future of Unionism in Tennessee. Until late summer, all Union sympathizers had worked together; afterwards they pulled in opposite directions. The division among Unionists became so deep that it assured the doom of any broadly based, popular Union party in the state. Johnson led one faction, known as the radicals, which favored a vigorous war effort and supported the Lincoln administration. The radicals, despite the state's exemption from the effects of the Emancipation Proclamation, insisted upon abolition in Tennessee and advocated a policy of harsh treatment of rebels, such as denying them political rights. Also part of the radicals' platform was a system of reward and favorable treatment for those who had, from the beginning, remained steadfastly loyal to the national government.

Conservative Tennessee Unionists did not oppose military government per se, but the military governor's new, radical program appalled them. They continued to favor lenient treatment of rebel sympathizers and were willing to make peace with the South, or at least accept the Southern states back into the Union with no conditions attached. They especially deplored the administration's advocacy of emancipation which, to men with conservative minds, reeked with revolution.

Among the leading conservatives were Campbell, Bailie Peyton, and Emerson Etheridge. Campbell, a veteran of the Seminole and Mexican Wars, had joined the Whig Party and served for six years in the House of Representatives. In 1851, running on a platform fully supporting the compromise measures of 1850, he was elected governor, and in 1860 he favored John Bell and vigorously opposed secession. When the war began, he was the most distinguished Middle Tennessean to remain loyal, even though Confederate authorities offered him a high military command.[17]

Peyton, almost as well known as Campbell, had participated in the Mexican War and had become a prominent Middle Tennessee Whig, serving three terms in Congress and as a Whig presidential elector in 1860. Etheridge, from Dresden, Tennessee, was another eminent Whig who, like Campbell and Peyton, had served in Congress. When the war began he took a firm stand for the Union. Forced to flee the state, he went to Washington where he became clerk in the House of Representatives. Throughout the war he had a large following in Tennessee.[18]

The actions of the Nashville Union Club (or League), an offshoot of the Union League which had been founded in the North in 1862 as an arm of the Republican party, clearly revealed the split among Unionists, particularly over emancipation. The Union Club, formed in late January 1863, was, in effect, a Johnson club designed to support the governor. Mayor John Hugh Smith was its president, and its secretary was Horace Harrison, Johnson's appointee as U.S. district attorney for Middle Tennessee.[19]

Within a week after its founding, the club exposed its radical posture by unanimously adopting a resolution which opposed the appointment of any person to any office in the state who had not always been an unconditional Union man.[20] Thus, "deluded fellow citizens" would no longer be welcomed into Unionist ranks on equal terms, and Johnson's promise to grant "a full and complete amnesty for all past acts and declarations" was revoked. Special consideration would henceforth be given to those who had adhered to the Union at all costs, a policy which was despised by conservative Unionists who still sympathized with their erring brethren.

In April 1863, the club adopted a constitution and a declaration of principles which formalized the radical character of the organization. The constitution stated that no one could become a club member who had not been loyal since the rebellion began and pledged all possible aid to federal authorities in reestablishing control in Tennessee. Even more important was the declaration which, while calling for a vigorous prosecution of the war, set forth a threefold program that was followed well into the Reconstruction era. First, it revoked Johnson's earlier promise to protect property and demanded that traitors be punished economically by being deprived of their slaves and all other property. It also stated that rebels should suffer politically through the denial of political rights.[21]

Finally, the declaration encouraged immigrants from the North and Europe to settle in Tennessee on the assumption that .these Union-loving citizens would take the political and social places of those who had sided with the rebellion.[22] Nashville Unionists confidently expected that the loss of slaves in Tennessee would "be more than made up by the increased price of land under the new immigration." They argued, as the Nashville correspondent for the *New York Times* put it, "that the beautiful vine lands on their hills will draw in the German emigrant; that the Western and Eastern farmer will be tempted to their fertile valleys, where all productions of the temperate zone flourish bountifully, and that the capital of the seaboard will seek out their wonderful water-power, and the veins of exquisite marble in their mountains."[23]

Native Nashville Unionists had good reason to put high hopes on immigration because a sizable bloc of the German population in Nashville supported the radical position. The Germans formed their own Union League in Nashville in August 1863, and four months later adopted a formal set of resolutions which indicted slavery as "contrary to reason and repulsive to humanity," a "hideous spot on the proud escutcheon of the American Union" which brought blessings to neither "the white nor to the black population of the country." The Germans called for the immediate, unconditional abolition of slavery throughout the whole Union and "for the confiscation of rebel property being made unconditionally, and without any reservation whatever."[24]

It is difficult to determine exactly how widespread radical Unionism was in Middle Tennessee. In late April 1863, the *Daily*

Union reported a membership of almost eight hundred in the Nashville Union Club and several months later "C.L.B.," writing in the *New York Times*, put the figure at seven hundred.[25] The latter figure is probably a reasonably accurate estimate. It is definitely known that many of the club's members were not even residents of the city and that there was a close connection among the army, Governor Johnson, and the club. For example, on the evening of August 29, 1863, the club held a meeting at the state capitol to celebrate— prematurely, as it turned out—the capture of Fort Sumter. The assemblage was addressed by an East Tennessee colonel and a Michigan captain, and then the crowd moved on to Johnson's residence where both the governor and the general in command in Nashville spoke to the serenaders.[26]

Conservative Unionists believed in the Union but did not believe in the policy enunciated by the Union Club and the military governor. One such man was William S. Cheatham, who was a member of the Nashville city council before the war and who had stayed with the Union. When Johnson appointed a new city government, Cheatham became an alderman. He also became a charter member of the Nashville Union Club, but in a public letter in late May 1863, he explained that the club "advocated views from which I dissent." He desired the state to "emerge from the present horrible civil commotion with unsullied honor and her institutions as our Fathers made them." Any attempt to change these institutions was akin to desecration and sacrilege.[27]

Etheridge so strongly opposed tampering with slavery that when he was offered a federal judgeship, he flatly rejected it because of Lincoln's stand on emancipation, which he considered "treachery to the Union men of the South." Any Southern man, said Etheridge, "would be disgraced to accept any appointment under the President unless in . . . military service."[28] There were deep philosophical differences behind his opposition to Lincoln and Johnson. The administration's proposal to end slavery was truly revolutionary, and Etheridge was no revolutionary. Neither were many other Tennessee Unionists, and the extent to which they were willing to go to show their displeasure with the Lincoln-Johnson regime became clear in August 1863.

August 4 was a constitutionally set election date in Tennessee. In July, Johnson's supporters requested him to issue writs of election but, remembering his futile experience with elections in 1862, he declined on the grounds that sufficient Union strength could not be mustered until East Tennessee was redeemed. However, Etheridge proceeded, on his own initiative, to hold a gubernatorial election in Shelby and Bedford Counties, and Campbell was "elected" governor. Johnson simply ignored this embarrassing incident, and though Etheridge journeyed to Washington to persuade Lincoln to recognize Campbell, nothing came of it. Having temporarily lost in Tennessee, Etheridge carried his anti-administration campaign to Washington. At the opening of the Thirty-eighth Congress, he attempted to use his influence as acting clerk of the House of Representatives to create a controlling coalition of Democrats and conservative border state Unionists in the House. Although the "Etheridge Conspiracy" failed, Etheridge continued his crusade against the revolutionary designs of the Lincoln administration.[29]

By the fall of 1863, little hope existed for concerted effort among Tennessee Unionists toward reestablishing a loyal state government. Indeed, there was no longer any agreement on what a loyal state government should be. One faction of loyalists maintained that such a government had to be controlled exclusively by unconditional Union men committed to emancipation. The other faction, led by prewar Whigs whose political rivalry with Democrat Andrew Johnson long antedated the war, desired a return to the *status quo ante bellum*. King Solomon himself could not have reconciled these conflicting views.

III

Despite the rift in Unionist ranks, Johnson was in good cheer in September 1863, because Burnside's capture of Knoxville in early September seemed to signify the permanent expulsion of Confederate forces from most of Tennessee. With staunchly pro-Union East Tennessee now under federal control, Johnson again thought about holding elections.[30] Lincoln, too, perceived the possibilities now open to Johnson and urged him not to lose a moment's time in reinaugurating a loyal state government. In reply, Johnson wanted assurance that he had full authority to reorganize a civil government and therefore requested specific instructions from the president "to exercise all power necessary and proper to secure to the people of Tennessee a republican form of government." Two days after Johnson requested this specific grant of authority, he received it.[31]

Because of renewed Confederate offensive operations in East Tennessee in early November, it was impossible to mobilize the support of loyal East Tennessee behind any election effort, and high hopes for rapidly returning Tennessee to the Union were smashed. But the exchange of letters between the president and his subordinate in September 1863 is important because it shows how much they thought alike on the key issues in Tennessee.

Lincoln and Johnson agreed that only unconditional Union men should have political power in Tennessee. The president emphasized that firm friends of the Union must control the new government, that the "whole struggle for Tennessee will have been profitless to both State and Nation if it so ends that Governor Johnson is put down and Governor Harris is put up. It must not be so." All but trustworthy loyal men should be excluded from the work of Reconstruction.[32]

The two men also agreed that emancipation should be a precondition for Reconstruction and that Tennessee should never be permitted to return to the Union under its old constitution. "I see that you have declared in favor of emancipation in Tennessee," Lincoln wrote to Johnson, "for which may God bless you. Get emancipation into your new State government constitution and there will be no such word as fail for your case."[33] The military governor assured the president he had "taken decided ground for emancipation—for immediate emancipation, from gradual emancipation. Now is the time for settlement of the question." And as he wrote to General Hurlbut in Memphis, "reconstruction is the time [slavery] should be left out and no longer constitute an institution established by law."[34] Thus, like the president, Johnson and his followers—many of them slaveholders—believed "the destruction of Negro Slavery in this country, is an accomplished and immutable fact, and we are willing to accept it as such."[35] Black people could never be returned to their former position and, as Johnson phrased it, "the main thing now is to what status they shall occupy."[36]

Finally, the mid-September letters demonstrate that neither Johnson nor Lincoln viewed the military governor's position as hopeless despite growing disaffection among some Unionists. Johnson would not deviate from his hard-line policy because, after all, he knew he could depend on the president and East Tennessee to sustain him. With such support, he probably calculated he needed only minimal backing in Middle and West Tennessee to reconstruct the state successfully. By relying so heavily upon East Tennessee, Johnson could be sure of the unconditional loyalty of the reorganized state government, and by 1864 this was an all-consuming goal for the military governor and his radical supporters. Traitors, said Johnson, "should take a back seat in the work of restoration. If there be but five thousand men in Tennessee, loyal to the Constitution, loyal to freedom, loyal to justice, these true and faithful men should control the work of reorganization and reformation absolutely."[37]

IV

On December 8, 1863, Lincoln issued his Proclamation of Amnesty and Reconstruction which contained the famous ten percent plan and offered amnesty to individual Southerners. Taking the amnesty oath gave a person full political and property rights, except slave ownership. The president's proclamation provoked a heated debate in Tennessee between those who considered the amnesty offer just and liberal and those who thought it unjust and illiberal. One Middle Tennessee woman commented that the amnesty oath was "creating considerable excitement. Sentiment is very much divided, even among the loyal about it."[38] Conservative Unionists took heart because Lincoln's benevolent policy, if followed, might well put them in control in Tennessee, but radicals, reluctant to extend suffrage to any but unconditional Unionists, were unhappy with Lincoln's pronouncement.

Radicals feared the amnesty plan might undermine their position in Tennessee. The *Daily Times and True Union* expressed the sentiments of many staunch Unionists in regard to the amnesty oath: "Such a process is a cheap way for treason to avoid punishment. . . . Why should loyal people needlessly place themselves in the power of men who so recently have been their deadly foes?" Rebels had "no right to demand citizenship as a recompense for oath-taking."[39] It galled radicals to see men under indictment for treason and conspiracy have the indictments withdrawn the moment they took the oath, and it also irked them that men could have confiscation proceedings discontinued merely by taking an oath.[40] "If rebels are suffered for nearly three years to do all they can to break down the Government," moaned one of Johnson's correspondents, "and then when they are conquered, come forward and take a hypocritical oath to save property, an awful doom awaits the loyal portion of the American people."[41]

What especially irritated radicals was that many people took Lincoln's oath in bad faith, with no demonstration of genuine repentance. "A number of rebels come to Nashville daily and take the oath of amnesty," wrote the *Daily Union*. "Some of them take it with 'wry faces.' The fact is, they are like the fellow that, on a wager, eat the crow. They can 'eat crow'; but d————d if they have a hankering for it!"[42] Or, as one radical put it, "No patriotism, no love of country and kind, no noble sentiment of returning loyalty" accompanied the oath-taking.[43]

Nashville radicals soon asked Johnson if he could persuade Lincoln to make the Amnesty Proclamation less favorable to rebels. In mid-May 1864, Johnson wrote Lincoln that the amnesty provisions of the December 8 proclamation will be "seriously detrimental in reorganizing the state government. . . . " All amnesty did was keep alive the rebel spirit—it reconciled no one. Johnson requested that Tennessee be excepted from the operation of the proclamation and suggested all pardons for Tennesseans be granted upon the direct application to the president by those desiring it. "The influence will be better and they will feel a much greater obligation to the Government."[44]

Lincoln did not formally exempt Tennessee from the proclamation, but even before Johnson had made his appeal, the president had allowed him to alter substantially the operation and effect of the amnesty oath in Tennessee. A month after the issuance of the proclamation, Johnson wrote to Horace Maynard about the county elections to be held in some parts of the state in March. With good reason, Johnson feared the "disloyal influence, cloaked with a citizenship extended by the President in his amnesty proclamation, would assume control of the ballot-box in the March elections." Consequently, the governor desired to subject all "who have not been loyal" to "the severest test."[45]

Shortly thereafter, he issued his own proclamation which spelled out what he meant. All who wanted to vote in March had to swear a rigid oath to support and defend the Constitution and "to ardently desire the suppression of the present rebellion against the Government of the United States, the success of its armies and the defeat of all those who oppose them." Further, they had to swear they would "hereafter heartily aid and assist all loyal people in the accomplishment of these results."[46]

Johnson's oath, because it was so much stronger, virtually denied suffrage to ex-Confederates who had taken the president's amnesty oath. Even many conservative Unionists would have to swear falsely to take it, since many of them did not honestly "ardently desire" the suppression of the rebellion. If Johnson's plan prevailed, the March elections would be totally in the hands of unconditional Union men. Conservative Unionists and ex-rebels soon made their opposition

known. Would Lincoln sustain Johnson, or would he declare his own
amnesty oath sufficient evidence of loyalty and the only qualification
necessary to enjoy suffrage?

A week after Johnson issued his proclamation, Maynard explained to Lincoln two major criticisms of the president's proclamation, its "excessive liberality to rebels" and its "placing in the same
category repentant rebels & men always loyal." The "expressions of
repugnance" by loyal men at being placed on a par with ex-rebels were
"too strong to be disregarded." To obviate this criticism, said
Maynard, the military governor had devised his own oath which was
"quite satisfactory to the Union men, but greatly to the disgust of
secesh & semi-secesh." Maynard concluded by advising the president
that he would probably be asked to intervene in the matter. "This I
hope you *will not do*."[47]

Maynard was a good prophet. On February 20, 1864, Warren
Jordan, a conservative Unionist from Cheatham County, wrote Secretary of State William Seward asking whether, in county and state
elections, the citizens of Tennessee had to "take the oath prescribed by
Governor Johnson, or will the President's oath of amnesty entitle
them to vote?" Lincoln responded personally, saying that "In County
elections you better stand by Gov. Johnson's plan. Otherwise you will
have conflict and confusion."[48] The president saw no conflict between
his oath and Johnson's since he knew the governor's purpose was "to
restore the State government and place it under the control of citizens
truly loyal to the Government of the United States." If Johnson's plan
would create such a government, then Lincoln was ready to bow to the
governor's judgment.[49]

A correspondent for the *New York Times* reported that the ballot-
ing resulted in "the triumphant election" of the unconditionally loyal
Union candidates, but in actuality the March elections were a mock-
ery. As the *Daily Union* admitted, "We might as well speak out
plainly, and confess to the world, that what was called an election . . .
at least so far as Nashville is concerned, was a serious farce." Although
federal bayonets were not in sight at the polls, small guards waited
nearby to prevent disturbances; even so, the vote was very light—
only about two thousand votes in Davidson County—and the results
were too rigged to be satisfactory since many voters were non-resident
soldiers and government employees. In other areas of the state as well,
the elections took place under military supervision and protection.[50]

The March election in Nashville illustrates two important
points. One is that after two years of federal control, the city was no

more loyal than when Buell's troops first entered it. Johnson's best efforts had come to naught. Secondly, the military governor's plan, not the president's, was the one that controlled the election. Both men were so deeply committed to the creation of an unconditional Union government that Johnson willingly subverted a presidential program, and Lincoln knowingly acquiesced. Continued intransigence by Tennesseans merely seemed to strengthen the resolve of Lincoln and Johnson to make Tennessee a thoroughly loyal state—no matter what the cost.

V

The March 1864 elections demonstrated that staunch Unionists were to be favored with special political privileges. The changing nature of two Boards of Claims established in Nashville by military authority also demonstrated that loyal Unionists were going to receive special economic consideration as well.

For at least the first year of federal occupation, grave risks from Confederate forces attended all foraging done by Union troops. Consequently, foraging parties loaded their wagons and returned to Nashville as quickly as possible, often failing to give correct forage vouchers and receipts. Now, as the occupation gained permanence, an "incessant inpouring of '*Irregular Accounts*'" flooded the various army departments. Something had to be done to aid the departments in the time-consuming work of settling these accounts, and to conciliate— as far as was proper—those who had suffered.[51]

In mid-March 1863, Rosecrans established a Board of Commissioners to investigate and report "the amount of damage sustained by citizens and inhabitants, from the occupation or destruction of their property by the forces of the United States." Two military officers and three Nashville citizens, Russell Houston, William Driver, and Horace H. Harrison, sat on the board. The choice of these three civilians was probably Johnson's because all were prominent in the unconditional Union party he was trying to build.[52]

Initially Rosecrans instructed the board not to consider the question of loyalty or disloyalty, but several weeks later, in amended instructions, he required all persons presenting claims to file an explicit statement of citizenship. Those who acknowledged themselves to be United States citizens would have their claims considered first. People flocked to the board to present claims, and by November 1, 1864, almost fifteen hundred had submitted claims totaling $2,620,367.02.[53]

The radicals did not approve of the work of the board because, they complained, many of the claimants were notoriously disloyal. The *Daily Union* declared "that the Government should proclaim the determination to receive no claim for charges from rebel sympathizers"; disloyal claimants should "feel to their dying day, the foolish criminality of their treason." The board, said William Driver, "under the mild conciliating order of General Rosecrans soon found that nearly all claimants for sums of any considerable amount were Rebels." He estimated that three-fourths of all amounts claimed belonged to disloyal people who had "done all in their power to destroy our government."[54]

This situation persisted until the fall of 1864 when General Thomas dissolved the Rosecrans board and established one of his own, composed of four military officers and Driver. His board was to "take evidence as to the loyalty of claimants"[55] and "award damages only to those of whose loyalty they are satisfied." Since Driver, who believed it was folly "to hope by mild means to kill treason," was the only board member qualified to pass on a claimant's loyalty, radicals could now breathe easier.[56] When wealthy secessionists henceforth presented claims, Driver simply marked them rebel or disloyal, "which should," he said, "forever void all claims they may have filed against the government of the United States as they have done all in their power to destroy that Government."[57]

Thus, by the fall of 1864, radicals were grim and serious in their efforts to keep ex-Confederates and conservatives subservient. Only unconditional men were to profit—politically and economically—from the reestablishment of civil government. Rewards should accrue only to those who "deserved" them. Taking an amnesty oath was not enough because past action, not promises for the future, was the proof of loyalty. Erring and deluded fellow citizens no longer merited consideration, their property and political rights were no longer guaranteed respect. Andrew Johnson's position in the fall of 1864 was a long way from the policy set forth in March 1862.

VI

The presidential election of November 1864 brought another crisis to Tennessee Unionism. Johnson's nomination for vice president made it very desirable for Tennessee to vote for the Republican ticket in the election. A sizable vote in the state would vindicate the policy pursued by both men; furthermore, the Republicans might need every electoral vote they could get to claim victory. However, the split among Tennessee Unionists made a large Lincoln-Johnson vote doubtful. In fact, there was real worry about whether they could win a free and open election. Mussey, who was in charge of recruiting black troops in Nashville, feared that "the men who own these Slaves and 'Conservative Union' men and those who have taken the Amnesty Oath will vote together and against the Administration. The result of an Election is today feared by the Union men of the State."[58]

They had good reason to be concerned. In September a "Constitutional Union Club," dedicated to the election of General McClellan, the Democratic peace candidate, was established in Nashville, and McClellan electors, including Campbell, Peyton, and Etheridge, were selected. Conservative Unionists were so confident of success that one Nashville paper, the *Daily Press*, openly favored McClellan and savagely criticized the military governor.[59]

On the other side, one radical who considered McClellanites worse than rebels suggested sending them south beyond federal lines,[60] a proposal which was too extreme for Johnson, although he was not opposed to vigorous action. On September 30 the governor issued another proclamation setting forth a new test oath for prospective voters which was even more stringent than the one that had controlled the March elections. A voter had to swear to uphold the Constitution, to "sincerely rejoice in the triumph of the armies and navies of the United States," and to "cordially oppose all armistices or negotiations for peace" with the South. The proclamation also permitted soldiers to vote without oath or registration, and they were to vote at polls opened for their convenience.[61] The formula employed in March was thus to be reused in November. The new oath would disfranchise ex-Confederates and many conservative Unionists; soldiers would again go to the polls to swell the aggregate vote and ensure that the "right" side would win.

Radicals were also thought to have employed violence in their cause. For example, on October 21 over one hundred McClellan soldiers from the hospitals, the invalid corps, and the army in the suburbs, about three hundred government employees, and about one hundred citizens held a meeting in Nashville. Without any warning, about thirty soldiers from Battery D, First Tennessee Light Artillery, "yelling like demons, with loaded weapons, and charging bayonets," burst through the doors and broke up the meeting.[62] The Tennessee troopers, who went unpunished, later claimed that no one, including Johnson, knew of their intentions to disrupt the meeting.[63] Although there is no concrete evidence that radicals planned the disruption, it is hard to believe they did not.

The combination of Johnson's oath and his terror tactics drove conservatives to appeal to the president for protection. Lincoln curtly rejected their formal protest, saying he expected to let McClellan's friends manage their side of the election in their way, and he would manage his side in his way. Upon receiving this unsatisfactory answer, Tennessee conservatives again wrote Lincoln deploring the despotic powers assumed by Johnson and the use of violence to stifle free speech and the right to assemble. Since military power overawed them and their appeals to the president were in vain, the conservatives announced the withdrawal of the McClellan ticket in Tennessee. "There will be no election for President in Tennessee in 1864," they wrote. "You and Governor Johnson may 'manage your side of it in your own way,' but it will be no *election*."[64]

Once again the president sustained Johnson, again the unconditional Union party in Tennessee won, and again the election bordered on being a farce. In Nashville the Lincoln-Johnson vote was only 1,317, and 25 McClellan supporters somehow managed to sneak in their ballots.[65] In the end, the electoral votes of Tennessee were unnecessary for Republican victory, and Congress rejected them on the grounds that the state was in rebellion and could not have held a legal election.

VII

Events in Tennessee reached a climax in the winter of 1864–65 because the governor was more eager than ever to establish a loyal government in Tennessee. As one of Johnson's contemporaries recalled, Johnson "had been elected Vice President, and his term as Military Governor was to end on or before March 3d. His ambition was to carry to Washington his own State, as a reconstructed member of the Union, and present it as a rich jewel to the nation."[66]

Johnson directed Union executive committees in the three divisions of the state to issue calls for a convention to meet in Nashville on December 19, 1864, for the express purpose of restoring civil government. Hood's invasion delayed the meeting, but following the virtual annihilation of Hood's army, the convention met on January 9, 1865.

It was attended by five hundred unconditional Unionists, many of whom were irregularly elected and some who simply came on their own responsibility. Most of the delegates represented the old Whig party and had little or no political or judicial experience. Federal soldiers—that is, Tennesseans serving in Tennessee units—comprised more than half the membership. Although this convention probably did not truly represent Unionist sentiment in the state, it adopted a constitutional amendment abolishing slavery and set up a schedule for restoring civil rule. Both the amendment and the schedule were to be submitted to the people for ratification on February 22. The convention also provided for the election of a governor and general assembly on March 4, and William G. Brownlow of East Tennessee was nominated for governor.[67]

Johnson, ecstatic over the convention's work, was particularly delighted by the adoption of the antislavery amendment.[68] But he could not have been pleased by the small number of Nashvillians who voted for it. The city ratified the amendment by a vote of only 1,349 to 4. The *Daily Times and True Union* noted it was shameful that a town of 25,000 permanent residents gave so few votes "to the cause of the Union and civil law."[69] Here was final proof that Nashville remained a disloyal city.

The state as a whole approved both the amendment and the schedule, and, in accordance with the schedule, an election in which voters chose a general assembly and elected Brownlow as governor took place on March 4. Since slightly over ten percent of the number of voters in 1860 participated in the election, Tennessee now qualified for readmission to the Union under Lincoln's ten percent plan. On April 5 Brownlow assumed office. There is, of course, a rich irony in the passing of the mantle of the governorship from Johnson to Brownlow. Throughout the antebellum era, Democrat Johnson and Whig Brownlow had convulsed East Tennessee politics with their bitter internecine strife, and the intense rivalry flourished again during Reconstruction, this time on a national stage. But the war had temporarily thrust them together, their love for the Union overwhelming their political hatred of each other. Politics—and war—do indeed make strange bedfellows.[70]

The day before Brownlow's election, Johnson resigned as brigadier general of volunteers and military governor of Tennessee to accept the vice presidency. His performance in Tennessee elicited plaudits from Secretary Stanton and General in Chief Halleck, and outwardly the new vice president had fulfilled his primary duty as military governor.[71] Tennessee now had a loyal *state government*. But, dominated by a small faction of radical Unionists, it still lacked broad support throughout the state. Johnson had not fostered a feeling of loyalty among the *people*, the majority of whom had little love for Johnson and his stringent policy toward "traitors." The new government gave the illusion of loyalty, but the governor and the president had defined loyalty so narrowly that their political action became repressive rather than inspirational. In reality, loyalty—the way Johnson and Lincoln defined it—was no more widespread in March 1865 than it had been three years before.

NOTES

1. William T. Sherman, *Memoirs of General William T. Sherman By Himself*, 1: pp. 226, 337; Howard K. Beale and Alan W. Brownsword, eds., *Diary of Gideon Welles, Secretary of the Navy under Lincoln and Johnson*, 1: p. 85.

2. *Appleton's Annual Cyclopaedia and Register of Important Events* (1862), p. 764.

3. *Ibid.*, p. 765.

4. Connally F. Trigg to AJ, 1, 7 April 1862, AJP, Presidential Papers Microfilm.

5. AJ to Stanton, 17 April 1862, and AJ to Lincoln, 5 June 1862, both in *OR*, 2, 3, pp. 457, 642–43.

6. Stanton to AJ, 7 June 1862, *ibid.*, p. 659; P.H. Watson to AJ, 4 August 1862, *ibid.*, 2, 4, pp. 335–36.

7. AJ to Secretary of War, 9 August 1862, and AJ to Gen. L. Thomas, 9 August 1862, both in *ibid.*, 2, 4, p. 362.

8. Robert H. White, ed., *Messages of the Governors of Tennessee*, 5: p. 375; Thomas B. Alexander, *Political Reconstruction in Tennessee*, p. 25; Joseph Fowler to AJ, 26 February 1862, AJP.

9. *Nashville Daily Union*, 20 May 1862.

10. *Ibid.*, 21 May 1862.

11. *Nashville Daily Union*, 24 May 1862; [?] to AJ, October 1862, and parole of honor by Foster, 3 November 1862, both in AJP; *Nashville Dispatch*, 22 November 1862.

12. Herschel Gower and Jack Allen, eds., *Pen and Sword*, p. 625.

13. Roy P. Basler, ed., *The Collected Works of Abraham Lincoln*, 5: pp. 302–3.

14. *Ibid.*, pp. 470–71.

15. *Appleton's Annual Cyclopaedia* (1862), p. 769; James Welch Patton, *Unionism and Reconstruction in Tennessee, 1860–1869*, pp. 37–38. Lincoln also badly wanted elections in North Carolina, Louisiana, and Arkansas during the fall of 1862; see Herman Belz, *Reconstructing the Union*, p. 105.

16. W.H. Sidell to Col. J.B. Fry, 1 August 1862, *OR*, 1, 16, 2, pp. 242–43; AJ to Gen. J.T. Boyle, 4 August 1862, and AJ to Thomas, 16 August 1862, both in AJP.

17. Allen Johnson, Dumas Malone, and Harris E. Starr, eds., *Dictionary of*

American Biography, 3: p. 466; Joshua W. Caldwell, *Sketches of the Bench and Bar of Tennessee*, pp. 190–98.

18. Caldwell, *Sketches*, pp. 241–45; Alexander, *Political Reconstruction*, pp. 87, 158.

19. *Nashville Daily Union*, 25 January 1863.

20. Letter of the three-man committee of the Nashville Union Club, 31 January 1863, AJP.

21. *Nashville Daily Union*, 23 April 1863.

22. *Ibid*.

23. Letters from "C.L.B.," August 1863, in the *New York Times*, 13, 21 August 1863.

24. *Nashville Daily Press and Times*, 11 August 1863; *Nashville Daily Union*, 29 December 1863.

25. *Nashville Daily Union*, 23 April 1863; letter from "C.L.B.," August 1863, in the *New York Times*, 13 August 1863.

26. David Millspaugh Diary, 29, 31 August 1863, David Millspaugh Papers, MHC.

27. *Nashville Dispatch*, 22 May 1863.

28. Quoted in James G. Randall, *Lincoln the President*, 2: p. 175.

29. Stanley J. Folmsbee, Robert E. Corlew, and Enoch L. Mitchell, *History of Tennessee*, 2: pp. 79–80; Herman Belz, "The Etheridge Conspiracy of 1863."

30. Charles A. Dana, *Recollections of the Civil War, with the Leaders at Washington and in the Field in the Sixties*, p. 106.

31. Lincoln to AJ, 11 September 1863, and AJ to Lincoln, 17 September 1863, both in *OR*, 3, 3, pp. 789, 819; Basler, ed., *Works of Lincoln*, 6: p. 469.

32. Lincoln to AJ, 11 September 1863, *OR*, 3, 3, p. 789.

33. *Ibid*.

34. AJ to Lincoln, 17 September 1863, *ibid*., p. 819; AJ to Hurlbut, 3 October 1863, AJP.

35. Statement submitted to Stanton by John W. Bowen and others, 26 September 1863, RG 94, The Negro in the Military Service of the United States, #1607–09. Also see the letter from "C.L.B.," August 1863, in the *New York Times*, 13 August 1863.

36. AJ to Hurlbut, 3 October 1863, AJP.

37. Speech given by AJ in Nashville, mid-June 1864, reported in the *New York Times*, 16 June 1864.

38. Sarah Ridley Trimble, ed., "Behind the Lines in Middle Tennessee, 1863–1865," p. 67. Also see the *Nashville Daily Union*, 29 December 1863.

39. *Nashville Daily Times and True Union*, 26 May 1864.

40. *Ibid*., 5, 9, 12 May, 9 July 1864; *Nashville Daily Union*, 23 February 1864.

41. William A. Lorrells to AJ, 23 June 1864, AJP.

42. *Nashville Daily Union*, 2 March 1864.

43. *Ibid*., 10 January 1864.

44. S.C. Mercer to AJ, 20 February 1864, and AJ to Lincoln, 17 May 1864, both in AJP.

45. AJ to Horace Maynard, 14 January 1864, AJP; letter from a Nashville correspondent, 3 March 1864, in the *New York Times*, 13 March 1864.

46. *Nashville Daily Times and True Union*, 20 February 1864.

47. Basler, ed., *Works of Lincoln*, 7: pp. 183–84.

48. Warren Jordan to Seward, 20 February 1864, and Lincoln to Jordan, 21 February 1864, both in AJP.

49. Basler, ed., *Works of Lincoln,* 7: p. 209.

50. *New York Times,* 13 March 1864; *Nashville Daily Union,* 8 March 1864; *Nashville Dispatch,* 6 March 1864; E.H. East to AJ, 8 March 1864, and A.C. Gillem to AJ, 11 March 1864 (two letters). All in AJP.

51. RG 92, Report of the Nashville Board of Claims.

52. *Ibid.;* Henry Stone to Board of Examiners, 12 March 1863, RG 393, Entry 908.

53. RG 92, Journal of the Driver Board; letter to Board of Claims, 6 April 1863, RG 393, Entry 908; RG 92, Report of the Nashville Board of Claims.

54. *Nashville Daily Union,* 26 July 1863; RG 92, Report of the Nashville Board of Claims.

55. RG 92, Report of the Board of Claims.

56. *Nashville Dispatch,* 24 May 1862.

57. RG 92, Report of the Nashville Board of Claims.

58. See the essay by Mussey in RG 393, Entry 1142. Though undated, this was apparently written in August 1864.

59. *Nashville Daily Press and Times,* 21 September, 11, 12 October 1864.

60. *Ibid.,* 5 November 1864.

61. Basler, ed., *Works of Lincoln,* 8: pp. 65–68.

62. *Nashville Daily Press and Times,* 24 October 1864.

63. *Ibid.,* 26 October 1864.

64. Basler, ed., *Works of Lincoln,* 8: pp. 58–65.

65. White, *Messages,* 5: p. 386.

66. Oliver P. Temple, *Notable Men of Tennessee From 1833 to 1875, Their Times and Their Contemporaries,* p. 411.

67. *Ibid.,* p. 409; Alexander, *Political Reconstruction,* pp. 16–18, 26; Stanley J. Folmsbee, Robert E. Corlew, and Enoch L. Mitchell, *Tennessee, A Short History,* p. 346.

68. AJ to Lincoln, 13 January 1865, *OR,* 3, 4, p. 1050.

69. *Nashville Dispatch,* 23 February 1865; *Nashville Daily Times and True Union,* 28 February 1865.

70. Folmsbee, Corlew, and Mitchell, *A Short History,* p. 346; Ralph W. Haskins, "Internecine Strife in Tennessee."

71. AJ to Stanton, 3 March 1865, and Stanton to AJ, 3 March 1865, both in AJP; Halleck to Francis Lieber, 18 April 1865, Francis Lieber Papers, The Huntington Library. Between AJ's resignation and Brownlow's inauguration, Edward H. East, the secretary of state, performed the duties of the governor's office; see Patton, *Unionism and Reconstruction,* p. 84.

Chapter 6

THE ARMY AND
THE BLACK MAN

Slavery, the one Tennessee institution permanently affected by military occupation, *officially* ended in the state on March 4, 1865, when the "people" adopted a constitutional amendment abolishing it. In reality, slavery had already been abolished by the activities of the United States Army because wherever the army went in Tennessee, slavery simply disintegrated. By the fall of 1863, a growing number of Tennesseans recognized slavery's demise, despite the state's exemption from the Emancipation Proclamation.

Although the institution died during the war, the overall attitude and intellectual outlook which supported slavery did not change. The army altered the institution, the external shell; but racism, the inner core, remained untouched. Only a small minority in Nashville, mostly people of Northern birth, took abolition seriously and tried to overcome their racial fears and prejudices.

I

Slaves came to Nashville with the first settlers, and as agricultural operations expanded in the area, the number of slaves increased accordingly. By 1860 there were 14,790 slaves and 1,209 free blacks in a total population of 57,055 in Davidson County. The number of slaveholders in the county was 2,153 and most of them owned fewer than 100 acres and fewer than 5 slaves each. In the years immediately preceding the war, Davidson County slaveowners were primarily farmers, not planters, and they regarded their slaves as "handy men" rather than producers of staples.[1]

In 1860 slightly more than seven hundred free blacks—and probably that many more nominal slaves—lived in Nashville. While some of these men and women had accumulated considerable wealth, their position was not pleasant because the trend in Tennessee was for whites to treat free blacks as if they might become slaves once again. Some members of the legislature of 1859–60 made an intensive effort to banish free blacks from the state, and one scholar has conjectured that these people would have been forced to leave the state or return to slavery had the war not intervened.[2]

When the federal army arrived in Middle Tennessee, slave reaction was initially mixed. Some slaves remained remarkably loyal to their masters, but others immediately asserted their freedom by deserting their owners and seeking, as one slave woman phrased it, "a new home and a new destiny with strangers."[3] As the union occupation became more firmly established, the number of fugitives who sought protection behind Union lines grew while those who remained on nearby farms and plantations became increasingly insolent and disobedient, at least in the eyes of their white masters. Middle Tennessee slaveowners soon came to fully expect that their slaves would just pick up and leave.[4]

However, being within federal lines did not guarantee security for either slaves or free blacks because masters were not without recourse in attempting to recover their "property." Recapturing slaves within the city and spiriting them away to the Deep South became a profitable venture. Several members of the city police, as well as the sheriff of Davidson County, engaged in this lucrative business. Slaveowners solicited the aid of the night police or the sheriff in catching their fugitive slaves; the police would arrest the blacks and turn them over to the supposed owner for a sizable reward.[5] So infamous was the practice that the provost marshal warned the city marshal that if any "of the policemen of Nashville are again caught engaged in arresting, as fugitives, any slaves of *rebel* masters, I will take the case into my own hands, and give them a term in the city prison."[6]

Slaveowners could also appeal to military officers for the recovery of fugitives. A brigadier general stationed in Nashville in the fall of 1862 recalled that slaveowners gave him no rest. Every master who called on him, said the general, was "a prodigy of patriotism and devotion to the Union. He wants his negro, as he says, not for his value, but to gratify a longing mother, who ardently desires that her son shall return to her and to slavery. The kind-hearted owner only wishes to oblige her."[7]

Some of the military men in the vicinity often willingly helped slaveowners and displayed little sympathy for black people. Within the first ten days of occupation, Buell helped several masters retrieve their escaped slaves, and in mid-March he ordered General Mitchel to allow no more fugitives to enter or remain within his lines. Rosecrans believed officers could not harbor slaves of loyal masters except under extreme circumstances, and allowed masters to recover their slaves.[8] Even after Johnson made abolition a war aim in Tennessee, Major General Lovell H. Rousseau, following the expressed desire of General Thomas,[9] decreed that military authorities should have as little to do with slaves as possible, "it being considered best to allow masters and slaves to settle their own affairs without military interference." Rousseau, who commanded the Districts of Nashville and of Tennessee from November 1863 to November 1865, disliked children and elderly black men and women who came to Nashville where they became a charge to the government, "consuming rations of the soldiers, whilst they are utterly useless to the authorities."[10] Hence, when slaveowners came to Nashville seeking fugitives, Rousseau often gave direct written orders to have the escaped slaves returned.[11]

The policy of returning fugitives was contrary to the Lieber Code which stated that if a slave held by the enemy is "captured by or comes as a fugitive under the protection of the military forces of the United States, such person is immediately entitled to the rights and privileges of a freeman." To return such a person "into slavery would amount to enslaving a free person, and neither the United States nor any officer under their authority can enslave any human being."[12]

Rousseau's behavior appalled men of antislavery sentiments. Mussey, the New England abolitionist engaged in organizing black troops in Nashville, was highly critical of the general. And a two-man Senate committee appointed to investigate the condition of black refugees in the Department of the Cumberland concluded that Rousseau was "wholly unfit for his present command, or for any command where the care and safety of colored refugees can, by possibility, become the subject of his official action."[13]

If being within federal lines did not guarantee freedom for black men and women, even less did it ensure fair treatment. Blacks were especially mistreated during the first eighteen months of Union rule, when Confederate forces threatened the city most seriously and before Johnson's policy toward slavery in Tennessee had been clarified. The most pressing need of the occupation forces was the construction of defensive works around the perimeter of the city, an enterprise which required large amounts of labor. Under the guise of military necessity, army officials often ruthlessly impressed blacks to work on the fortifications.

The first impressment took place in August 1862, when Buell's chief of staff directed the Nashville post commander "to call in regular form upon slave owners for hands to work, and put as many on the works as can be employed." The call went out for one thousand slaves, with each slaveholder in Davidson County being required to furnish a specified number. The master had to provide his impressed slaves with daily subsistence, axes, and spades, while the length of service and the manner and terms of payment were to be determined at the pleasure of the government.[14]

A second impressment in October 1862 was more general in nature. Nashville's commanding officer ordered the city patrols to "impress into service every Negro you can find in the Streets of this City who can not prove that he is owned by any person loyal to the government of the United States and residing in and about the City." Such blacks were to be turned over to Buell's chief engineer, Captain James St. Clair Morton, for work on the fortifications. Nothing was said about length of service or payment of wages; nor was any special protection afforded the numerous free blacks residing in the city. Military patrols simply began arresting as many black men as they could.[15]

A third major impressment took place in August and September of 1863 when Union authorities needed twenty-five hundred men to work on the Nashville and Northwestern Railroad, which was being built under Johnson's direction. By now the military had developed sophisticated impressment techniques. For instance, the patrols would wait until Sunday morning and then raid the crowded black churches. And the troopers did not hesitate to use violence and threats. During one church raid, they shot and killed a black man and threatened others with a similar fate if they tried to escape.[16]

The inhumane treatment the forced laborers received from the army only compounded the brutality of their impressment. Fair treatment, at a minimum, would have included reasonable living conditions and regular wages. In theory the blacks received both, but in practice they got neither. Between August 1862 and April 1863, the amount due blacks for work on the fortifications was $85,858.50, but of this sum only $13,648.00 was paid. Furthermore, although the army employed fewer than three thousand black men during this time, between six hundred and eight hundred of them died—an extraordinary mortality rate caused by the inadequate shelter and insufficient diet provided by the army. The only kindness the army seems to have exhibited was to provide free coffins for those who died during their ordeal.[17]

The army did have legitimate problems in trying to pay impressed laborers. Disbursing officers did not know whether to pay the blacks or their masters. If the blacks were slaves of loyal Tennesseans, the pay supposedly went to the master; if slaves of disloyal persons, then the blacks were to receive the money themselves. But it was often impossible to determine whether the blacks belonged to loyal or disloyal owners. Also, there was no way for relatives or families to draw the pay the government owed deceased blacks. As one disbursing officer said, if "a wife comes with a certificate issued to her deceased husband for labor, we have to refuse payment, for the reason there is no one authorized to sign his name to the receipt roll."[18]

No doubt the blacks laboring upon the fortifications knew little about these impediments. What they did know was that they were not being well cared for and they were not being paid. The Senate committee investigating refugee conditions in Tennessee found blacks demoralized by "the extraordinary delays in paying the wages of the labor of the refugees, where the wages are finally paid, and the criminal neglect or refusal to pay at all, as often occurs when the labor has been performed on the defences [*sic*] of Nashville. . . . "[19]

Surely the laborers had good reason to be demoralized: it seemed that they had fled their old masters only to be reenslaved by new ones, the Union army officers. Yet there was a difference. Under the new masters the blacks were, at least in theory, free, and the blacks recognized the difference despite their deprivations and degradation. As one bewildered white Middle Tennessean put it, the "negroes will run to [the Yankees] from good homes of kind masters & bear more oppression than they ever knew before, get *no pay* & yet love the Yankee for his meanness."[20] And Captain Morton reported that the "negroes have as a general rule been faithful and diligent—far more so than could reasonably have been expected, considering the circumstances of exposure and privation of proper clothing, blankets, etc. under which they were at first employed." Morton also noted that once, when Nashville was in imminent danger of attack, the blacks "cheerfully and zealously turned out, after a hard day's labor, and labored all night, or nearly so, strengthening the defenses." The weary workers even volunteered to maintain part of the Union lines with axes and other tools if the rebels attacked.[21]

Throughout the summer of 1863, the army blatantly mistreated and exploited black people in the Rock City, and yet blacks still retained a large amount of spirit and enthusiasm for the Union cause. It was a foolhardy policy which did not take advantage of this élan. And in the fall of that year, as the new season crowned the wooded hills surrounding Nashville with tinges of red and gold, the winds of change blew through the city's streets.

II

The relationship between the army and blacks in the city underwent a fundamental transformation in the fall of 1863 for two reasons. First, Nashville had become a much more secure stronghold, surrounded by imposing fortifications and bristling with cannons pointed in all directions. With the defenses nearing completion and the Army of Tennessee driven away from the area, the need for labor slackened, although it by no means disappeared. More importantly, the government had decided to recruit black troops in the Department of the Cumberland, a decision which was merely one more step in the change in national policy from exploiting blacks as laborers to employing them as troops. This change in policy, begun in 1862 by enterprising Union commanders who organized black troops without regard to War Department orders or administration policy, gained considerable momentum after the Emancipation Proclamation signaled Lincoln's willingness to accept black soldiers.[22]

In March 1863, the War Department dispatched Adjutant General Lorenzo Thomas to the Mississippi Valley to raise as many black regiments as possible. The systematic recruitment of black soldiers along the Mississippi, initiated by Thomas, soon expanded into the interior of Tennessee, reaching the banks of the Cumberland when Major George L. Stearns arrived in Nashville in September 1863.

Stearns, a wealthy Boston merchant who had long been an advocate of emancipation, was on intimate terms with leading Massachusetts abolitionist-politicians such as Governor John Andrew and Senator Charles Sumner. Stearns had been a strong supporter of John Brown and had given him generous financial aid throughout the late 1850s, including money for the abortive Harper's Ferry raid. During the secession crisis, Stearns opposed any compromise with the South, and following the Emancipation Proclamation, he enlisted black troops for Massachusetts regiments. He soon received an adjutant general's commission with the rank of major and was given the authority to recruit blacks anywhere in the country. In mid-August 1863, Stanton ordered this enthusiastic and energetic recruiter to Middle Tennessee to organize the large number of blacks congregated in the rear of Rosecrans' army, an assignment which greatly pleased Stearns and his antislavery friends.[23] "I am most happy to go," he wrote. "I have determined either to burn slavery out, or be burnt by it myself. . . . [T]his war [is] a *civilizer*, not a *barbarism*. The use of the musket [is] the first step in the education of the black man."[24]

Shortly after Stearns began operations in Nashville, Mussey, a thirty-year-old regular army officer and ex-Dartmouth College student, was detailed to duty as mustering officer for black troops and was directed to cooperate with Major Stearns in the organization of black regiments. When Stearns resigned in January 1864, Mussey assumed command of the work of organizing black troops in the Nashville vicinity.[25] Like Stearns, Mussey had opposed all compromise with the South during the secession crisis. He cursed mightily about a rumored withdrawal from Fort Sumter, and actually looked forward to war because he believed it would inevitably be fought over slavery.[26] "If we would conquer in this war," he wrote in midsummer 1862, "we must value the Union as everything and Slavery as nothing. We must abandon the Institution to its fate. . . . Oh this war— fraught with so much suffering and sorrow—I can rejoice in it—for it is a war for Freedom and Human Rights."[27]

Mussey was particularly eager to help organize black soldiers, a task which he viewed as the "sacred work of raising a fallen Race."[28] Only by making soldiers of black men, he thought, could slavery be destroyed and blacks be elevated to the position of citizens.[29] In the spring of 1863, he wrote that he was willing to risk his reputation with a black regiment, and from the fall of that year until the end of the war, Mussey commanded the 100th United States Colored Infantry (U.S.C.I.), which contained the first black men openly recruited in Kentucky.[30]

In organizing black troops in the Department of the Cumberland, Stearns and Mussey had to surmount several obstacles. Some military men, especially Sherman, opposed raising black troops, or at least viewed it merely as a more systematic way to exploit black labor than earlier impressments had been. Sherman had been consistently pro-Southern and pro-slavery since the 1830s, and although he deplored secession, he had no quarrel with the South's peculiar institution and hoped the fratricidal conflict would remain a white man's war. Before undertaking his march to the sea, he bluntly stated that he cared "not a straw for niggers." "I have the question put to me often," he said, "Is not a negro as good as a white man to stop a bullet? Yes; and a sand-bag is better. . . ."[31] Sherman believed that almost all troops should be white and that blacks best served the army as teamsters, pioneers, and servants. He candidly confessed his preference for three hundred blacks armed with tools to a thousand armed with rifles.[32] In sum, Sherman was unsympathetic to the idea that, as Mussey had phrased it, "the Negro is to be made a man by first being made a soldier. . . .[33]

Stearns and Mussey encountered opposition not only from some high ranking military personnel, but also from some Middle Tennessee civilians. Although the organization of black regiments began shortly after radical Unionists started advocating emancipation in Tennessee, many Unionists who generally followed Johnson's leadership doubted the propriety of freeing the slaves and using them as troops. To overcome this opposition, Stearns, who realized "public opinion will change slowly or rapidly as we drive on the work," undertook a vigorous public relations campaign. He made personal appeals, organized public meetings, submitted newspaper articles on the subject, and employed two agents full-time to further influence public opinion.[34]

By late fall 1863, both Mussey and Stearns were optimistic. Mussey wrote to a close friend that all Union men of the state, whether slaveholders or not, supported their work. "The people—generally —feel the insecurity of slave property," he said, "and are submitting to their fate gracefully."[35] Stearns believed the leading slaveholding Union men of Tennessee now clearly saw "that their political and social existence *here* depends on the abolition of slavery and the control of the state by Union men. Therefore they have entered most heartily into my plans for the organization of colored regiments and are daily in consultation with me."[36]

However, in gaining additional support among Tennessee Unionists, Stearns and Mussey had encountered opposition from Johnson, who was potentially the most formidable barrier to the successful completion of their task. When Stearns first arrived in Nashville, he immediately visited Johnson and found that the military governor was "well disposed, understands the subject, and will co-operate and advise me." But several days later, Stearns wrote that

Johnson was afraid of him and opposed his enterprise. The Bostonian dispatched a note to Stanton saying that if he took all the able-bodied men willing to enlist, he could get large numbers, but that Johnson objected to his work.[37]

Johnson opposed Stearns for two reasons. Although the governor did not oppose the formation of black regiments, he preferred to use the blacks primarily as laborers and only secondarily as soldiers. "We need more laborers now," he explained to Lincoln and Stanton, "than can be obtained for the prosecution of works that are indispensable to sustain the rear of General Rosecrans' army." Yet "Major Stearns proposes to organize and place them in camp, where they, in fact, remain idle. This will to a very great extent impede the progress of the works and diminish the number of hands employed. All the negroes will quit work when they can go into camp and do nothing."[38]

Here, then, was a major disagreement between Stearns and Johnson. The former wanted black troops used as soldiers, to share labor and combat assignments equally with white troops, while the latter wanted black soldiers to serve as laborers, thus freeing more whites for combat duty. Stearns wanted to organize black men because they were men and entitled to full equality, including military service; Johnson wanted to do it because it was an expedient thing to do to help the army.

Just as important, Johnson viewed Stearns as a challenge to his political authority in Tennessee. The question of emancipation and the use of black soldiers had both military *and* political implications. Because Johnson believed he was verging upon a reorganization of the state in the fall of 1863, it was important for the black troop problem to be handled with extreme care. Stearns and Mussey, with their crusading zeal, had taken "some improper and injurious steps" which Johnson feared would hamper the restoration of civil government by alienating loyal Tennesseans.[39]

For example, Johnson did not want persons from other states to become officers in black regiments when he could "find more men in Tennessee ready and willing to command than we can raise regiments to command in Tennessee." It would have a much better influence upon the public mind, thought Johnson, if Tennesseans handled the whole matter. Thus, Johnson resented the interlopers and demanded complete personal control over the raising and use of black troops. As he told Stanton and Lincoln, "I must be frank in stating my opinion that Major Stearns' mission, with his notions, will give us no aid in organizing negro regiments in Tennessee."[40]

As in so many other disputes involving Johnson, the Lincoln administration supported the military governor. When Stanton received the first inkling of difficulty between Stearns and Johnson, he telegraphed the major not to act contrary to Johnson's wishes in regard to enlistments without prior approval from the War Department. If he could not work with the governor, then he should leave Nashville and proceed to Cairo, Illinois, to await orders. The secretary of war also assured Johnson that Stearns was his subordinate, "bound to follow your directions, and may be relieved by you whenever his action is deemed by you prejudicial." The War Department relied totally upon Johnson's judgment in matters relating to *all* the people of Tennessee, white or black, bond or free.[41]

Ironically, having been granted supreme authority over the recruitment of black regiments, Johnson soon relinquished to Stearns nearly full control over the process. Exactly why he did this is not clear, but evidently Stearns employed the same persuasiveness on Johnson that he used on other Tennessee Unionists to convert them to his cause. Stearns told Stanton that he never quarreled, "having a much better mode of obtaining what I want." Within a month after their disagreement over the use of black troops, Stearns reported that "Governor Johnson, as soon as he understood me, came heartily into my plans. . . ."[42] Johnson had placed Stearns' affairs on a firm basis which gave the latter virtual control of the project, and Stearns described the governor as "a very pleasant and desirable co-worker, not caring to assume authority for its sake, and having enough business on his hands without interfering with mine."[43]

Apparently Johnson, with his political and military authority no longer threatened by the Boston merchant-turned-soldier, could afford to be magnanimous; and Stearns, fully aware he could not successfully contest Johnson's power, made an honest effort to work with, rather than against, the military governor. The result was an amiable compromise. For instance, when Stearns organized his first six hundred black soldiers, he requested orders for their deployment from the Engineers Corps. The commander of the corps forwarded the request to Johnson who ordered them to work on the rebuilding of the Northwestern Railroad which traversed guerrilla-infested country and where, as Johnson noted, they would have to work *and* fight.[44]

When Stearns resigned and returned East, the same cordial working relationship between Stearns and Johnson continued between Mussey and Johnson. Mussey got along so well with Johnson that he served as his private secretary from Lincoln's assassination until November 1865, when he and the new president split over the conduct of Reconstruction. When Stearns visited Nashville in early 1864, he found that Mussey was "devoted to his work and so far as I can see makes my place good."[45]

The crucial turning point in the relationship between the army and blacks in Nashville had been passed. When Johnson delegated authority over the recruitment of black regiments to Stearns and then Mussey, it meant freedmen's affairs would be in the hands of men motivated by a sincere concern for black people, rather than men solely interested in exploiting black labor.

III

Lincoln established the general guidelines for recruiting blacks in Middle Tennessee. All blacks who enlisted would be free when their terms of service expired; the slave of a loyal citizen could be enlisted with his master's consent; either Johnson or Rosecrans could order enlistments by conscription or the voluntary enlistment of slaves of loyal citizens without the consent of the masters; owners who lost slaves in this manner were eligible for compensation "not to exceed the sum authorized by law as bounties for volunteer service."[46] Stearns, after getting Johnson's approval, issued specific instructions for recruitment in the Department of the Cumberland which followed the president's dictates.[47] In one respect these instructions proved inadequate: the bounty, which did not compensate for the loss of a slave, enticed few loyal masters to allow the enlistment of their slaves. Johnson soon asked Lincoln for authority to offer loyal slaveowners an additonal $300 bounty, and Lincoln quickly approved.[48]

With enlistment procedures clarified, the next step was the procurement of officers. Since only white men could become commissioned officers in black regiments, care needed to be exercised in the selection of officers. Many white soldiers who otherwise cared not a whit for black people realized that a commission in a black regiment offered an opportunity for rapid advancement. Even Halleck advised his young friends in the army to enter black units because the "attention of the government & of the country is strongly drawn upon these troops and any officer who fights well with them will have rapid promotion—more rapid, I think, than if fighting with white troops, for the reason that he will be more prominently noticed."[49] Stearns and Mussey, however, opposed commissioning white officers who sought only personal glory and higher rank and pay. They demanded that white officers be motivated by a genuine desire to uplift the black race.[50]

Consequently, Stearns established an examining board in Nashville to weed out men who were not dedicated to the ideas that black troops deserved to be considered equally with white troops and that soldiering was an irrevocable step toward black citizenship. Despite this precaution, some white officers in black regiments turned out badly; but others were excellent selections fully in accord with the programs of Mussey and Stearns with respect to the future of the freedmen. One such individual was Thomas J. Morgan, who spent five rather anxious hours before the board.[51]

When Confederate batteries fired on Fort Sumter, Morgan was a twenty-one year old senior at Franklin College in Indiana. He served as a private in the Seventh Indiana Volunteer Infantry for three months and then reenlisted as a first lieutenant in the Seventieth Indiana and saw service in Kentucky and Tennessee. With "the strong conviction that the negro was a man worthy of freedom, and possessed of all the essential qualities of a good soldier," he "early advocated the organization of colored regiments,—not for fatigue or garrison duty, but for field service."[52]

After the board passed Morgan, Stearns assigned him to temporary duty in camp in Nashville, and then on November 1, 1863, ordered him to Gallatin, Tennessee, to organize the Fourteenth U.S.C.I. A careful examination of the recruits there convinced him "that these men, though black in skin, had men's hearts, and only needed right handling to develop into magnificent soldiers. Among them were the same varieties of physique, temperament, mental and moral endowments and experiences as would be found among the same number of white men." The "importance of giving colored troops a fair field and full opportunity to show of what mettle they were made" so strongly impressed him that he "lost no chance of insisting upon our *right* to be ordered into the field."[53]

Morgan and Mussey both deplored the excessive camp duty their soldiers received, and during the summer of 1864, they severely criticized General Thomas' refusal to give black troops a larger share of combat duties. Both men believed the ultimate status of the black man was to be determined by his conduct on the battlefield, not in camp and garrison duty. The commanding general became so distressed at Mussey's attacks on his deployment of troops that he ordered Mussey arrested until he made a retraction and apology, or until he was court-martialed. Mussey quickly apologized and was returned to duty. Morgan, too, ran afoul of Thomas, who threatened the Hoosier with discharge from the service if he did not restrain his criticisms.[54]

"Dusky Lincolnites" responded enthusiastically to the chance to become soldiers under officers like Morgan and Mussey. Black regiments filled up so rapidly throughout Tennessee that a year after recruiting operations had begun, Mussey advised that no more regiments should be formed in the state. Recruiting could continue to fill existing regiments, he said, but too few black men remained to warrant the formation of new ones. Ten black regiments had been wholly or partially filled in the Nashville vicinity, including eight of infantry, one of light artillery, and one of heavy artillery. Many other regiments, of course, had been formed in other sections of the state.[55]

Black troops, despite the best efforts of their officers, continued to endure a number of inequities. They were paid less than white troops, were usually ignored on social occasions, and invariably performed a disproportionate amount of fatigue and garrison duty. Yet because of the influence of men like Stearns, Mussey, and Morgan, their situation had improved markedly from the earlier period of forced impressment and exploitation.[56]

Nothing demonstrated this more clearly than the events prior to and during the Battle of Nashville. When Confederate forces threatened the city in December 1864, the army treated blacks very differently from the way they had been treated during the crisis days of 1862–63. In the new emergency, the Nashville post commander, reflecting the new emphasis on equality, ordered the provost marshal to impress up to a thousand "loafing or unemployed negroes *or white men* [emphasis added]" and put them to work on the fortifications.[57] More significantly, blacks not only served as laborers, but also took their places in the front ranks. Eight black regiments, formed into two brigades and incorporated into the Provisional Detachment commanded by Major General James B. Steedman, participated in the battle. The black regiments engaged in some of the most severe fighting: 630 were killed, wounded, and missing out of the Union total of 3,057.[58]

Mussey and Morgan, naturally, were jubilant that white soldiers had admitted blacks into "the Fraternity of fellow soldiers."[59] But they were not the only people impressed with the blacks' courageous behavior. General Steedman, a lifelong Democrat, reported he "was unable to discover that *color* made any difference in the fighting of my

troops. All, white and black, nobly did their duty as soldiers. . . ."[60]
The Union commander in Nashville, General Thomas, had once re-
marked that he thought blacks might fight behind breastworks, but
not out in the open. Now, as he rode over the battlefield, seeing the
intermingled white and black bodies strewn over the enemy's earth-
works, he turned to his staff and said, "Gentlemen, the question is
settled; negroes will fight."[61]

For idealists and humanitarians like Stearns, Mussey, and Morgan, who increasingly controlled freedmen's affairs in Tennessee after
the fall of 1863, it was essential that black men fight, bleed, and die.
They believed blacks earned the right to equal treatment forever once
they fought in defense of the Union. As Stearns said, when you put
weapons in the hands of black men "you at once increase their self
respect and give them confidence in their abilities to support themselves and their families. . . . With one hundred thousand Colored
men taught the use of the musket it will not be possible to re-enslave
them." And as Morgan wrote, "The manly qualities of the negro soldiers evinced in camp, on the march and in battle, won for them
golden opinions and made their freedom a necessity, and their citizenship a certainty."[62]

IV

With every minie ball fired in anger, with every bayonet thrust, with
every wound received or given, black soldiers strengthened their
claim to equal citizenship. While the war progressed, the army in and
around Nashville made efforts to facilitate the transition from slavery
to freedom and to prepare black people for postwar citizenship. The
army provided relief for black refugees, initiated educational programs for blacks, and tried to institute a system of contract labor.
Thus, many of the responsibilities assigned to the postwar Bureau of
Refugees, Freedmen, and Abandoned Lands (Freedmen's Bureau) actually began under army auspices during the war, thereby insuring an
essential continuity between the army's wartime and postwar activities on behalf of the black race.

By the summer and fall of 1863, the hordes of black refugees who
crowded into Nashville lived amidst indescribable filth, squalor, and
deprivation. The *Daily Times* feared many blacks would starve or
freeze to death during the winter and the city agent of the Pest House,
Spencer Chandler, worried about smallpox ravaging the black popula-

tion. Joseph G. McKee and M. M. Brown, agents for a northern benevolent society, expressed similar concerns and reported that it was impossible for most blacks in the city to find remunerative employment, leaving them with but two choices: either depend on public charity or resort to crime as a means of subsistence.[63]

The *Daily Times,* Chandler, and Brown and McKee all agreed that the military authorities had to intervene to relieve the suffering, and they urged that a contraband camp be established at some healthful locality outside the city.[64] When the army did not respond immediately, reliance had to be placed upon private charity. In December 1863, concerned white people held a meeting to organize a society for the relief of freedmen, and northern benevolent societies, such as the Pennsylvania Freedmen's Aid Association, the Western Freedmen's Aid Society, and the American Missionary Association, provided as much aid as they could.[65] But by late winter, it was obvious that these private resources alone were inadequate, and on February 4, 1864, Adjutant General Thomas ordered the creation of a contraband camp in the Nashville vicinity. The Quartermaster's Department and other staff departments were to issue all materials and supplies "necessary for the wants of these people on the requisition of the officer in charge of the camp." Thomas appointed Captain Ralph Hunt of the First Regiment of Kentucky Volunteers to command the camp.[66]

Initially the camp did not prosper. The two-man Senate committee investigating the condition of freedmen in Tennessee concluded that "this colored refugee camp has been, and is, grossly neglected in all things necessary to the reasonable care and comfort of its inmates." The two senators had "never witnessed an aggregate of wretchedness and misery equal to that we were here called to look upon." The main problem was Captain Hunt, a grafter who kept a store in Nashville where he sold many of the supplies he requisitioned for the contraband camp. Hunt's immediate successors were little better and in many cases "used their authority not only not to ameliorate their condition, but to add to their sufferings. . . ."[67] Evidently blacks purposefully began to avoid the camp because in early April, the Provost Guard began forcing them into it.[68]

Thus, during much of the war, the army in Nashville failed to provide adequate relief for suffering black refugees. The experiment in easing their physical miseries floundered primarily because unsympathetic men conducted it. After a year of effort and considerable government and private aid, the majority of black people spent the last winter of the war "half-clad, half-fed, and half-housed," and in consequence suffered a high mortality rate.[69]

Despite the wretchedness of the Nashville camp and other similar camps the Senate committee visited in Kentucky, Tennessee, and Alabama, the committee did not regard the concept of government aid to refugee blacks as a total failure. "The policy, or rather purpose, of the government in attempting to provide for the wants and ameliorate the condition of these unfortunate refugees," it said, "is a wise and philanthropic one, growing out of individual necessities on the one hand, and the highest possible public duty on the other." Even in the best hands, the camp would have experienced difficulties because government aid to blacks was a novel experiment, an enterprise without precedent. Thus far the experiment showed "more what *might be* accomplished under judicious management than what *has been* accomplished. In its very failures it is full of suggestions and instruction as to what might be done for the present comfort and ultimate welfare of the refugees under well-devised and well-regulated agencies of this kind." The key to future success was to have "sound-judging, sagacious, energetic, and philanthropic men" conduct the experiment.[70]

Mussey possessed exactly those qualities which the committee deemed necessary for successful operation of the government's welfare project. Officially, he had nothing to do with the contraband camp, but he was eager to participate in the experiment. In the fall of 1864, Mussey proposed the creation of a superintendent of freedmen in Tennessee who would have wide latitude in dealing with freedmen's problems. No doubt in making the proposal Mussey believed he would make an ideal superintendent, and so it was no surprise when, in February 1865, he was appointed to the superintendency of freedmen in East and Middle Tennessee. Black people now had a true friend in a position of considerable power. Mussey's appointment enabled blacks to hope for a more enlightened continuation of the government's experiment in the postwar period.[71]

Although the amelioration of physical distress remained a promise for the future, the wartime army achieved more positive immediate results in introducing black people to formal education. Wherever the army advanced into the South, the military encouraged and protected schools in black regiments, in occupied towns and contraband camps, and on abandoned plantations.[72] This was true in Middle Tennessee as well as in other major occupied regions. As one correspondent in the area wrote, the army was "a missionary school of *ideas and facts to the colored race.*"[73]

A Union soldier from Michigan who was stationed in Nashville expressed the feelings of many Unionists on the relationship between emancipation and education. Something more than mere abolition was necessary, he thought, since freeing the slaves "only half completes the work. It is like turning the hogs out of your kitchen. They must be taken care of or they will break into your parlors." Ex-slaves, he wrote, "must be thoroughly educated or they must be colonized before anything can be effected."[74]

No one believed this more firmly than Stearns and Mussey, both of whom rejected colonization but placed tremendous faith in education. "Major Stearns' policy," said Mussey, "was wise and large. He deemed the question of colored troops to involve the question of the elevation and improvement of the race. . . ."Stearns tried to instill and foster a desire for education among black people, especially soldiers. He directed chaplains of black regiments to make the education of the men in those regiments the principal part of their duties; by February 1865, each black unit had some educational arrangements under the charge of their chaplains.[75]

Stearns and Mussey also aided the northern benevolent societies in their educational efforts. By the spring of 1865, various societies, with strong support from the army and from Governor Johnson, maintained several schools in Nashville which catered daily to hundreds of eager pupils. The joint benevolent society-army schools were far from perfect, suffering from cramped accommodations, too few teachers, and shortages of books and stationery.[76] Some buildings originally designated as schools had to be converted to shelters simply to house refugees who might otherwise die from exposure.[77] As the Nashville commander noted, before attempting to educate blacks it was necessary first "to provide for their shelter and thus their existence. . . ." But Mussey tried to correct all these deficiencies, and in the meantime, black people in Nashville—soldiers and civilians alike—were at least getting a taste of education.[78]

During the war, the army in Middle Tennessee also took the first hesitant steps toward replacing forced labor with a contract labor system. On April 18, 1863, Stanton sent Johnson a detailed set of supplemental instructions which contained the genesis of the conversion. Among other things, the secretary of war ordered Johnson to "take possession of all abandoned lands and plantations that may come within your power, and lease them for occupation and cultivation upon such terms as you deem proper. . . ." He was also to "take in charge all abandoned slaves or colored persons who have been held in bondage, and whose masters have been, or are now, engaged in rebellion" and "provide for their useful employment and subsistence." Able-bodied blacks could be employed, for reasonable wages, on fortifications and other public works; the military governor should take measures to secure employment and compensation for all those not employed on public works or fortifications.[79]

The implication of these instructions was obvious: if Johnson had both land and laborers, then he should put the blacks to work on plantations for regular wages. In case Johnson missed this implication, Stanton elaborated on the subject for him. The blacks, Stanton wrote, "had better be set to digging their subsistence out of the ground." The governor should put as many contrabands as possible on abandoned plantations. "If some still remain," Stanton continued, "get loyal men of character to take them temporarily on wages to be paid to the contrabands themselves."[80]

Johnson disregarded these instructions at first because he believed he needed all the able-bodied men he could get to work on the fortifications. Furthermore, after September 1863, Major Stearns' recruitment activities reduced the number of available black men for such experimentation still more. Instituting a plan of contract labor also required a great deal of time and effort, and the military governor had little of either to spare. As a result, blacks who avoided impressment as well as those who had no desire to become soldiers remained idle.

But pressure to put idle black people to work on plantations intensified during the winter of 1863–64. It had been several years since Middle Tennessee produced a regular crop and now, with the state seemingly cleared of Confederate forces, it was time to put the region back on the road to agricultural prosperity. The *Dispatch* spoke for many Nashvillians in a piece on unemployed blacks. Let persons willing to employ black people "take them, upon proper guarantees, and put them to work where they can be making a support for themselves instead of being fed and cloathed [*sic*] at Government expense. Crop time is coming."[81]

On February 4, 1864, the same day the contraband camp was established, Adjutant General Thomas responded to this logic by issuing regulations for the government of freedmen in the Department of the Cumberland. All black men capable of bearing arms would be mustered into service, while other blacks would "be required to perform such labor as may be suited to their several conditions, in the respective staff departments of the army, on plantations or farms, leased or otherwise, within our lines, as wood-choppers, teamsters, or in any way that their labor can be made available." Loyal citizens could apply to the commandant of the contraband camp for permission to hire black people through written contracts. The contracts were for at least one year and the employer had to agree to pay, feed, and treat humanely all the blacks he hired. If enough loyalists could not be found, then district commanders could "designate such abandoned or confiscated plantations or farms as they may deem most suitable to be worked by the negroes, upon such terms as in their judgment shall be best adapted to the welfare of this class of people. . . ." Thomas' order gave district commanders specific authority to lease abandoned plantations to loyal citizens, and it also established a wage scale for employed blacks.[82]

Major General Thomas promised Stearns, who took a great interest in the contract labor project, "that in so far as it can be consistently done, any aid that may tend to promote the success of your proposed experiment in the cultivation of Tennessee lands, by Freed Colored labor, will be afforded you from this Department."[83] By early March, black refugees in the Nashville vicinity were "being colonized upon lands, by which it is believed they will be able to support themselves wholly or in part. A system of compensated labor is gradually taking the place of Slavery in this region which promises good results. . . ."[84] To the south, around Pulaski, a few officers also took a creditable interest in the undertaking, and some blacks went to work under the adjutant general's order.[85]

But basically Thomas' edict remained a theoretical framework rather than a working plan in Middle Tennessee. In the Rock City, the irresponsible administrators of the contraband camp took so little interest in the project that hundreds of blacks remained unemployed, languishing in delapidated Silby tents. Furthermore, even if the camp commanders had been the most high-minded individuals, any wartime efforts to convert from slave to free labor would have yielded only meager results. The uncertainties and confusion of wartime conditions simply did not allow for a stable labor system in the region.

Looking at history in perspective, it is lamentable that the embryonic programs of aid, education, and wage labor made so little progress during the conflict. By present day standards of right and wrong, just and unjust, it is obvious that greater advancement toward racial equality and justice would have been desirable. Yet, could the military have done more?

When considering the army's wartime relationship with blacks, it is important to remember that the army was engaged in a war. The army's primary responsibility was to win, and virtually all other considerations had to be subordinated to that task. While the fighting raged, the army could devote little energy to projects not directly associated with carrying on the war. Military necessity had to take precedence over any reformist goals, unless these goals could be harnessed to the military effort. This fact is so elemental it is easily overlooked.

It must also be emphasized that all of these programs were experimental. In providing relief for black refugees, creating black schools, and trying to establish a wage labor system, the army was not only the cutting edge of enormous social change, but it was also venturing into activities that were normally reserved for civil authorities. Certainly errors were made; but by their very nature, experiments frequently yield errors. Admittedly, positive achievements in aid, education, and labor were few; but the army developed important ideas which gave direction for the postwar energies of the nation in dealing with freedmen, easing the transition from war to peace for the ex-slaves.

Because of these fundamental conditions, it is surprising not that the army did so little, but that it did so much under such trying circumstances and while laboring under the additional burden of generations of accumulated racism. John Eaton, Jr., whom Grant selected to contend with the contraband problem in the upper Mississippi River Valley, stated this explicitly. Working with the freedmen was, he said, "a benevolent enterprize of the largest consequences to be conducted not merely in the midst of hostile passions, and prejudices, but under the cannon's mouth and amid the rattle of musketry."[86] Long after the war, Eaton still believed that, in the face of all its other wartime duties and problems, the army "accomplished practically all that could be done to free, feed, shelter, and protect the Negro and to give him medical attendance."[87]

Toward the end of the war, Mussey reflected on the subject of government supervision of the freedmen. "Where," he asked, "should this supervision be? In the hands of the Civil or Military authorities? While the question undoubtedly is properly a Civil question, the actual facts are that unless the Military exercise this supervision none will be exercised. . . ." Mussey knew that in Tennessee civil authority "rested in and flows from the Military Governor whose authority is supported by the machinery of Armies rather than that of Courts."[88] In postwar Tennessee, the state government continued to be supported by armies rather than courts, and the army retained a large degree of control over the supervision of freedmen's affairs. Wartime experimentation by military authorities gave Reconstruction America a blueprint for action—if the national government cared to follow it.

NOTES

1. Caleb Perry Patterson, *The Negro in Tennessee, 1790–1865,* p. 11; Thomas P. Abernethy, *From Frontier to Plantation in Tennessee,* p. 208; Chase Curran Mooney, "Slavery in Davidson County, Tennessee," pp. 32, 57; Mary Emily Robertson Campbell, *The Attitudes of Tennesseans Toward the Union, 1847–1861,* pp. 258–59, 263.

2. J. Merton England, "The Free Negro in Ante-Bellum Tennessee," *JSH*, pp. 37–38; *idem*, "The Free Negro in Ante-Bellum Tennessee," (Ph.D. dissertation), pp. 153–54, 178, 184–85, 229–31.

3. Ridley Wills, II, "Letters From Nashville, 1862, I," p. 76; Susannah to my dear and honored master [William G. Harding], 25 August 1862, Harding Family Papers, Joint University Libraries.

4. Sarah Ridley Trimble, ed., "Behind the Lines in Middle Tennessee, 1863–1865," p. 65; Lindsley Diary, 15 November 1863, Lindsley Family Papers, TSLA.

5. Report from the Office of Army Police submitted by William Truesdail to AJ, 16 February 1863, AJP, Presidential Papers Microfilm; John Fitch, *Annals of the Army of the Cumberland,* p. 508.

6. *Nashville Dispatch,* 27 February 1863.

7. John M. Palmer, *Personal Recollections of John M. Palmer,* p. 131.

8. Buell to J.R. Underwood, 6 March 1862, and Buell to Mitchell, 11 March 1862, both in RG 94, The Negro in the Military Service of the United States, #476, #480; C. Goddard to Brig. Gen. M.B. [*sic*: D.] Mason, 27 February 1863, RG 393, Entry 908; Maj. Frank J. Bond to Mrs. M.E. Benton, 27 July 1863, RG 393, Entry 867.

9. Whipple to Rousseau, 4 February 1864, RG 393, Entry 908.

10. *Nashville Dispatch,* 19 February 1864.

11. *Sen. Ex. Docs.,* 38th Cong., 2d sess., no. 28, pp. 15–17.

12. *OR*, 3, 3, p. 153.

13. Mussey to Stearns, 17 August 1864, RG 393, Entry 1142; *Sen. Ex. Docs.,* 38th Cong., 2d sess., no. 28, p. 18.

14. James B. Fry to Maj. Sidell, 6 August 1862, RG 94, Negro in the Military Service, #569; *Nashville Dispatch,* 22 August 1862.

15. Order by Gen. J.S. Negley to the Commander of City Patrols, 14 October 1862, Vertical File Material #1208, OHS; *Nashville Dispatch,* 16 October 1862.

16. *Nashville Dispatch,* 23 August 1863; Lindsley Diary, 20 September 1863; Frank Preston Stearns, *The Life and Public Services of George Luther Stearns,* p. 310; statement by Armstead Lewis, *OR*, 3, 3, pp. 840–41.

17. Stearns, *Stearns,* pp. 324–25; *Sen. Ex. Docs.,* 38th Cong., 2d sess., no. 28, p. 13; Lt. George Burroughs to AJ, 8 October 1863, AJP.

18. Capt. J.S.C. Morton to AJ, 5 December 1863, AJP; *Sen. Ex. Docs.,* 38th Cong., 2d sess., no. 28, p. 14.

19. *Sen. Ex. Docs.,* 38th Cong., 2d sess., no. 28, p. 21.

20. Trimble, ed., "Behind the Lines," p. 65.

21. Capt. J.S.C. Morton to Mussey, 4 December 1863, AJP.

22. Dudley Taylor Cornish, *The Sable Arm,* is the best overall treatment of the use of black troops in the Civil War.

23. J.M. Forbes to Rosecrans, 28 August 1863, William S. Rosecrans Papers, University Research Library.

24. Stearns, *Stearns,* p. 308.

25. *Ibid.,* p. 324; John Eaton, *Grant, Lincoln and the Freedmen,* p. 121; Mussey to Maj. C.W. Foster, 10 October 1864, *OR,* 3, 4, p. 763.

26. Mussey to William Henry Smith, 17 March [1861], William Henry Smith Papers, OHS.

27. Mussey to William Henry Smith, 6 July 1862, *ibid.*

28. Mussey to C.B. Morse, 15 August 1864, RG 393, Entry 1142.

29. Mussey to William Henry Smith, 6 October [1863?], Smith Papers.

30. Mussey to Joseph Barrett, 31 May 1863, R. Delevan Mussey Papers, Lincoln Miscellaneous Manuscript Collection, The University of Chicago Library; Mussey to William Henry Smith, 10 June 1863, Smith Papers; Mussey to Maj. C.W. Foster, 10 October 1864, *OR,* 3, 4, p. 765.

31. Robert K. Murray, "General Sherman, The Negro and Slavery." The quotations are from p. 128.

32. Sherman to Lorenzo Thomas, 21, 26 June 1864, both in RG 94, Negro in the Military Service, #2639, #2645–46; M.A. DeWolfe Howe, ed., *Home Letters of General Sherman,* pp. 252–53, 327–28.

33. [Mussey] to Capt. George B. Halstead, 8 June 1864, RG 393, Entry 1141. Rousseau also had little faith in black soldiers; see Thomas J. Morgan, "Reminiscences of Service with Colored Troops in the Army of the Cumberland, 1863–1865," p. 31.

34. Stearns to Stanton, 24 October 1863, RG 94, Negro in the Military Service, #1694–95; Mussey to Maj. C.W. Foster, 10 October 1864, *OR,* 3, 4, p. 772.

35. Mussey to Joseph Barrett, 13 November 1863, Mussey Papers. Also see Mussey to Salmon P. Chase, 18 October 1863, Salmon P. Chase Papers, LC.

36. Stearns, *Stearns,* p. 314. By January 1864, even Rousseau realized slavery was virtually dead in Tennessee; see Rousseau to Whipple, 30 January 1864, *OR,* 1, 32, 2, p. 268.

37. Stearns, *Stearns,* pp. 309–10; Stearns to Stanton, 16 September 1863, *OR,* 3, 3, p. 816.

38. AJ to Stanton, 17 September 1863, *OR,* 3, 3, pp. 819–20.

39. AJ to Rosecrans, 17 September 1863, AJP.

40. AJ to Stanton, 17 September 1863, *OR,* 3, 3, pp. 819–20.

41. Stanton to Stearns, 16, 18 September 1863, and Stanton to AJ, 18 September 1863. All in *ibid.,* pp. 816–17, 823.

42. Stearns to Stanton, 24 October 1863, RG 94, Negro in the Military Service, #1694–95.

43. Stearns to John M. Forbes, 18 October 1863, *ibid.,* #1695–97.

44. Stearns to Col. Innes (and endorsements on the letter), 7 October 1863, and AJ to Rosecrans, 12 October 1863, both in AJP. Stearns came to respect the governor

so much that he regretted Johnson was not nominated for the presidency in 1864; see Stearns to AJ, 9 June 1864, AJP.

45. Stearns to Senator Henry Wilson, 4 March 1864, RG 94, Negro in the Military Service, #2404–06.

46. Stanton to Stearns, 16 September 1863, *OR*, 3, 3, p. 816.

47. Stearns to Stanton, 25 September 1863, *ibid.*, p. 840.

48. AJ to Lincoln, 23 September 1863, AJP; *Nashville Dispatch,* 5 November 1863.

49. Halleck to Lieber, 27 December 1863, Francis Lieber Papers, The Huntington Library.

50. Circular issued by Mussey, 15 February 1864, RG 94, Negro in the Military Service, #2383.

51. [Mussey] to Brig. Gen. Tillson, 17 May 1864, RG 393, Entry 1141; Joseph T. Wilson, *The Black Phalanx*, p. 291. Also see Morris Stuart Hall Autobiography, Morris Stuart Hall Papers, MHC.

52. Morgan, "Reminiscences," pp. 7, 9.

53. *Ibid.,* pp. 10–11, 14, 24–25.

54. George Washington Williams, *A History of the Negro Troops in the War of the Rebellion, 1861–65, Preceded by a Review of the Military Service of Negroes in Ancient and Modern Times,* pp. 162–63; Chief of Staff [unsigned]to Mussey, 19, 30 June 1864; AAG [unsigned] to Morgan, 29 July, 9 August 1864. All in RG 393, Entry 908.

55. Francis Everett Hall to his sister, 8 November 1863, Francis Everett Hall Papers, MHC; Stearns, *Stearns,* pp. 313, 316; Mussey to Maj. C.W. Foster, 10 October 1864, *OR,* 3, 4, pp. 769–70; Wilson, *Black Phalanx*, pp. 465–66, 468, 470, 478; Bobby L. Lovett, "The Negro's Civil War in Tennessee, 1861–65."

56. See Mussey's eloquent letter in the *Nashville Daily Times and True Union,* 6 July 1864, about discrimination against black troops during a Fourth of July celebration.

57. Capt. L. Howland to Hunter Brooke, 3 December 1864, RG 393, Entry 861.

58. *Battles and Leaders of the Civil War,* 4: pp. 462–63, 473; Frank A. Handy Diary, 15 December 1864, William R. Perkins Library, Manuscript Department.

59. Mussey to AJ, 16 December 1864, RG 393, Entry 1142. Also see Mussey to Capt. C.P. Brown, December 1864, RG 94, Negro in the Military Service, #3504–06, and Morgan, "Reminiscences," pp. 44–45.

60. Quoted in Williams, *Negro Troops,* p. 290.

61. Wilson, *Black Phalanx,* pp. 295, 304.

62. Stearns to William Whiting, 27 April 1863, RG 94, Negro in the Military Service, #1206-07; Morgan, "Reminiscences," p. 6. For similar sentiments see Robert B. Warden, *An Account of the Private Life and Public Services of Salmon Portland Chase,* p. 644, and Henry V. Freeman, "A Colored Brigade in the Campaign and Battle of Nashville," p. 400.

63. *Nashville Daily Times and True Union,* 17 September 1863; *Nashville Dispatch,* 9 July 1863; Joseph G. McKee and M.M. Brown to AJ, 3 November [1863], AJP.

64. *Ibid.*, all three sources.

65. *Nashville Daily Union,* 15 December 1863; essay by Mussey enclosed with Mussey to AJ, 20 February 1865, AJP.

66. *Sen. Ex. Docs.*, 38th Cong., 2d sess., no. 28, pp. 1–2.

67. *Ibid.*, pp. 3–5, 9, 23.

68. *Nashville Daily Times and True Union*, 11 April 1864. Not all contraband camps were as wretched as the one in Nashville; see Cam Walker, "Corinth."

69. Letter from "C.V.S.," 28 January 1865, in the *New York Times*, 8 February 1865.

70. *Sen. Ex. Docs.*, 38th Cong., 2d sess., no. 28, p. 19.

71. Mussey to Maj. C.W. Foster, 10 October 1864, *OR*, 3, 4, p. 771; essay by Mussey enclosed with Mussey to AJ, 20 February 1865, and Mussey to Capt. C.P. Brown, 13 February 1865, both in AJP.

72. Robert Stanley Bahney, "Generals and Negroes."

73. *American Missionary*, August 1863.

74. John W. Nicholson to his wife, 20 March [1865], John W. Nicholson Papers, MHC.

75. Mussey to Maj. C.W. Foster, 10 October 1864, *OR*, 3, 4, p. 771. Also see Mussey to AJ, 20 February 1865, AJP; Daniel Chapman, to "Mr. Editor," 9 December 1863, no. H8854, and Statement by Ira Bristol, 7 June 1864, no. H8897, both in AMAM,T, Amistad Research Center, Dillard University.

76. Mussey to AJ, 20 February 1865, AJP.

77. Capt. L. Howland to Capt. John F. Isom, 21 September 1864, RG 393, Entry 861.

78. Brig. Gen. [Miller] to Brig. Gen. Webster, 19 September 1864, *ibid.*

79. Stanton to AJ, 18 April 1863, *OR*, 3, 3, pp. 122–23.

80. Quoted in Clifton R. Hall, *Andrew Johnson, Military Governor of Tennessee*, pp. 207–8.

81. *Nashville Dispatch*, 29 January 1864.

82. *Sen. Ex. Docs.*, 38th Cong., 2d sess., no. 28, pp. 2–3.

83. Capt. and AAG [unsigned] to Stearns, 6 March 1864, RG 393, Entry 908.

84. Brig. Gen. and Chief of Staff [unsigned] to Mr. J.W. Evans, 2 March 1864, *ibid.*

85. Diary of Walter T. Carpenter, 26 February 1864, OHS.

86. Eaton to Henry Cowles, 13 March 1863, no. H8832, AMAM,T.

87. Eaton, *Grant, Lincoln and the Freedmen*, p. 125.

88. Essay by Mussey enclosed with Mussey to AJ, 20 February 1865, AJP.

Chapter 7

"THE CITY GOVERNMENT
EXISTED BY
MILITARY AUTHORITY"

Three masters, an unequal triad, ruled Nashville during the Civil War: the military government; the commanding general of the Department of the Cumberland; and the city administration. The main struggle for power within the city was between Andrew Johnson and the commanding general, a contest which, by late 1863, had been decided in Johnson's favor. However, the overriding importance of these two masters should not obscure the municipal government's role throughout the occupation.

The city government in Nashville at the time of the war consisted of a mayor, board of aldermen, and board of common council, all elected by the people. The two boards meeting in convention composed the city council, which elected all other city officials. During the war, Johnson appointed all the aldermen and councilmen who in turn elected the mayor as well as other city officers.

William Birkhimer, an authority on military government, has pointed out that in conquered territory "whatever of the civil authorities are permitted to perform their functions, it is . . . , for the benefit of the conquered as an act of grace on the part of the conqueror and at most for his convenience." By allowing local municipal administration and law to operate, the conqueror is relieved of having to perform the functions of civil government. Furthermore, an indigenous civil administration "tends to secure the happiness of the governed and consequently their contentment." The conqueror is left free to pursue other objectives, while the business activities and social relations of the people are disturbed as little as possible. Of course, city officials retained in office would be strictly subordinate to military authorities and often their actions would be dictated by their military superiors.[1]

The theory of mutual accord between conqueror and conquered usually broke down in practice. In New Orleans, federal military authorities were willing to allow the municipal government to continue in office, but city officials proved uncooperative and were deposed and replaced by military personnel within a month. In Memphis, the prewar mayor, John Park, remained at his post after the city's capture. However, he was both inefficient and disloyal, and in 1864 the military suspended him and established military government in the city.[2]

The difference in Nashville was Andrew Johnson. Had Buell or Rosecrans been the final arbitrator, the course of events might have paralleled that in New Orleans or Memphis. But Johnson, who was committed to the restoration of civil government in Tennessee, considered it politically important to have a municipal government functioning in the state capital. True, when Nashville officials refused to take an oath of allegiance, Johnson swiftly ousted them, but he did not replace civil government with direct military rule. Instead he appointed loyal civilians to fill the positions of deposed officials and thus maintained at least the facade of civil rule.

I

The change in personnel between the elected city government in existence just before the war and the Johnson-appointed government of April 1862 was almost complete. On the board of aldermen, the military governor replaced all but one man (William S. Cheatham), and on the board of common council, he replaced everyone (though one member of the Board, William Shane, did become city recorder in the new government). Only about half a dozen initial Johnson appointees had served in the city administration during the preceding decade.[3]

While the occupation continued, Johnson reappointed city officials every September, the normal time for city elections. His last municipal appointees, who served until shortly after the end of the war, evidenced a striking continuity with his first appointees. Five of his original eight aldermen still served in that body when Lee surrendered to Grant. Only four of the original sixteen councilmen still sat on that board, but two others had moved up to the board of aldermen.

Furthermore, one alderman (Cheatham) had become a councilman, a demotion which may have resulted from his opposition to Johnson's program.[4]

Nashville's mayor under the Johnson regime was John Hugh Smith, an antebellum Whig and wartime convert to Republicanism. Admitted to the Nashville bar in 1843 and elected mayor in 1845, Smith served seven years as mayor before moving on to the state general assembly in 1853 as Davidson County's representative. In 1859 he again ran for mayor of Nashville, but lost by a mere twenty-two votes. Taking a strong pro-Union stand in the secession crisis, Smith praised Johnson's equally steadfast position. In 1862 Johnson appointed Smith as an alderman, and then the city council elected him mayor—an unlikely eventuality without the governor's prior approval. After all, Smith was the perfect man to give legitimacy to the new municipal government. Not only was he obviously popular in Nashville, but since he and Johnson were from different political parties, it gave a bipartisan appearance to the effort to revive loyalty in the city.[5] Smith knew that accepting the mayor's office was not going to increase his popularity, but believed that "when reason and loyalty" returned, he would be thanked for continuing civil government and thus preventing martial law.[6]

For all intents and purposes, however, the city was under martial law during the war, and the men serving in the city administration entertained few illusions about their position. Almost from the start, they were made aware that they were in the hands of Andrew Johnson and the military. In early May 1862, the board of aldermen passed two acts to suppress disloyalty in the city and forwarded them to the common council for approval. The council, instead of acting swiftly, tabled the bills and was jolted into action later in the month only after Mayor Smith informed the councilmen that if they "refused to make loyal men of the citizens of Nashville, Governor Johnson would find the means to do so." The council promptly passed both bills with minor amendments, which the aldermen accepted.[7]

By June the common council had learned its lesson. When a councilman introduced a bill to repeal an act prohibiting the sale of liquor in the city, another councilman quickly reminded him that the act was originally passed at the request of the military authorities. The second councilman urged consultation with these officials before repealing the act, a course of action readily agreed upon.[8]

Military officers remained extremely sensitive to challenges to their authority. For example, in February 1863, the army applied for the use of Brennan's foundry which was needed for military purposes, but which was already under libel in the hands of U.S. Marshal Glascock, who opposed the army's request even after the army gave him the proper vouchers. Nashville military authorities forwarded the matter to the commanding general, explaining that Glascock might simply be trying "to keep his record right and to appear as doing nothing involuntarily towards relieving himself of the responsibility of the trust imposed on him," but that he might also be initiating "an issue between the U.S. Civil and Military authorities. . . ."[9] The commanding general, while stressing the necessity of preserving civil-military harmony, informed Glascock he would have to yield, and the foundry became military property.[10] Two years later, when City Recorder Shane proclaimed the military authorities had no right to issue orders which conflicted with his interpretation of city ordinances, the provost marshal bluntly lectured him "that such a position is altogether untenable and that such comments are not to be allowed."[11]

Thus, the city government remained under the army's heel, and most Nashvillians realized the true situation. In September 1862, Alderman Scovel, the Unionist real estate dealer who had been persecuted by the Confederates before the federal occupation, admitted that "the City Government existed by military authority."[12] Less than a month before Appomattox, Alderman William Driver acknowledged that city council's status had not changed, that it held "the position of a military board."[13] About the same time the *Daily Union*, looking forward to the return of peace, reminded members of the city government they would "not much longer be above respecting the voice of the people."[14]

II

Nashville was a miserable place during the war, plagued by rats, flies, and mosquitoes. On hot summer afternoons flies were often so plentiful that the simple task of writing a letter became an onerous chore.[15] By night, clouds of mosquitoes, with a seemingly "insatiable appetite for human blood," patrolled the city's airways, sorely tempting men "to use *an extra adjective,* in giving [their] opinion of the long legged little rascals."[16] During dry spells, dust from the city's streets billowed into the sky, actually blocking out sunlight and, occasionally even blinding pedestrians when the wind was strong.[17] Rain, how-

ever, was not always welcome because it flooded the streets with
"Nashville mud a kind of cross between tar and grease."[18] Winter
brought little relief to the beleaguered city. Cold and snow caused
great suffering, especially among the poor, because shelter, clothing,
and fuel were in short supply and very expensive. A vicious crime
wave seized the city, making residents afraid to venture out at night.
The streets fell into disrepair and became clogged with filth and trash.
As drinking and prostitution flourished, the city's health declined
markedly, and an erratic but generally depressed economy made all
the misery even harder to bear. The capstone of the city's wartime
wretchedness was a disastrous flood in the spring of 1865 which made
Nashville look like an island in a vast lake and did immense damage to
buildings, roads, fences, bridges, and livestock.[19]

The city government struggled with these problems throughout
the war. Although the city supposedly had its regular income from
taxes and court fees, in December 1862 Mayor Smith reported to the
board of aldermen that the city treasury was unable "for want of
means, to pay the officers, employees, and the indispensable ordinary
expenses of the city." There was, he said, an "inability or indisposi-
tion, or both, amongst the tax payers to pay their taxes."[20] In short,
before the occupation was a year old, the municipal government
lacked sufficient funds to deal with the serious problems which beset
the city. Since the only place to turn for assistance was to the military
governor or to other military authorities, the army soon became involved in trying to solve municipal problems. Without the army's
cooperation the city would have been in a more deplorable condition
than it was when the war ended. It was, of course, to the army's
benefit to have a clean, healthy, orderly city. What was good for the
populace was also good for the military.

Providing fire and police protection were two of the most important joint municipal-military efforts. Fire protection was especially
vital to the army because Nashville was such a huge supply depot. By
March 1863, the military was convinced that the city's fire department was inadequate, and the post commander ordered it, at the
expense of the national government, to double its effective force and to
purchase any amount of hose needed. When the city fire committee
consulted military authorities about the purchase of two thousand feet
of hose, it learned that the army itself would make the purchase for the
city. Military officials eventually decided it would be safer to handle
the entire matter themselves, and so the chief quartermaster in
Nashville organized his own fire department.[21]

The lion's share of the responsibility for policing the city also fell to the army, partly by choice but primarily because the municipal government abdicated most of its responsibility. When one of the city policemen died in mid-August 1862, the board of aldermen and the common council considered filling the vacancy but decided it was unnecessary to pay a new policeman while there was a provost guard in the city. A month later the aldermen even contemplated dismissing the city's entire detective police.[22]

By the fall of 1862, with only eighteen policemen on night duty to protect the city, greater military assistance was desperately needed. In November the *Dispatch* suggested that the post commander detail between forty and sixty men to patrol the city at night under the guidance of the city police. The city council accepted the suggestion and appointed Mayor Smith to consult with General Rosecrans, who agreed to help. He divided Nashville into three districts for the purpose of police administration and detailed a squad of soldiers for each district. By Christmas they were patrolling the streets, commanded by Nashville night police. The press initially praised the new police arrangement, but within two weeks problems developed because the soldiers who were assigned to police duty began to roam the city during the day, drinking, robbing, and insulting citizens.[23] Furthermore, joint policing led to complications when soldiers and government employees were arrested and punished, thereby straining civil-military relations.[24]

Throughout the war, the best efforts of the army and the municipal government to police the city failed. "The city," complained the *Daily Times and True Union* in November 1864, "swarms with a host of burglars, brass-knuck and slingshot ruffians, pickpockets and highwaymen, who have flocked hither from all parts of the country." It was plain, the paper continued, "that neither the military nor the municipal police is near as strong as it should be." Several months later, the same newspaper reported that the "carnival of blood still reigns unchecked in Nashville," and a northern correspondent sadly commented that murderers and crooks filled the city.[25] The register of arrests made by the city patrol in 1864–65 easily confirms these descriptions and criticisms.[26]

Another problem which the municipal administration failed to solve was the filthy, unhealthy condition of the Rock City. Trash and garbage threatened to engulf Nashville by the middle of 1863, prompting the *Daily Press* to ask, "Shall we be stunk to death?"[27] In prewar years, Nashville's streets had been cleaned by workhouse criminals and slaves hired by the year, but by 1863 slave labor was no longer available, workhouse criminals had been "liberated" by Union recruiting officers, and the city had no money to pay laborers.[28] Therefore Mayor Smith had to appeal to individual citizens to clean their own premises, warning that if they did not voluntarily respond, "a more expeditious power will be applied."[29]

Citizens failed to respond and a more expeditious power—the military—was applied. In January 1864, the post commander, noting that municipal regulations had failed to keep the city clean, ordered the occupant of every house to clean the pavement or sidewalk in front of his building by 9 a.m. daily. Government wagons would pick up the piles of debris.[30] In March the commander placed Captain W. D. Chamberlain of the Twenty-ninth Massachusetts Volunteer Infantry in charge of the cleanup operation. The captain pursued his task with vigor, and within a month the city showed a definite improvement.[31]

However, once the city was thoroughly scrubbed, the army's cleaning apparatus apparently fell into disuse. In late May, the provost marshal commented that during an evening stroll through the most respectable portion of the city, a person could "detect at least a score of well defined odors, besides stinks innumerable proceeding from stagnant surface water, festering pools and unclean privies throughout the city."[32] Finally, in November the post commander reacted to the renewed assault on nasal sensibilities and ordered the provost marshal to devise a plan for cleaning the city's sidewalks and streets.[33] Little progress could be made because military authorities soon had to focus all attention on repelling Hood's invasion, and in the early months of 1865, complaints about the city's filth again appeared in the press. Particularly serious was the large number of unburied horse carcasses in the city cemetery, on the main streets, and near the city water works. Army personnel again assumed primary responsibility for cleaning the city, although this time, with the war rapidly winding down, municipal laborers aided the military.[34]

Some citizens were unhappy about the city's abdication of responsibility in the matter of sanitation. A Nashville doctor complained that the "praiseworthy exertions" of the military authorities had evoked no concert of action from the municipal government. The physician believed the city government should be the leader in the cleanup of the city, not a bystander on the sidelines, a sentiment which was echoed by the *Daily Union*.[35] Such criticisms were unfair because the civilian government had neither the money nor the manpower to keep the city clean. Furthermore, individual citizens were not entirely without blame. One Union soldier informed his sister that the army had taken charge of cleaning the city because the "people have grown careless and slovenly and it has rendered it highly necessary for such a thing to be done."[36] Under the circumstances, the army was the only agency available with the resources to clean the community.

The army also became the guardian of the city's health when specific problems arose. For example, smallpox epidemics swept through Nashville almost yearly during the war, and since the municipal authorities seemed incapable of dealing with the problem, another important municipal function was relegated to the military by default. On November 21, 1863, the post commander established two different locations where army medical officers would provide free vaccinations, and he ordered all persons—citizens and soldiers—to have themselves vaccinated immediately.[37] Despite this order, the epidemic continued unabated. Early in the new year, the commander ordered that all smallpox cases be promptly reported to the acting assistant surgeon. Afflicted invididuals would be transported to a smallpox camp, established by the army, for treatment. Finally, in near desperation, the commander told the provost marshal to arrest any persons who were not vaccinated at the end of one week from the date of his order and convey them outside the picket lines of the post.[38]

It is impossible to tell whether the army's efforts finally curtailed the epidemic, or whether it simply died out naturally. Nor does it matter. What is important is that the army became entangled in yet another municipal problem because city officials lacked the resolve and resources to tackle it themselves.

III

The army took on other heavy burdens when it tried to control two severe and closely related problems: drinking and prostitution. "Nashville whiskey," said the *Dispatch* in the summer of 1862, "appears to have a very bad effect upon the soldiers in our midst." Large numbers of drunken soldiers were omnipresent, "creating a disturbance, stealing fruit, and committing all kinds of unlawful acts."[39] The paper urged the provost marshal to take action, and in late August he issued the first in a never-ending series of orders designed to bring drinking under control and thereby preserve the public peace and safety.[40]

During the course of the war, the army tried just about everything—total prohibition, a strict liquor licensing system, threats, and, in a few instances, even bayonets—but it was to no avail. Frequent arrests and jail sentences ranging from five to twenty days did little to deter people from selling liquor illegally; and as for soldiers, the military could issue all the orders it wanted, but they were still going to get drunk and raise havoc.[41] Soldiers and government employees, "maddened by the liquor," committed "excesses of the most disgraceful nature" almost daily.[42] The best the army could do was arrest offenders; it could not prevent people from becoming offenders.

The army was no more successful at ending prostitution in Nashville. In 1860 city census takers, for unknown reasons, counted two hundred and seven women who admitted they were prostitutes.[43] The city fathers were aware their community housed a large number of them, and several days before the firing on Fort Sumter, an alderman introduced a bill calling for something to be done about the problem. But no doubt the aldermen forgot about the bill in the commotion brought on by the war. Then, several months after the federal occupation began, Alderman Cheatham introduced a new bill to control prostitution but, as in so many other municipal matters, the city council proved incapable of energetic and decisive action.[44]

Prostitution flourished in a section of the city known as "Smokey Row," which was "a foul breathing hole of hell . . ., belching forth its pestilential breath."[45] One young soldier stationed in Nashville described the women who inhabited "Smokey Row" as abominable, low, vile, mean, lewd, wanton, dissolute, licentious, vicious, immoral, and wicked, and then explained apologetically that he would need a dictionary "to find words enough, and then I could not find them bad enough, to express my hatred of these beings calling themselves women. . . ."[46] But, alas, such sentiments among Union soldiers were rare indeed. In fact, there was an "old Saying that No Man Could be a Soldier unless he had gone through Smokey Row."[47]

It was also said that "Smokey Row killed more soldiers than the warr [*sic*]."[48] Because of the attractions of "Smokey," the army units stationed in Nashville suffered severely from venereal disease as hundreds, and probably thousands, of men jammed into army hospitals for treatment. During 1863 "an unmitigated source of annoyance" to the post commander was "the constant complaints of the various commanders of Corps, Divisions, Brigades, Regiments, and Companies and the Surgeons of Regiments as to their men being kept in the Post and the various Field Hospitals of the Department for the treatment of venereal disease."[49]

In midsummer 1863, elements of the Nashville press urged civil and military authorities to do something about the scandalous women who were ruining the health of so many soldiers. The complaints of Union officers and righteous citizens attracted the attention of the commanding general of the Department of the Cumberland who demanded the adoption of a plan to deal with the problem. The Nashville post commander decided to banish the prostitutes. In early July, army patrols began rounding up licentious females in order to put them aboard steamers and send them North. Within a few days, the patrols corralled some three hundred of them, and they expected to collect another one hundred and fifty.[50]

Although the press praised the plan, and even suggested the military should do more to restore Nashville's good order and security, the deportation scheme ran into problems. Since the army limited the plan to white women, some people feared black strumpets would quickly replace the white ones. Also, the patrols inadvertently arrested several respectable Nashville ladies while rounding up the prostitutes, a mistake which did little to enhance the army's prestige among native Nashvillians. Still another hitch developed when many prostitutes suddenly married, instantly transforming themselves into "decent" women and thus gaining exclusion from the deportation order. Some who married on the spur of the moment had previously figured prominently in police proceedings against prostitutes.[51]

Overshadowing all these problems was a much larger one: there was no place to unload the prostitutes. The steamer with its feminine cargo went to Louisville, but authorities there refused to accept any such commercial articles. The boat pushed on to Cincinnati, but the thought of hundreds of whores flooding the city appalled the city fathers there, too, and they rejected the cargo. In the end, the secretary of war intervened and directed the steamer to return to Nashville where its human cargo once again prowled the streets.[52]

Sickness in the army garrison increased at once, and the old complaints were renewed. Provost Marshal George Spaulding of the Eighteenth Michigan Infantry devised a new scheme for controlling prostitution: rather than abolish it, the army would license it. Spaulding proposed that prostitutes be compelled to report to a medical officer for an examination. If free of venereal disease, the woman would pay a license fee and submit to periodic medical examinations, but if a woman was diseased or became diseased, she would be sent to a special army hospital for rehabilitation before being permitted to return to work. The money collected from license and examination fees would support this hospital, as well as another facility for diseased soldiers.[53] The army's new program went into effect in the fall of 1863 when authorities obtained an old brick building in a secluded part of the city and converted it into an examination room and hospital "for the reception of valetudinarian females from the unhealthy purlieus of Smokey."[54]

In October 1864, $600.59 was received from the Prostitute Hospital, while expenditures by the surgeon in charge, W. M. Chambers, were $585.59; for the month of January 1865, these figures had climbed to $1,281.00 received and $1,210.77 expended.[55] By January 1865, almost four hundred women had been licensed. However, some of these had left the city, ten had died, a few had married, and still others had simply ceased to report for examinations. Thus, as the last year of the war began, the number of licensed females reporting for examinations was actually less than two hundred and fifty. Over one hundred other women had reported for their initial examination, but then failed to obtain a license. Two hundred and seven prostitutes had been treated for venereal disease.[56]

Surgeon Chambers believed that the prostitutes themselves were highly satisfied with the program and that most of them would regret seeing it abolished. The army also profited because the program virtually eliminated the venereal disease problem. Colonel Spaulding's plan saved thousands of men from the sick lists, thereby promoting the efficiency of the army. The plan worked so successfully that army surgeons from other cities traveled to Nashville to examine its operation.[57]

There is no evidence that the army tried to control liquor and prostitution as a moral crusade. Instead, military authorities acted out of self-defense. Drunken and diseased soldiers were of little value to the army, and the problems caused by drinking and whoring interfered with efficient military operations. The army had to intervene to prevent the wholesale demoralization of troops stationed in Nashville.

IV

Perhaps the most burdensome wartime problem in Nashville was economic stagnation and dislocation, a difficulty which actually antedated the federal occupation of Middle Tennessee. General crop fail-

ures in the late 1850s and early 1860s and the political tensions and
uncertainty following Lincoln's election had initiated the economic
distress. The business directory for 1860–61 spoke of "the stringency
which has for some time prevailed in financial and commercial circles,
and the comparative quiet which has reigned in the various departments of trade."[58] In mid-summer 1860, Henry Clay Yeatman, a
budding entrepreneur, complained that "there is very little doing in
the way of business," and after Lincoln's victory, he noted that business prospects were "very unpromising as it appears certain that one or
more of the Southern states will certainly leave the confederacy."[59]

Business remained very sluggish after Tennessee seceded, partly
because shippers could not use the Louisville and Nashville Railroad,
the city's main transportation link to the North. Furthermore, Southerners purposely avoided ordinary commercial ties. And, of course,
with the enemy threatening the borders of Tennessee, trade was compressed into even narrower channels. In the fall of 1861, Nashville's
mayor spoke of "the depressed condition of property and trade," "the
stringency of the money market," and the small profits being reaped
by merchants and businessmen.[60] These economic problems led to a
rapid increase in prices which, naturally, struck hardest at the poor.
"Something must be done, and that quickly," urged the *Republican
Banner*, "for the relief of the poor of Nashville. The amount of suffering in our city, at this moment, is scarcely known to the community at
large."[61]

Thus, when Union troops entered the city, it was already in deep
economic trouble, with the cotton and tobacco trade being particularly hard hit. Between September 1861 and June 1862, cotton warehouses in Nashville received only 8,672 bales, less than half the
amount received during the same months in the preceding year. By
July 1862, not a single bale was for sale in the city. The tobacco trade
was in even worse straits, with receipts less than a third of what they
had been the previous year.[62] Nashville's once prosperous wholesale
and retail grocery market was also in serious trouble, driving food
prices abnormally high. In mid-August, the *Dispatch* quite accurately
predicted that "it will require a long time to regain the prosperity we
have heretofore enjoyed."[63]

Nashville failed to recover economically until well into the Reconstruction period. The disruption of Middle Tennessee's labor supply, the devastation of the area by contending armies, the military
control of the transportation system, and the rapid depreciation of
Southern state currencies all contributed to the economic woes of war.
But perhaps most importantly, a steady stream of presidential, Treas-

ury Department, and military regulations hampered all attempts to revive the economy.

Middle Tennessee exhibited signs of devastation within a month after Union troops occupied it, and the region became increasingly desolate as the war progressed. Certainly Southern troops caused some of the devastation,[64] but much of the ruin resulted from Union foraging and indiscriminate pillaging. A Union brigadier general, who marched and fought throughout Middle Tennessee in the summer and fall of 1862, noted that federal troops "have lived upon the country, and have really desolated it . . ., the country is exhausted." Under the foraging system, he continued' "all suffer, rich and poor; of all methods of providing for any army this is the most wasteful."[65] In the spring of 1863, another soldier wrote how sad it was to see such beautiful country so completely ruined, and wondered how people could still live in the area. "There are no fences left at all. There is no corn and hay for the cattle and horses, but there are no horses left anyhow and the planters have no food for themselves."[66] By 1864 so few farm animals remained in the region that few crops could be produced, and some residents whose corncribs and smokehouses had been emptied by Union foragers faced the threat of starvation.[67]

Legal impressments and foraging were bad enough, but Union pillaging and robbing compounded the problem. Prowling soldiers committed "grave outrages and wrongs" on helpless citizens, indiscriminately burned homes and barns, and destroyed shrubbery, stone walls, and fences for no apparent reason.[68] In these and other ways, undisciplined Union troops made life miserable within Union lines. One female rebel sympathizer declared, with some exaggeration, that "the Goths, vandals, and Huns all combined were not more merciless or savage than the Yankees." "Our life here in this subjugated country," she said, "is not life—it is mere existence—breathing, eating & drinking."[69]

Reports of wanton destruction by Union soldiers alarmed Francis Lieber. "It does incalculable injury," he stated. "It demoralizes our troops; it annihilates wealth irrecoverably, and makes a return to a state of peace more and more difficult."[70] Some Nashville Unionists realized that the inexcusable destruction of property stirred a spirit of revenge. "This wholesale plundering and pillaging through the country while it causes great suffering among the people," wrote a Unionist to Johnson, "drives thousands to desperation, and causes a great many to enter the southern army—will also greatly *demoralize* the Federal soldiers."[71]

Union officers, aware of the problem, issued orders designed to bring soldiers under control,[72] but the new regulations were not very effective. As late as January 1865, Nashville commander Brigadier General John F. Miller lamented that robbing and marauding troops spared neither women nor the elderly in their depredations and were "fast becoming enemies of the human race."[73] Combined with legal foraging and impressments, this senseless harassment and destruction contributed to the desolation of Middle Tennessee.

Military control of transportation also added to the economic distress. In November 1862, the *Daily Union* reported that persons "desiring to send goods over the Louisville and Nashville Railroad are in a great fever, because the Government monopolizes the freight trains for Army use. . . ." The *Dispatch* agreed that the virtual impossibility of transporting supplies over the Louisville and Nashville was having a damaging effect on the business community.[74] The army also controlled water transportation to and from Nashville, and could arbitrarily prevent private freight from being conveyed on it. Merchants complained about the difficulties of transportation, but could do nothing to help the situation. Army officers knew that prohibiting the shipment of private goods by rail and water would raise a howl of protest, but often the military situation allowed no alternative.[75]

Depreciation of Southern state currencies created financial chaos in Nashville. When the federals occupied the city, businessmen refused to receive these currencies at par in ordinary transactions. Although the *Dispatch* initially carried on an earnest campaign to bring Tennessee and other Southern currencies up to par, by September 1862 the discount on non-Tennessee Southern currencies became so great that even the *Dispatch* would not accept them as payment for debts.[76] By the summer of 1863, some branches of the municipal government refused to accept Tennessee currency as payment for taxes and fines. The depreciation of these currencies became still greater when the government ordered all purchases of cotton and tobacco paid for in greenbacks.[77] Panic-stricken Nashville merchants held public meetings to discuss the confused state of local currencies, and they appealed to Johnson for help. Although both Johnson and the merchants met with bankers on the subject, nothing could halt the decline of Southern currency. The result was a severe monetary stringency which made ordinary business transactions difficult.[78]

And, too, the vast number of regulations governing trade hampered the economy of Middle Tennessee. The president and Congress had original authority to regulate and license trade with the Confederacy, but the government failed to establish a balanced, unified policy concerning trade with the enemy and instead vacillated between nearly complete prohibition and almost free intercourse. As the government pursued its unsteady path, a maze of Congressional acts and presidential proclamations flowed from Washington, which, in turn, had to be interpreted by the Treasury Department and its agents and also by military commanders. The resultant web of ever-changing orders and regulations often confounded merchants.[79]

Even when Nashville businessmen understood government regulations, they were not happy with them. For example, Treasury Department regulations issued during the summer of 1863 restricted Nashville's wholesale trade and limited the city to "a little *picayune* retail business."[80] Merchants feared this would prevent their usual customers from making purchases in Nashville, their "natural and legitimate" market, and would drive them to rival cities for their supplies.[81]

Dismayed merchants, supported by the city's press, campaigned to have the restrictions removed in order to regain the city's trade. Eventually, through the intervention of Governor Johnson, authorities relaxed the restrictions on Nashville's wholesale trade.[82] While this provided temporary relief, the basic problem of confusing and complex regulations remained. The cotton trade, said the *Daily Union* in December 1863, "is only sick of too much dieting and doctoring. Fresh air and freedom of limb would restore it in a few weeks to vigorous health and great usefulness." The "entire cotton nursing system, as well as the network of Chinese restrictions thrown around every other branch of trade" should be discarded.[83] Early in 1864, General Grant loosened restrictions on the cotton trade and, true to the *Daily Union's* prediction, cotton flowed into Nashville throughout the spring.[84]

But restrictions on other branches of trade remained intact. In the fall of 1864, merchants again protested the undue restraints on trade, and in mid-April 1865, Mayor Smith suggested that the city council appeal to General Thomas and Governor Brownlow to have all military restrictions removed from the city's trade.[85] Thus, through the spring of 1865, Treasury Department and military regulations repressed trade, contributing to Nashville's serious economic problems.

The most obvious aspect of the city's economic dislocation was inflation. Prices for both luxuries and necessities remained high, making life miserable for black and white refugees. When the municipal government proved unable to provide relief for these unfortunate people, the army tried to ease their condition in several ways. The Quartermaster's Department employed hundreds of female East Tennessee refugees, thus keeping them off public charity. Military barracks were temporarily turned over to refugees so they would at least have a place to sleep, and the army issued thousands of rations every week to save them from starvation. As a last resort, military authorities provided free transportation to the North for white refugees, where they might escape the high prices and make a new beginning in life.[86]

Late in the war, the army also attempted to set prices for fuel and provisions. The provost marshal tried at least twice to establish maximum prices for a number of essential items, but his orders had little effect and often made a bad situation worse.[87] For instance, flour was selling for $25 a barrel when the provost marshal set the price at $15 a barrel. This "did not abate the price but suddenly put the article out of market. Nobody had any to sell."[88] Shortages became so severe that the army contemplated seizing the supplies which were being held back and selling them at the fixed price.[89]

Despite the army's efforts to help, refugees remained in deplorable condition, without adequate food, fuel, clothing, or shelter. Illness was widespread, and during the winter of 1864–65, a number of children died from cold and exposure.[90] The military simply did not have the manpower or time to give proper attention to the plight of refugee civilians, white or black.

V

During the war, the municipal government had only limited effectiveness in practical matters. Overwhelmed by problems created and intensified by military occupation, it could not provide fire and police protection or protect the health and morals of its citizens. It had no power to solve the economic problems which beset the city. Unable to be of much help itself, the city government willingly allowed the army to assume a dominant role in community affairs. Protest against military usurpation would have been futile in any case, since members of the city government held their positions by the grace of military power.

However, maintaining at least the illusion of civil authority did have several important benefits. It gave a certain legitimacy—feeble though it may have been—to Johnson's political role and hence was vital for the purpose of propaganda. Furthermore, the civil government's wartime existence made the transition from war to peace remarkably easy. When the war ended, municipal authorities exhibited a tremendous vitality and sense of purpose. It is doubtful that they could have asserted themselves so forcefully had they started from scratch in 1865 after a three-year gap in civil government.

However, the military did not solve Nashville's municipal troubles either. While fighting continued, most of the army's efforts to cope with community problems ended in failure or, at best, only partial success. The simple fact is that while the chaos of war reigned in Middle Tennessee, Nashville's difficulties were insoluble. Only peace could bring an end to the city's distress, because only then would problems magnified by wartime conditions be reduced to a manageable size.

NOTES

1. William E. Birkhimer, *Military Government and Martial Law*, pp. 60, 274. Also see A.H. Carpenter, "Military Government of Southern Territory, 1861–1865," p. 481, and Doris Appel Graber, *The Development of the Law of Belligerent Occupation, 1863–1914*, p. 273.

2. Gerald M. Capers, Jr., *Occupied City*, pp. 60–66; Joseph Howard Parks, "Memphis Under Military Rule, 1862–1865," pp. 32, 56.

3. [John Wooldridge], *History of Nashville, Tenn. . . . ,* pp. 123–24.

4. *Ibid.*, p. 124.

5. Stanley Frazer Rose, "Nashville and Its Leadership Elite, 1861–69," pp. 66–67; Herschel Gower and Jack Allen, eds., *Pen and Sword*, pp. 535–36; *Singleton's Nashville Business Directory for 1865*, pp. 112–13.

6. *Nashville Dispatch*, 11 June 1862.

7. *Ibid.*, 29 April, 8, 9, 23 May.

8. *Ibid.*, 14 June 1862.

9. Maj. W.H. Sidell to Lt. Col. Goddard, 20 February 1863, and Sidell to Capt. Laporte, 28 February 1863, both in RG 393, Entry 867.

10. AAAG Henry Stone to Glascock, 21 February 1863, RG 393, Entry 908.

11. Provost Marshal [Hunter Brooke] to William Shane, 28 February 1865, RG 393, Entry 1655.

12. *Nashville Dispatch,* 24 September 1862.

13. *Nashville Daily Press and Times*, 22 March 1865.

14. *Nashville Daily Union*, 19 February 1865.

15. Francis Everett Hall to his mother, 15 June 1863, Francis Everett Hall Papers, MHC.

16. Frank A. Handy Diary, 18 August, 6 September 1864, William R. Perkins Library, Manuscript Department.

17. *Ibid.*, 25 October 1864, 23 March 1865; *Nashville Daily Union*, 16 March 1865.

18. Handy Diary, 26 November [1864].

19. *Ibid.*, 3, 4 March 1865; *Nashville Daily Union*, 9 March 1865.

20. *Nashville Dispatch*, 11, 13 December 1862.

21. *Nashville Daily Union*, 20 March 1863; *Nashville Dispatch*, 23 December 1863, 15 January 1864; *House Ex. Docs.*, 39th Cong., 1st sess., no. 1, pt. 1, p. 598.

22. *Nashville Dispatch*, 13, 15 August, 14 September 1862.

23. *Ibid.*, 19, 26, 28 November, 11, 12, 21 December 1862, 4 January 1863.

24. Lt. and Assistant Provost Marshal [unsigned] to James Kelly, 22 January 1864; Provost Marshal [Spaulding] to James Kelly, 30 January 1864; Provost Marshal Horner to A.C. Clark, 25 March 1864; Provost Marshal Horner to City Recorder Shane, 15 May 1864; Lt. and Assistant Provost Marshal [unsigned] to Shane, 5 August 1864. All in RG 393, Entry 1655.

25. *Nashville Daily Times and True Union*, 21 November 1864, 7 February 1865; *New York Times*, 12 March 1865. Also see Francis Everett Hall to his mother, 11 April 1864, Francis Everett Hall Papers.

26. RG 393, Entry 1659.

27. *Nashville Daily Press and Times*, 4 September 1863. Also see the letter from "C.L.B.," August 1863, in the *New York Times*, 21 August 1863.

28. *Nashville Dispatch*, 28 January 1864.

29. *Ibid.*, 12 June 1863.

30. *Ibid.*, 27 January 1864.

31. *Nashville Daily Union*, 24, 30 March, 7 May 1864; *Nashville Daily Times and True Union*, 4 May 1864.

32. Provost Marshal Horner to Capt. Nevin, 24 May 1864, RG 393, Entry 1655.

33. Capt. L. Howland to Capt. Hunter Brooke, 6 November 1864, RG 393, Entry 861.

34. Capt. L. Howland to Capt. W.C. Thorpe, 20 March 1865, and Brig. Gen. [Miller] to Brevet Brig. Gen. J.L. Donaldson, 28 March 1865, both in *ibid.*; *Nashville Daily Union*, 7, 17 January, 14 February 1865; *Nashville Daily Times and True Union*, 28 February 1865.

35. *Nashville Daily Union*, 28 January, 22 March 1864.

36. Francis Everett Hall to his sister, 11 April 1864, Francis Everett Hall Papers.

37. *Nashville Daily Union*, 27 November 1863.

38. *Nashville Dispatch*, 27 January 1864; *Nashville Daily Times and True Union*, 22 February 1864.

39. *Nashville Dispatch*, 28, 29 August 1862.

40. *Ibid.*, 1 September 1862.

41. RG 393, Entry 1659.

42. Capt. L. Howland to Provost Marshal Hunter Brooke, 15 October 1864, RG 393, Entry 861. Similar attempts by the army to control liquor in New Orleans also failed; see Capers, *Occupied City*, p. 205.

43. David Kaser, "Nashville's Women of Pleasure in 1860," pp. 379–82.

449 *Republican Banner*, 10 April 161; *Nashville Dispatch*, 11 June 1862.

45. *Nashville Daily Press and Times*, 13 August 1863.

46. Franklin H. Bailey to his mother, 17 November 1863, Franklin H. Bailey Papers, MHC.

47. Memoirs of Benton E. Dubbs, Civil War Collection, TSLA.

48. *Ibid.*

49. Sanitary Report of the Condition of the Prostitutes of Nashville, Tennessee, by W.M. Chambers (Surgeon U.S. Volunteers and Medical Examiner), William P. Palmer Collection, The Western Reserve Historical Society. Prostitution and venereal disease flourished wherever Union armies went; see Gerald M. Capers, Jr., *Occupied City*, pp. 204–5, and *idem, The Biography of a River Town—Memphis*, p. 160.

50. *Nashville Dispatch*, 20 June 1863; Sanitary Report; *Nashville Daily Press and Times*, 10 July 1863.

51. *Nashville Daily Press and Times*, 10, 14, 16 July 1863; *Nashville Dispatch*, 9, 12 July 1863.

52. *Appleton's Annual Cyclopaedia and Register of Important Events*, (1864), p. 770.

53. *Ibid.*; Sanitary Report; *Nashville Daily Union*, 21 August 1863.

54. *Nashville Daily Press and Times*, 4 September 1863.

55. Financial Report of Provost Marshal Hunter Brooke for October 1864 and January 1865, RG 393, Entry 1655.

56. Sanitary Report.

57. Sanitary Report; *Appleton's Annual Cyclopaedia* (1864), p. 770.

58. *Nashville City and Business Directory for 1860–61,* preface. Also see Gower and Allen, eds., *Pen and Sword*, p. 572.

59. Yeatman to his wife, 13 July, 14 November 1860, Yeatman-Polk Collection, TSLA. Also see A.J.D. Thurston to AJ, 11 March 1861, AJP, Presidential Papers Microfilm, and the *Nashville Union and American*, 2 February 1861.

60. *Republican Banner*, 2 October 1861. Also see *ibid.*, 25 April, 4 July 1861.

61. *Ibid.*, 30 November 1861.

62. *Nashville Dispatch*, 22 June, 6 July 1862.

63. *Ibid.*, 10 August 1862. Also see *ibid.*, 31 July 1862.

64. Mark Cockrill to AJ, 21 August 1862, AJP; Rosecrans to Braxton Bragg, 4, 10 December 1862, both in RG 393, Entry 908.

65. John M. Palmer, *Personal Recollections of John M. Palmer,* pp. 137–38.

66. Fanny J. Anderson, ed., "The Shelly Papers," p. 187.

67. John A. Pitts, *Personal and Professional Reminiscences of an Old Lawyer*, pp. 103–4; Rousseau to W.D. Whipple, 30 January 1864, *OR*, 1, 32, 2, p. 269; Henry A. Potter to his mother, 2 December 1862, Henry Albert Potter Letters, MHC.

68. Orders of Rosecrans, 28 July 1863, printed in the *New York Times*, 5 August 1863. Also see Pitts, *Reminiscences,* p. 106; J.P. Garesché to Maj. Gen. A.M. McCook, 24 November 1862, RG 393, Entry 908; Brig. Gen. [Miller] to Maj. Polk, 26 November 1864, RG 393, Entry 861.

69. Sarah Ridley Trimble, ed., "Behind the Lines in Middle Tennessee, 1863–1865," pp. 63, 79.

70. Thomas Sergeant Perry, ed., *Life and Letters of Francis Lieber*, p. 334.

71. [?] to AJ, [?] October 1862, AJP.

72. See, for example, the *Nashville Daily Union*, 30 July 1862.

73. [Miller] to Maj. Beaumont, 13 January 1863 [*sic*: the date was actually 1865], RG 393, Entry 861.

74. *Nashville Daily Union*, 28 November 1862; *Nashville Dispatch*, 5 December 1862. Also see the *Nashville Daily Union*, 24, 25 March 1863; C. Goddard to Gen. R.B. Mitchell, 13 December 1862, RG 393, Entry 908.

75. *Nashville Daily Times and True Union*, 26 February 1864; *Nashville Daily Press*

and Times, 29 September 1864; Rachel Sherman Thorndike, ed., *The Sherman Letters*, pp. 227–28.

76. *Nashville Dispatch*, 14 April, 10 May, 6 September 1862. Also see the *Nashville Daily Union*, 22 April 1862.

77. *Nashville Dispatch*, 10 July, 9 August 1863.

78. *Nashville Daily Press and Times*, 15 August 1863; *Nashville Daily Union*, 13, 18 August 1 63.

79. Birkhimer, *Military Government,* p. 223; Carpenter, "Military Government," p. 479; Ellis Merton Coulter, "Commercial Intercourse with the Confederacy in the Mississippi Valley, 1861–1865," pp. 378, 395.

80. *Nashville Daily Press and Times*, 14 August 1863.

81. *Ibid.*, 6 September 1863. Also see the *Nashville Dispatch*, 3 September 1863.

82. *Nashville Daily Union*, 15 August 1863; *Nashville Daily Press and Times*, 8 September 1863; *Nashville Daily Times and True Union,* 15 September 1864.

83. *Nashville Daily Union*, 27, 30 December 1863.

84. *Ibid.*, 20 February 1864; *Nashville Daily Times and True Union*, 26, 29 February, 2, 4 April 1864.

85. *Nashville Daily Press and Times*, 29 September 1864, 12 April 1865.

86. *Nashville Daily Times and True Union*, 15 March, 11 April 1864; *Nashville Daily Press and Times*, 30 September 1863; Handy Diary, 10, 24 December 1864.

87. *Nashville Daily Times and True Union*, 29 November 1864, 25 January 1865.

88. *Nashville Daily Union*, 10 December 1864.

89. Handy Diary, 10 December 1864.

90. *Nashville Daily Union*, 24 November 1864.

Chapter 8

CONCLUSION AND
SUMMARY

By mid-1863 Nashville had become a garrison town, and as a result, civilian influence was decreasing and the impact of the army was increasing. But the climax of the Union military presence in the city came in the winter of 1864–65, beginning with Hood's forlorn siege which brought the war to the city's doorstep for the last time.

"The citizens of Nashville will long remember Hood," wrote a *New York Times* correspondent in late January 1865. "The sense of the injuries inflicted on them and their city by his recklessness and folly, will have more than a passing poignancy."[1] Hood's thrust into Middle Tennessee sent hundreds of new refugees pouring into the city, compounding the already staggering refugee problem and creating a severe test for military security. Many of the recent arrivals ("a lean, lank, gangling set of men" who looked "as though they would make 'A No. 1' material for Soldiers of Chivalry—alias Guerrillas") put military authorities on edge for fear of sabotage.[2]

More painful to bear than the further overcrowding and the heightened sense of military insecurity was the final desolation of the region. Hood's invasion completed the devastation which began when Confederate forces retreated from Middle Tennessee, and which was furthered by three years of Union occupation. Homes—some of them very fine ones—went up in flames along the rebel lines and between the lines of the two armies; gaping trenches and rifle pits disfigured "many a smiling yard and fruitful garden"; the few remaining fences and shrubs fell before the onslaught; and rebels made serious inroads into whatever livestock and forage had heretofore escaped Union foragers. True enough, reported "C.V.S.," even before "Hood came on his Quixotic errand, the condition of the city was anything but seemly and desirable. It had long ceased to challenge praise from visitors on the ground of its beauty. The marring hoof of war had trodden too deeply for that." And yet it did retain, "in spite of three or four years incessant trampling of iron heels, many bright signs to show what it had been in its palmiest days."[3] Now, however, even this small lingering remnant of beauty and charm had been destroyed, leaving only a "dreary waste."[4]

A visitor to the city could not help but be impressed with war's destructiveness; but other scenes would capture his attention, too. On the streets, the "fast women" riding in the finest hacks, elegantly dressed in the height of fashion, contrasted with a large segment of the female population dressed in mourning, since few of the city's resident families escaped personal loss during the war.[5] And, as rebel deserters flooded into Nashville to take the oath of allegiance, the solid blue of Union troops became increasingly tainted with gray until the streets presented a decidedly mixed complexion.[6] On every corner apple, nut, and fruit dealers hawked their produce, "making more clear money than a Major Gen'l in the Army can make." Small shops and liquor stores also profited from the presence of thousands of soldiers and government employees in the city. Indeed, by February 1865, with the war far removed from Middle Tennessee, trade of all kinds suddenly became so brisk that, as a Union officer put it, one would hardly guess "from the appearance of things, that there was any war within 1000 miles."[7]

If organized war seemed distant, a stop at the provost marshal's office or the undertaker's would demonstrate that violence was still close at hand. The record "of murder, robbery, & theft, as well as many smaller crimes" provided "an instructive but sad Commentary upon the character" of Nashville.[8] So serious was the crime wave in the last winter of the war that General Miller suspected professional thugs had entered government service "in order to cloak their true character." Miller directed the city patrol increased by one-third and pleaded with the provost marshal to devise some plan to bring government employees under control and to quell the rising tide of violence and crime.[9]

But the sheer immensity of the government's presence made the task all but impossible. The permanent Nashville garrison rose to over ten thousand men and officers in December 1864, and then remained at well over eight thousand through May 1865.[10] Furthermore, new regiments constantly moved in and out, staying a few days or weeks before setting out for distant battlefields.[11] And, of course, the city had become the logistical heart for the western theater of the war, necessitating the services of many thousands of civilian government employees.

In the business section, it was not unusual to see eight or ten steamers discharging enormous piles of hay, corn, pork, beans, and hard breads onto the wharves where they would then be loaded onto government wagons and hauled away to government warehouses. Slightly upriver, on the south bank of the Cumberland, several steam sawmills whirred constantly, churning out tens of thousands of board feet of lumber per day for the construction of government warehouses, barracks, stables, and shops.[12] The Commissary Department—"one of the hugest concerns connected with the army"—stockpiled millions of rations; the Ordnance Department provided millions of musket cartridges and hundreds of thousands of rounds of artillery ammunition; the Medical Department maintained approximately twenty hospitals, with the main field hospital covering two hundred acres. The U.S. Military Railroad establishment dwarfed all other departments. During Sherman's Atlanta campaign, for example, it controlled nearly fifteen hundred miles of track, two hundred and seventy-one locomotives, three thousand cars, and employed eighteen thousand men as mechanics, engineers, blacksmiths, conductors, brakesmen, and unskilled laborers.[13] To impose strict order and discipline upon this heterogenous mixture of soldiers and civilians was far beyond military capabilities.

Disciplined or not, this vast war-making complex, situated in the midst of Dixie itself, helped forge the Union victory which was beginning to be obvious to all by early 1865. The last gasping breaths of the "Bogus Confederacy" had come one after the other with dazzling rapidity: the fall of Atlanta, the capture of Savannah, Lincoln's reinauguration, the glorious news that Richmond and Petersburg had succumbed, and finally, Lee's surrender. The news of each of these events was followed by gleeful celebrations among the army personnel, government employees, and the small but steadfast Unionist element in Nashville. One-hundred-gun salutes, pealing church bells, trees adorned with red, white, and blue lanterns, cheering crowds, glowingly patriotic speeches by various dignitaries, meandering parades—all this and more proved that the Confederacy's cause was lost.[14]

The end of the war in Nashville, as in so many other places in the nation, was a strange mixture of joy and sorrow for Union-loving citizens. The exultation and celebration produced by Lee's surrender turned into gloom and dismay at the news of Lincoln's assassination. Saturday, April 15, was set aside as a day of festivities in honor of the final Union victory, but early in the morning, just as a massive parade was beginning, word of the president's death "flew over the city like wildfire." Instantaneously, joy became grief. Bands which had started the morning playing soul-stirring patriotic airs switched to solemn, mournful dirges. With arms reversed and colors trailing, the assembled soldiers marched back to camp. Flags which had been flying proudly over the city suddenly rode at half mast. Swiftly, too, indignation and hatred toward Southern sympathizers gripped the soldiers, and when a few citizens foolishly expressed pleasure at the president's assassination, they were shot down in the streets.[15]

Shooting a few innocent (though stupid) civilians would not bring Lincoln back. John Wilkes Booth had done his deed, and all that remained was to pay the late president proper last respects (which was done with a three- to four-mile-long funeral procession on April 19) and begin winding down the war.[16]

I

For Nashville the war closed on a grim note: fresh devastation all about; a complete breakdown of law and order; wartime hatreds stirred anew by Lincoln's murder. Yet signs of recovery appeared quickly, and the rapid demobilization of the military establishment provided visible evidence to all that the war was in fact over.

The arrival of spring helped hide the scars of war, showing that the desolation was only transitory and that the natural beauty and fertility of Middle Tennessee remained. By early April, fields were being plowed in preparation for putting in the spring crop, fruit trees blossomed, early forest trees sprouted new leaves, and the grass and clover fields soon provided a lush, green blanket for the landscape. In town, too, the renewal of peacetime life soon began. Throughout the summer, old, worthless buildings were removed, new ones sprang up in their places, and a variety of minor repairs and a liberal application of fresh paint erased the wear and tear of four years of strife and neglect.[17]

The North and South Nashville Street Companies were incorporated and began to sell capital stock; the Broad Street Bridge Company began rebuilding the old suspension bridge. By late summer, citizens could look forward to the reopening of the public schools, and the University of Nashville, which had limped through the war, exhibited signs of its prewar vigor. Most importantly, by fall the wholesale trade of Nashville showed daily improvement under the guidance of the newly formed chamber of commerce.[18] Thus, when the *Daily Press* proclaimed "A New Era for Nashville" in its headlines, most people probably nodded their heads in hearty approval.[19]

Alongside this civilian activity, the army was equally busy closing up shop, presenting strong "proofs of the discontinuance of the war."[20] In late April, the secretary of war stopped all enlistments for the volunteer forces and, amidst scandals in the Pay and Quartermaster's Departments in Nashville, the huge volunteer armies in the West began mustering out.[21] By midsummer, all the artillery surrounding the capitol, along with the munitions stored in the basement, had been removed, and practically all restrictions on trade had been lifted.[22] In late June, General Thomas authorized Tennessee citizens who had been sent North for the duration of the war to return home, and all deserters who had been allowed to go home, but had to report monthly to the nearest provost marshal, were relieved of that obligation.[23]

The office of the conductor of the military railroads for the Division of Tennessee went out of existence, as did the office of post surgeon. Officials dissolved practically all general courts martial and military commissions in the District of Middle Tennessee by August, and throughout the summer and fall, the army offered an endless variety of government property for sale to the public.[24] By mid-October, military news had "about dried up and nearly all the offices have closed."[25]

Meanwhile, the military role in municipal government waned. In late June, General Miller told Mayor Smith that "in the reduced state of the Military Establishment, and the restoration, in part at least, of the Civil Authorities," the military could no longer "regulate the Sanitary Conditions of the City. . . ." The people, he said, "must be brought to feel, that in returning to a peace establishment, they must assume responsibilities from which they have temporarily been relieved, & adopt measures for their own protection." A month later, Miller's successor, Brigadier General Charles C. Doolittle, informed Smith of General Thomas' intention "to have this city turned over as soon as possible to civil authorities entirely, the military being used for purely military duty." "The experiment of civil government," continued Doolittle, "must be made in Nashville at some time and it may as well be commenced now as at a future period."[26]

Despite these hopeful signs, several ill omens for the future appeared. As Tennesseans prepared for Congressional elections in early August, Nashville's Unionist press complained that ex-Confederates seemed "to think that the rebellion has made no alteration in the state of affairs" and that the "inflammatory appeals and coarse invectives of the Copperhead journals today read like slightly altered editorials from the same papers of 1860–61."[27] In late July, President Johnson assured Governor Brownlow that he could "call upon Major General Thomas for sufficient military force to sustain the civil authorities of the State," and Thomas informed the Brownlow government that the governor would be "fully sustained in carrying out the policy of the General and State Governments so long as troops remain on duty in the State."[28] During the Congressional elections, Doolittle dispatched small detachments of troops to several Middle Tennessee counties to protect loyal voters.[29]

Thus, although the fighting was over, emotions still ran high, and the army almost immediately assumed a political role in Tennessee which was to continue longer than anyone at the time imagined. During the next decade, the army in Middle Tennessee faced problems far more frustrating than trying to capture Morgan or Forrest, and more difficult than repelling Hood's army. Perhaps few people— military or civilian—realized in 1865, as war eased into peace, that years of bitter struggle lay ahead. But this is another story.

II

The occupation of Nashville clearly demonstrates that Reconstruction began in 1862, not 1865. Within two weeks after the city's capture, Lincoln appointed Andrew Johnson as military governor of Tennessee with the primary task of reestablishing a state government which would command widespread support and be loyal to the federal government. Certainly this was the essence of the whole Reconstruction process. Thus, Johnson's arrival in the capital marked the beginning of Reconstruction in Tennessee.

Lincoln and Johnson misunderstood Southern Unionism because they assumed that the people in the seceded states, especially in the Upper South, were basically loyal and that they had only been momentarily overwhelmed by a well-organized minority of secessionists. They could not believe that many Tennesseans felt any deep-seated love for, or allegiance to, the Confederacy. Once a Unionist rallying point had been established in Tennessee, both men expected Tennesseans to return to their former allegiance and quickly restore the state to the Union.

Therefore, Johnson planned to punish the leaders of the rebellion but to follow a conciliatory and magnanimous policy toward the majority of "deluded and erring" Tennesseans. Once those who had temporarily embraced secession renewed their allegiance, Johnson promised them equality with those who had remained loyal. To his surprise, practically no one hurried to accept forgiveness. Most Tennesseans interpreted leniency as an indication of weakness and continued to adhere to the Confederacy. In less than six months, Johnson concluded that his policy was a failure, and he therefore decided upon a new, sterner approach which demanded an increasingly vigorous prosecution of the war, the abolition of slavery in the state, and the denial of civil and political rights to secessionists. Proscription and punishment of the disloyal and favorable treatment of the unconditionally loyal replaced his previous concept of equal treatment for all. This harsher policy gained few converts, yet it also alienated many conservative Unionists who opposed Lincoln's emancipation plan and continued to believe in a moderate policy toward Confederate sympathizers. The stage was now set for the conflict between ex-Confederates and conservative Unionists on the one hand, and radical Unionists on the other—a conflict which dominated Tennessee's postwar political troubles.

Under the military governor's guidance, a loyal state government was formed in the spring of 1865, but because radical Unionists from East Tennessee were in control, it did not have widespread support in the state. Thus, Johnson did not achieve his goal of creating a loyal *and popular* government, and in this sense wartime Reconstruction in Tennessee must be judged a failure.

Why did Confederate sympathizers remain so opposed to renewing allegiance to the Union, even under Johnson's initially lenient terms? Obviously Southerners believed their cause was just, and a struggle dressed in the silks of truth, justice, and freedom is not lightly abandoned. Furthermore, the Union army was unable to completely destroy Confederate forces in Tennessee and thereby quash secessionists' hopes for deliverance. As long as there was a chance that Confederate armies might sweep back into Nashville, most Southern supporters saw little need to make anything more than temporary adjustments in behavior to appease federal authorities. A series of command disputes with senior military officers, especially Buell and Rosecrans, also frustrated Johnson's efforts. Instead of presenting a united front against secession, the military governor and the commanding generals spent much time and energy struggling with each other for ultimate control in Tennessee. Disputes among Union authorities encouraged disloyalty because they seemed to indicate weakness and indecision in the federal government's determination to crush the Confederacy.

Many secessionists hesitated to desert the Confederacy because of Andrew Johnson himself. In the spring of 1862, Johnson, a prewar Democrat, was popular in staunchly Unionist East Tennessee, but not in Middle and West Tennessee where secessionist sentiment prevailed. During the secession crisis of 1860–61, Democrats in those two divisions of the state came to hate Johnson because of his pro-Union stand. Whigs had never cared for Johnson and now secessionist Whigs had even greater cause to dislike him, while pro-Union Whigs found themselves drawn into an uneasy alliance with an old political adversary. This unpromising political situation handicapped the military governor's efforts from the start. His original conciliatory policy might have succeeded in the hands of a loyal Whig, such as Campbell, but it seems that the absence of a preexisting political base upon which to build doomed any policy Johnson adopted.

Johnson tried to erect a political base in Nashville by deposing the pro-Confederate city government and appointing an entirely new one. Since almost all Nashville's leading citizens supported the South, he had to rely on men of little standing in the community who had little previous governmental experience. Only Mayor Smith was both popular and experienced in municipal affairs.

The first postwar municipal election, held in September 1865, demonstrated that the Nashville community had never considered Johnson's appointees anything but a puppet government. The voters returned only one Johnson appointee to office, but they elected Confederate sympathizers in abundance. For instance, the new mayor was W. Matt Brown, an antebellum Whig who became a postwar Democrat. Brown, who had been the city marshal when Johnson asked city officials to take an oath of allegiance, refused to swear the oath. Although he later claimed he never voted for secession and that he had always been a Union man, it is also true that Brown did not actively support Johnson's efforts. The second leading vote-getter for mayor was F. O. Hurt, an avowed secessionist who had served on the Committee of Vigilance and Safety during the Confederate rule of Nashville. Richard B. Cheatham, Nashville's mayor at the time of its capture who had refused to take the oath of allegiance, was elected to the board of aldermen and became president of the city council. Mayor Smith, who ran for reelection, received only 302 votes out of the more than 2,800 cast.[30]

The failure of Johnson's appointed government to attain popular standing meant that the city's disloyal population had to be kept under constant surveillance by the army, which employed a wide range of population control measures. While these may have momentarily changed the demeanor of many Nashvillians, they did not change any basic beliefs. Punishment and reprisal by the army did not convince citizens that the Southern cause was unjust. On the positive side, however, army surveillance did keep the populace from giving active aid to the rebels and prevented even the hint of rebellion among Nashvillians, thereby contributing to the stability of the military government.

The army no doubt would have preferred to stay out of municipal affairs completely. But when the city government abdicated responsibility for almost all municipal problems because it lacked both resources and community support, the army had no choice but to move in and grapple with problems such as fire and police protection, waste collection and disposal, health and morality, and economic dislocation. Although the army solved none of these problems entirely, it did not allow them to overwhelm the city—or, for that matter, the army. Had the military been less diligent, Nashville would have been a *very* sorry place indeed during the war.

The occupation of Nashville, although significant in an immediate sense because it kept the city secure as an important supply base for Union forces, had only limited impact on long-term change. When Confederate armies finally surrendered, the people of Nashville really felt no differently toward the Union than they had three years earlier. They renewed allegiance to Washington because their cause had been defeated militarily, not because they had been convinced their cause was wrong.

Slavery was the one institution permanently affected by the occupation. Since the Emancipation Proclamation specifically excluded Tennessee, slavery's demise there can be directly attributed to Johnson and the army. When Union soldiers entered Tennessee, slavery simply disintegrated as slaves fled from their masters and sought refuge behind Union lines. Furthermore, by September 1863, Johnson had made abolition a precondition for Reconstruction. Equal in importance to the actual destruction of the institution of slavery was the army's attempt to integrate black people into the mainstream of American life. The military's wartime social programs achieved little actual success because the army devoted its primary energies to winning the war, but the initiation of these programs smoothed the transition from war to peace for both blacks and whites.

The failure of wartime Reconstruction in Nashville was not due to lack of presidential support. No matter what policy Johnson followed, or which generals he quarreled with, he had Lincoln's approval. As Congress sought more control over the Reconstruction process, culminating in the Wade–Davis Bill of July 1864, Lincoln found himself more deeply committed to his military governors in order to maintain authority over Reconstruction. Nothing demonstrates his strong commitment to Johnson more than his willingness to subvert his own plan of Reconstruction of December 8, 1863. The amnesty provisions of Lincoln's proclamation went into only limited operation in Tennessee because Johnson required prospective voters to take a special oath before they could qualify to vote. The governor's oath prevented all Confederate sympathizers, and many conservative Unionists as well, from exercising political rights, and thereby left Reconstruction firmly in the hands of unconditional Unionists.

In the end, Tennessee was restored in the spring of 1865 by the combined use of the liberal ten percent portion of the president's plan and a rigid test of loyalty similar to the one proposed by Congressional supporters of the Wade–Davis Bill. What this means is that authorities often composed wartime Reconstruction policy on the spot; thus policy can best be understood on the operational level—that is, in Nashville rather than Washington. No matter what was said, proclaimed, or enacted in the nation's capital, what actually happened, at least in Nashville and throughout Tennessee, was often the result of policy improvised at the local level.

But the improvisation of policy at the local level during the war should not be surprising. When in the winter of 1860–61 Southern disciples of John C. Calhoun converted the South Carolinian's theories into practice, the Union was in a weak condition to meet the challenge successfully. The North's military might was latent, not actual; a new and untried political party controlled the government; no corpus of Constitutional law existed to guide the Lincoln administration in matters of martial law and military government.

Long before the North could fully mobilize, before Lincoln's leadership had demonstrated its solid fiber, and before actual experience could forge new concepts controlling wartime internal-security matters, Union armies had crashed through the Confederacy's defensive perimeter. Consequently, as federal authorities (especially military commanders and military governors) plunged into the contracting South, they lacked guidance from Washington in regard to a host of problems new to American experience. The two most pressing, and the most novel, of these problems were how to control a hostile civilian population and how to reconstruct a divided Union.

The capture of Nashville provided a stage upon which solutions to these vital problems could be acted out. It was difficult drama, thrusting the actors into previously unexplored areas affecting civilian persons and institutions. During three years of occupation, local authorities, often acting out of necessity rather than choice and interacting periodically with national authorities, hammered out answers to the array of unprecedented questions posed by the necessity for military conquest and national Reconstruction.

To be sure, the solutions were imperfect: a hostile citizenry had been cowed, not converted; black people had been freed, but not yet made equal; although a new, loyal state government existed, it was of questionable legitimacy; and Southern soldiers, defeated in battle by superior numbers and material resources, were only momentarily subdued in spirit. Now in 1865, as the nation returned to a peaceful condition, this wartime experience could not be erased. These imperfect solutions, often imperfectly arrived at amidst the terrible cacophony of war, inevitably formed the foundation for the *continuing* process of Reconstruction during the postwar era.

NOTES

1. Letter from "C.V.S.," 28 January 1865, in the *New York Times,* 8 February 1865.

2. Frank A. Handy Diary, 24 December 1864, William R. Perkins Library, Manuscript Department. Also see L. Howland to Capt. Hunter Brooke and Col. Mason, 30 November 1864, RG 393, Entry 861.

3. Letter from "C.V.S.," 28 January 1865, in the *New York Times,* 8 February 1865. Also see the Handy Diary, 8 December 1864, 12 January, 4 April 1865.

4. Handy Diary, 12 January 1865.

5. *Ibid.,* 6, 19 February 1865.

6. *New York Times,* 12 March 1865; *Nashville Daily Union,* 6 May 1865.

7. Handy Diary, 31 December 1864, 3 February 1865. Also see the entry for 3 December 1864.

8. *Ibid.*, 11 January 1865.

9. L. Howland to Col. Mason, 2 February 1865, and Brig. Gen. [Miller] to Hunter Brooke, 5 March 1865, both in RG 393, Entry 861.

10. RG 94, Returns From U.S. Military Posts, 1800–1916, Post Troops at Nashville, Tennessee, for December 1864 through May 1865.

11. Handy Diary, 28 February, 1 March 1865.

12. *Ibid.*, 22, 27 February 1865.

13. Letter from Benjamin C. Truman, 23 May 1865, in the *New York Times*, 2 June 1865.

14. Handy Diary, 12 September, 28, 31 December 1864, 4 March, 3 April 1865; J.W. Scully to AJ, 6 April 1865, AJP, Presidential Papers Microfilm.

15. Handy Diary, 15 April 1865; Martha Patterson to AJ, 15 April 1865, AJP; [Captain William H. Gay], "Lincoln's Assassination; How Nashville Heard the News," pp. 38–39.

16. Handy Diary, 19 April 1865.

17. *Ibid.*, 1 April 1865; *Nashville Daily Press and Times*, 22 June, 27 September 1865.

18. *Nashville Daily Union*, 6 June, 30 August, 19 September 1865; *Nashville Dispatch*, 19 September 1865; *Nashville Daily Press and Times*, 19 July, 27 September, 4 October 1865.

19. *Nashville Daily Press and Times*, 25 August 1865.

20. Letter from Benjamin C. Truman, 23 May 1865, in the *New York Times*, 2 June 1865.

21. Whipple to Rousseau, 1 May 1865, RG 393, Entry 908; *Nashville Daily Union*, 9, 18 July, 6, 7 September, 10 December 1865; *Nashville Daily Press and Times*, 19, 30 June, 2, 3 July 1865.

22. *Nashville Daily Press and Times*, 2, 29, 31 May, 26 June 1865; *Nashville Daily Times and True Union*, 2 May 1865.

23. *Nashville Daily Union*, 21 June 1865.

24. *Ibid.*, 2 August, 20, 21 September 1865; *Nashville Daily Press and Times*, 21 June, 7, 13 October 1865.

25. *Nashville Dispatch*, 15 October 1865.

26. [Miller] to Smith, 30 June 1865, and Doolittle to Smith, 24 July 1865, both in RG 393, Entry 861.

27. *Nashville Daily Press and Times*, 18 July 1865.

28. *Ibid.*, 22, 28 July 1865.

29. 1st Lt. and AAAG Lewis Bleakney to 188th O.V.I., 31 July 1865; Bleakney to 186th O.V.I., 31 July 1865; Bleakney to Sir, 1 August 1865. All in RG 393, Entry 861.

30. *Nashville Daily Union*, 22, 26 September, 1 October 1865; *Nashville Daily Press and Times*, 6 October 1865; Stanley Frazer Rose, "Nashville and Its Leadership Elite, 1861–69," p. 67; [John Wooldridge], *History of Nashville, Tenn. . . .*, p. 124. In Memphis the deposed mayor, John Park, was reelected in June 1865; see Ernest Walter Hooper, "Memphis, Tennessee," p. 53.

BIBLIOGRAPHY

I. PRIMARY SOURCES

Manuscripts

AJP (Presidential Papers Microfilm)
AMAM,T (Amistad Research Center, Dillard University, New Orleans)
Franklin H. Bailey Papers (MHC)
John Preston Watts Brown Collection (TSLA)
Buell-Brien Papers (TSLA)
Walter T. Carpenter Diary (OHS)
Salmon P. Chase Papers (LC)
Isaac Newton Demmon Papers (MHC)
Benton E. Dubbs Memoirs (Civil War Collection, TSLA)
John W. Fillmore Diary (OHS)
Francis Everett Hall Papers (MHC)
Morris Stuart Hall Papers (MHC)
Frank A. Handy Diary (William R. Perkins Library, Manuscript Department, Dur-
    ham, North Carolina)
Harding Family Papers (Joint University Libraries, Nashville)
Harding-Jackson Papers (TSLA)
Francis Lieber Papers (The Huntington Library, San Marino, California)
Lindsley Family Papers (TSLA)
McGavock-Hayes Papers (TSLA)
David Millspaugh Papers (MHC)
R. Delevan Mussey Papers (Lincoln Miscellaneous Manuscript Collection, The Uni-
    versity of Chicago Library, Chicago)
Thomas A. R. Nelson Papers (McClung Collection, Lawson McGhee Library, Knox-
    ville)
John W. Nicholson Papers (MHC)
William P. Palmer Collection (The Western Reserve Historical Society, Cleveland)

Henry Albert Potter Letters (MHC)
William S. Rosecrans Papers (University Research Library, Los Angeles)
William Henry Smith Papers (OHS)
Edwin M. Stanton Papers (LC)
Thaddeus Stevens Papers (LC)
Vertical File Material #1208 (OHS)
John Weissert Papers (MHC)
Yeatman-Polk Collection (TSLA)

Unpublished Government Records

RG 92, The Records of the Office of the Quartermaster General, NA.
    Journal of the Driver Board.
    Report of the Board of Claims.
    Report of the Nashville Board of Claims.
RG 94, The Records of the Adjutant General's Office, NA.
    Returns From U.S. Military Posts, 1800–1916: Nashville, Tennessee, December 1862–December 1873.
    The Negro in the Military Service of the United States, 1639–1886.
RG 393, The Records of the United States Army Continental Commands, 1821–1920, NA.
For easy reference, in the footnotes I have used the entry numbers contained in the *Preliminary Inventory of the Records of United States Army Continental Commands, 1821–1920* (4 vols. to date. National Archives & Records Service, General Services Administration, Washington).
  Volume I, Geographical Divisions and Departments and Military (Reconstruction) Districts.
    Entry 867. Departments of Cumberland and Ohio (P), 1861–68. General Records. Letters Sent. February 1862–June 1865.
    Entry 901. Departments of Cumberland and Ohio (P), 1861–68. Records of Staff Officers. Letters Sent by the Provost Marshal. September 1863–March 1864 and November 1864–June 1865.
    Entry 908. Department of the Cumberland and Division and Department of Tennessee (P), 1862–70. General Records. Letters Sent. November 1862–June 1865.
    Entry 1141. Department of the Cumberland and Division and Department of Tennessee (P), 1862–70. Organization of U.S. Colored Troops. Letters Sent by the Commissioner. March 1864–February 1865.
    Entry 1142. Department of the Cumberland and Divison and Department of Tennessee (P), 1862–70. Organization of U.S. Colored Troops. Press Copies of Letters Sent by the Commissioner. June 1864–January 1865.
  Volume IV, Military Installations, 1821–81.
    Entry 861. Barracks, Camps, and Posts. Nashville, Tennessee, 1863–77. General Records. Letters Sent. September 1864–January 1877.
    Entry 1655. Provost Marshal Field Organizations of the Civil War. Towns and Posts. Nashville, Tennessee, 1863–66. Letters Sent by the Provost Marshal. January 1864–February 1866.

Entry 1657. Provost Marshal Field Organizations of the Civil War. Towns and Posts. Nashville, Tennessee, 1863–66. Register of Oaths of Allegiance Administered and Bond Provided. June 1863–April 1865.

Entry 1659. Provost Marshal Field Organizations of the Civil War. Towns and Posts. Nashville, Tennessee, 1863–66. Register of Arrests Made by the City Patrol and of Rebel and Citizen Prisoners. 1864–65.

Published Government Documents

Congressional Globe, 36th Cong., 2d sess.; 37th Cong., 1st sess.

House Ex. Docs., 37th Cong., 3d sess., no. 1 (serial 1159). Report of the Secretary of War, 1 December 1862.

House Ex. Docs., 38th Cong., 2d sess., no. 1 (serial 1184). Report of the Secretary of War, 5 December 1863.

House Ex. Docs., 38th Cong., 2d sess., no. 83 (serial 1230). Report of the Secretary of War, 1 March 1865.

House Ex. Docs., 39th Cong., 1st sess., no. 1, pt. 1 (serial 1249) and pt. 2 (serial 1250). Report of the Secretary of War, 22 November 1865.

Sen. Ex. Docs., 38th Cong., 2d sess., no. 28 (serial 1209). Report of the Commissioners of Investigation of Colored Refugees in Kentucky, Tennessee, and Alabama, 28 December 1864.

Newspapers

American Missionary
Nashville Daily Press and Times
Nashville Daily Times and True Union
Nashville Daily Union
Nashville Dispatch
Nashville Union and American
New York Times
Republican Banner (Nashville)

Books and Articles

Alderson, T. William, ed. "The Civil War Diary of Captain James Litton Cooper, September 30, 1861 to January, 1865." *THQ* 15 (June 1956):141–73.

Anderson, Fanny J., ed. "The Shelly Papers." *Indiana Magazine of History* 44 (June 1948):181–98.

Appleton's Annual Cyclopaedia and Register of Important Events. 42 vols. New York: D. Appleton and Company, 1862–1903.

Basler, Roy P., ed. *The Collected Works of Abraham Lincoln.* 9 vols. New Brunswick: Rutgers University Press, 1953.

Battles and Leaders of the Civil War. 4 vols. New York: Thomas Yoseloff, Inc., 1956.

Beale, Howard K., and Brownsword, Alan W., eds. *Diary of Gideon Welles, Secretary of the Navy Under Lincoln and Johnson.* 3 vols. New York: W. W. Norton & Company, Inc., 1960.

Beatty, John. *Memoirs of a Volunteer, 1861–1863*. New York: W. W. Norton & Company, Inc., 1946.

Blaine, James G. *Twenty Years of Congress: From Lincoln to Garfield*. 2 vols. Norwich, Conn.: The Henry Bill Publishing Company, 1884.

Caldwell, Mrs. James E. *A Chapter from the Life of a Little Girl of the Confederacy*. Nashville: The Parthenon Press, [1936?].

Caldwell, Joshua W. *Sketches of the Bench and Bar of Tennessee*. Knoxville: Ogden Brothers & Co., 1898.

Chancellor, Sir Christopher, ed. *An Englishman in the American Civil War: The Diaries of Henry Yates Thompson, 1863*. New York: New York University Press, 1971.

Clayton, W. W. *History of Davidson County, Tennessee, with Illustrations and Biographical Sketches of Its Prominent Men and Pioneers*. Philadelphia: J. W. Lewis Co., 1880.

Dana, Charles A. *Recollections of the Civil War, with the Leaders at Washington and in the Field in the Sixties*. New York: D. Appleton and Company, 1898.

Dennett, Tyler, ed. *Lincoln and the Civil War in the Diaries and Letters of John Hay*. New York: Dodd, Mead & Company, 1939.

"Diary and Correspondence of Salmon P. Chase." *Annual Report of the American Historical Association for the Year 1902*. 2 vols. Washington: Government Printing Office, 1903.

Eaton, John. *Grant, Lincoln and the Freedmen: Reminiscences of the Civil War*. New York: Longmans, Green, and Co., 1907.

Fisher, Lieut.-Col. Horace N. "Reminiscences of the Raising of the Original 'Old Glory' Over the Capitol at Nashville, Tenn., on February 27, 1862." *The Essex Institute Historical Collections* 47 (January 1911):96–100.

Fitch, John. *Annals of the Army of the Cumberland*. Philadelphia: J. B. Lippincott & Co., 1864.

Freeman, Henry V. "A Colored Brigade in the Campaign and Battle of Nashville." *Military Essays and Recollections: Papers Read Before the Commandery of the State of Illinois, Military Order of the Loyal Legion of the United States,* vol. 2. Chicago: A. C. McClurg and Company, 1894.

[Gay, Captain William H.] "Lincoln's Assassination; How Nashville Heard the News." *THM* 5 (April 1919):38–39.

Gower, Herschel, and Allen, Jack, eds. *Pen and Sword: The Life and Journals of Randal W. McGavock*. Nashville: Tennessee Historical Commission, 1959.

Graf, Leroy P., and Haskins, Ralph W., eds. *The Papers of Andrew Johnson*. 4 vols. to date. Knoxville: The University of Tennessee Press, 1967–76.

Grant, Ulysses S. *Personal Memoirs of U.S. Grant*. 2 vols. New York: Charles L. Webster & Company, 1885–86.

Howe, M. A. De Wolfe, ed. *Home Letters of General Sherman*. New York: Charles Scribner's Sons, 1909.

Johnson, Richard W. *Memoir of Maj.-Gen. George H. Thomas*. Philadelphia: J. B. Lippincott & Co., 1881.

Miller, Randall M., ed. "Letters From Nashville, 1862, II: 'Dear Master'." *THQ* 33 (Spring 1974):85–92.

Moore, Frank, ed. *Speeches of Andrew Johnson, President of the United States*. Boston: Little, Brown, and Company, 1865.

Morgan, Mrs. Irby. *How It Was: Four Years Among the Rebels*. Nashville: Publishing House Methodist Episcopal Church, South, 1892.

Morgan, Thomas J. "Reminiscences of Service with Colored Troops in the Army of the Cumberland, 1863–65." *Personal Narratives of Events in the War of the Rebellion, Being Papers Read Before the Rhode Island Soldiers and Sailors Historical Society*, 3d. ser., no. 11. Providence: Rhode Island Soldiers and Sailors Historical Society, 1885.

Mott, Charles R., Jr., ed. "War Journal of a Confederate Officer." *THQ* 5 (September 1946):234–48.

Nashville City and Business Directory for 1860–61. Nashville: L. P. Williams & Co., 1860.

Palmer, John M. *Personal Recollections of John M. Palmer: The Story of an Earnest Life*. Cincinnati: The Robert Clarke Company, 1901.

Perry, Thomas Sergeant, ed. *The Life and Letters of Francis Lieber*. Boston: James R. Osgood and Company, 1882.

Pitts, John A. *Personal and Professional Reminiscences of an Old Lawyer*. Kingsport, Tenn.: Southern Publishers, Incorporated, 1930.

Rawick, George P., ed. *The American Slave: A Composite Biography (Volume 16: Kansas, Kentucky, Maryland, Ohio, Virginia and Tennessee Narratives)*. Westport, Conn.: Greenwood Publishing Company, 1972.

Reed, Seth. *The Story of My Life*. Cincinnati: Jennings and Graham, 1914.

Richardson, James D., ed. *A Compilation of the Messages and Papers of the Presidents, 1789–1897*. 9 vols. Washington: Government Printing Office, 1896–98.

Rusling, James F. *Men and Things I Saw in Civil War Days*. New York: Eaton & Mains, 1899.

Schurz, Carl. *The Reminiscences of Carl Schurz*. 3 vols. n.p.: The McClure Company, 1908.

Sherman, William T. *Memoris of General William T. Sherman By Himself*. 2 vols. Bloomington: Indiana University Press, 1957.

Simon, John Y., ed. *The Papers of Ulysses S. Grant*. 5 vols. to date. Carbondale: Southern Illinois University Press, 1967–73.

Singleton's Nashville Business Directory for 1865. Nashville: R. H. Singleton, 1865.

Temple, Oliver P. *Notable Men of Tennessee From 1833 to 1875, Their Times and Their Contemporaries*. New York: The Cosmopolitan Press, 1912.

Thorndike, Rachel Sherman, ed. *The Sherman Letters: Correspondence Between General and Senator Sherman From 1837 to 1891*. New York: Charles Scribner's Sons, 1894.

Trimble, Sarah Ridley, ed. "Behind the Lines in Middle Tennessee, 1863–1865: The Journal of Bettie Ridley Blackmore." *THQ* 12 (March 1953):48–80.

The War of the Rebellion: A Compilation of the Official Records of the Union and Confederate Armies. 4 ser., 70 vols. in 128 vols. Washington: Government Printing Office, 1880–1901.

White, Robert H., ed. *Messages of the Governors of Tennessee*. 6 vols. Nashville: The Tennessee Historical Commission, 1952–63.

Wills, Ridley, II, ed. "Letters From Nashville, 1862, I: A Portrait of Belle Meade." *THQ* 33 (Spring 1974): 70–84.

[Wooldridge, John]. *History of Nashville, Tenn. . . . .* Nashville: Publishing House of the Methodist Episcopal Church, South, 1890.

II. SECONDARY SOURCES

Books and Articles

Abernethy, Thomas P. *From Frontier to Plantation in Tennessee*. Chapel Hill: University of North Carolina Press, 1932.

Alexander, Thomas B. *Political Reconstruction in Tennessee*. Nashville: Vanderbilt University Press, 1950.

————. *Thomas A. R. Nelson of East Tennessee*. Nashville: Tennessee Historical Commission, 1956.

————. "Neither Peace Nor War: Conditions in Tennessee in 1865." *ETHSP*, no. 21 (1949):33–52.

————. "Whiggery and Reconstruction in Tennessee." *JSH* 16 (August 1950): 291–305.

Ambler, Charles H. *Francis H. Pierpont: Union War Governor of Virginia and Father of West Virginia*. Chapel Hill: University of North Carolina Press, 1937.

————. *Sectionalism in Virginia From 1776 to 1861*. Chicago: University of Chicago Press, 1910.

Andrews, J. Cutler. *The South Reports the Civil War*. Princeton: Princeton University Press, 1970.

Armistead, George H., Jr. "'He is a Great Rascal,' A Sketch of Byrd Douglas." *THQ* 27 (Spring 1968):37–40.

Baumgardner, James L. "Abraham Lincoln, Andrew Johnson, and the Federal Patronage: An Attempt to Save Tennessee for the Union?" *ETHSP*, no. 45 (1973):51–60.

Beale, Howard K. *The Critical Year: A Study of Andrew Johnson and Reconstruction*. New York: Harcourt, Brace and Company, 1930.

Belissary, Constantine G. "Industry and Industrial Philosophy in Tennessee, 1850–1860." *ETHSP*, no. 23 (1951):46–57.

Belz, Herman. *Reconstructing the Union: Theory and Policy During the Civil War*. Ithaca: Cornell University Press, 1969.

————. "The Etheridge Conspiracy of 1863: A Projected Conservative Coup." *JSH* 36 (November 1970):549–68.

Bentley, George R. *A History of the Freedmen's Bureau*. Philadelphia: University of Pennsylvania, 1955.

Birkhimer, William E. *Military Government and Martial Law*. Washington: James J. Chapman, 1892.

Blassingame, John W. "The Union Army as an Educational Institution for Negroes, 1862–1865." *The Journal of Negro Education* 34 (Spring 1965):152–59.

Bowers, Claude G. *The Tragic Era: The Revolution After Lincoln*. Boston: Houghton Mifflin Co., 1929.

Brock, W. R. *An American Crisis: Congress and Reconstruction, 1865–1877*. New York: St. Martin's Press, 1963.

Burt, Jesse C. *Nashville, Its Life and Times*. Nashville: Tennessee Book Company, 1959.

————. "East Tennessee, Lincoln, and Sherman." *ETHSP*, no. 34 (1962):3–25, and no. 35 (1963):54–75.

———. "Sherman's Logistics and Andrew Johnson." *THQ* 15 (September 1956): ₁95–216.

Campbell, Mary Emily Robertson. *The Attitudes of Tennesseans Toward the Union, 1847–1861.* New York: Vantage Press, 1961.

Capers, Gerald M., Jr. *The Biography of a River Town—Memphis: Its Heroic Age.* Chapel Hill: University of North Carolina Press, 1939.

———. *Occupied City: New Orleans Under the Federals, 1862–1865.* n.p.: University of Kentucky Press, 1965.

Carpenter, A. H. "Military Government of Southern Territory, 1861–1865." *Annual Report of the American Historical Association for the Year 1900*, 467–98. Washington: Government Printing Office, 1901.

Christ Church Nashville, 1829–1929. Nashville: Marshall & Bruce Co., 1929.

Clark, Charles B. "Politics in Maryland During the Civil War." *Maryland Historical Magazine* 37 (December 1942): 378–99.

Cleaves, Freeman. *Rock of Chickamauga: The Life of General George H. Thomas.* Norman: University of Oklahoma Press, 1949.

Connelly, Thomas Lawrence. *Army of the Heartland: The Army of Tennessee, 1861–1862.* Baton Rouge: Louisiana State University Press, 1967.

———. *Autumn of Glory: The Army of Tennessee, 1862–1865.* Baton Rouge: Louisiana State University Press, 1971.

Cornish, Dudley Taylor. *The Sable Arm: Negro Troops in the Union Army, 1861–1865.* New York: Longmans, Green, & Co., 1956.

Coulter, Ellis Merton. *William G. Brownlow, Fighting Parson of the Southern Highlands.* Chapel Hill: University of North Carolina Press, 1937.

———. "Commercial Intercourse with the Confederacy in the Mississippi Valley, 1861–1865." *Mississippi Valley Historical Review* 5 (March 1919): 377–96.

Cox, Lawanda, and Cox, John H. *Politics, Principle, and Prejudice, 1865–1866: Dilemma of Reconstruction America.* New York: Atheneum, 1969.

Crabb, Alfred Leland. *Nashville: Personality of a City.* Indianapolis: The Bobbs-Merrill Company, Inc., 1960.

———. "The Twilight of the Nashville Gods." *THQ* 15 (December 1956): 291–305.

Davenport, F. Gavin. *Cultural Life in Nashville, 1825–1860.* Chapel Hill: University of North Carolina Press, 1941.

Davis, George B. "Doctor Francis Lieber's Instructions for the Government of Armies in the Field." *American Journal of International Law* 1 (January-April 1907):13–26.

Dorris, Jonathan Truman. *Pardon and Amnesty Under Lincoln and Johnson: The Restoration of the Confederates to Their Rights and Privileges, 1861–1898.* Chapel Hill: University of North Carolina Press, 1953.

Dunning, William A. *Reconstruction, Political and Economic, 1865–1877.* New York: Harper & Brothers, 1907.

England, J. Merton. "The Free Negro in Ante-Bellum Tennessee." *JSH* 9 (February 1943):37–58.

Fertig, James Walter. *The Secession and Reconstruction of Tennessee.* Chicago: University of Chicago Press, 1898.

Fitzgerald, O. P. *John B. McFerrin: A Biography.* Nashville: Publishing House of the M. E. Church, South, 1889.

Folmsbee, Stanley J.; Corlew, Robert E.; and Mitchell, Enoch L. *History of Tennessee.* 2 vols. New York: Lewis Historical Publishing Company, Inc., 1960.

————. *Tennessee, A Short History.* Knoxville: University of Tennessee Press, 1969.

Folsom, Burton W., II. "The Politics of Elites: Prominence and Party in Davidson County, Tennessee, 1835–1861." *JSH* 39 (August 1973): 359–78.

Frank, Fedora S. *Five Families and Eight Young Men (Nashville and Her Jewry, 1850–1861).* Nashville: Tennessee Book Company, 1962.

Franklin, John Hope. *Reconstruction After the Civil War.* Chicago: University of Chicago Press, 1961.

Freidel, Frank. *Francis Lieber, Nineteenth-Century Liberal.* Baton Rouge: Louisiana State University Press, 1947.

————. "General Orders 100 and Military Government." *The Mississippi Valley Historical Review* 32 (March 1946): 541–56.

Futrell, Robert J. "Federal Military Government in the South, 1861–1865." *Military Affairs* 15 (Fall 1951): 181–91.

Gabriel, Ralph H. "American Experience with Military Government." *American Political Science Review* 37 (June 1943): 417–38.

Gerteis, Louis S. *From Contraband to Freedmen: Federal Policy Toward Southern Blacks, 1861–1865.* Westport, Connecticut, and London: Greenwood Press, Inc., 1973.

Govan, Gilbert E., and Livingood, James W. "Chattanooga Under Military Occupation, 1863–1865." *JSH* 17 (February 1951): 23–47.

Graber, Doris Appel. *The Development of the Law of Belligerent Occupation, 1863–1914.* New York: Columbia University Press, 1949.

Graf, LeRoy P. "Andrew Johnson and the Coming of the War." *THQ* 19 (September 1960): 208–22.

Hall, Clifton R. *Andrew Johnson, Military Governor of Tennessee.* Princeton: Princeton University Press, 1916.

Hamer, Philip M. *Tennessee: A History, 1673–1932.* 4 vols. New York: American Historical Association, Inc., 1933.

Haskins, Ralph W. "Internecine Strife in Tennessee: Andrew Johnson Versus Parson Brownlow." *THQ* 24 (Winter 1965): 321–40.

Henry, J. Milton. "The Revolution in Tennessee, February, 1861, to June, 1861." *THQ* 18 (June 1959): 99–119.

Hesseltine, William B. *Lincoln's Plan of Reconstruction.* Tuscaloosa: The Confederate Publishing Company, Inc., 1960.

Horn, Stanley F. *The Decisive Battle of Nashville.* Knoxville: University of Tennessee Press, 1956.

————. "Nashville During the Civil War." *THQ* 4 (March 1945): 3–23.

————. "Dr. John Rolfe Hudson and the Confederate Underground in Nashville." *THQ* 22 (March 1963): 38–52.

Hume, Leland. *Early History of the Nashville Public Schools.* Nashville: n.p., n.d.

Hyman, Harold Melvin. *Era of the Oath: Northern Loyalty Tests During the Civil War and Reconstruction.* Philadelphia: University of Pennsylvania Press, 1954.

————. "Deceit in Dixie." *Civil War History* 3 (March 1957): 65–82.

————, and Thomas, Benjamin. *Stanton: The Life and Times of Lincoln's Secretary of War.* New York: Alfred A. Knopf, Inc., 1962.

————. *A More Perfect Union: The Impact of the Civil War and Reconstruction on the Constitution.* New York: Alfred A. Knopf, Inc., 1973.

Johnson, Allen; Malone, Dumas; and Starr, Harris E., eds. *Dictionary of American Biography.* 21 vols. and index. New York: Charles Scribner's Sons, 1928–44.

Kaser, David. "Nashville's Women of Pleasure in 1860." *THQ* 23 (December 1964): 379–82.

Klingberg, Frank W. *The Southern Claims Commission*. Berkeley: University of California Press, 1955.

Lamers, William M. *The Edge of Glory: A Biography of General William S. Rosecrans, U.S.A.* New York: Harcourt, Brace & World, Inc., 1961.

Lovett, Bobby L. "The Negro's Civil War in Tennessee, 1861–1865." *The Journal of Negro History* 41 (January 1976): 36–50.

McCarthy, Charles H. *Lincoln's Plan of Reconstruction*. New York: McClure, Phillips & Co., 1901.

McFeely, William S. *Yankee Stepfather: General O. O. Howard and the Freedmen*. New Haven: Yale University Press, 1968.

McKinney, Francis F. *Education in Violence: The Life of George H. Thomas and the History of the Army of the Cumberland*. Detroit: Wayne State University Press, 1961.

McKitrick, Eric L. *Andrew Johnson and Reconstruction*. Chicago: University of Chicago Press, 1960.

———, ed. *Andrew Johnson: A Profile*. New York: Hill and Wang, 1969.

McRaven, Henry. *Nashville, "Athens of the South."* Chapel Hill: Scheer & Jervis, 1949.

Massey, Mary Elizabeth. *Refugee Life in the Confederacy*. Baton Rouge: Louisiana State University Press, 1964.

May, J. Thomas. "Continuity and Change in the Labor Program of the Union Army and the Freedmen's Bureau." *Civil War History* 17 (September 1971): 232–45.

Milton, George Fort. *The Age of Hate: Andrew Johnson and the Radicals*. New York: Coward, McCann, Inc., 1930.

Mitchel, F. A. *Ormsby MacKnight Mitchel, Astronomer and General: A Biographical Narrative*. Cambridge, Mass.: The Riverside Press, 1887.

Mooney, Chase C. *Slavery in Tennessee*. Bloomington: Indiana University Press, 1957.

Moore, John Trotwood, and Foster, Austin P. *Tennessee, The Volunteer State, 1769–1923*. 4 vols. Chicago: S. J. Clarke Publishing Company, 1923.

Murray, Robert K. "General Sherman, The Negro and Slavery: The Story of an Unrecognized Rebel." *Negro History Bulletin* 22 (1959): 125–30.

Neal, John Randolph. *Disunion and Restoration in Tennessee*. Freeport, N.Y.: Books For Libraries Press, 1971 (first published in 1899).

Owsley, Frank L., and Harriet C. "The Economic Structure of Rural Tennessee, 1850–1860." *JSH* 8 (May 1942): 161–82.

Parks, Joseph Howard. *John Bell of Tennessee*. Baton Rouge: Louisiana State University Press, 1950.

———. "Memphis Under Military Rule, 1862 to 1865." *ETHSP*, no. 14 (1942): 31–59.

Partin, Robert Love. *The Secession Movement in Tennessee*. Nashville: George Peabody College for Teachers, 1935.

Patterson, Caleb Perry. *The Negro in Tennessee, 1790–1865*. Austin: University of Texas Bulletin, no. 2205, 1922.

Patton, James Welch. *Unionism and Reconstruction in Tennessee, 1860–1869*. Chapel Hill: University of North Carolina Press, 1934.

Plaisance, Aloysius F., and Schelver, Leo F., III. "Federal Military Hospitals in Nashville, May and June, 1863." *THQ* 29 (Summer 1970): 166–75.

Potter, David M. *Lincoln and His Party in the Secession Crisis*. New Haven: Yale University Press, 1942.

Rable, George C. "Anatomy of a Unionist: Andrew Johnson in the Secession Crisis." *THQ* 32 (Winter 1973): 332–54.

Randall, James G. *Constitutional Problems Under Lincoln*. New York: D. Appleton and Company, 1926.

———. *Lincoln the President*. 4 vols. New York: Dodd, Mead & Company, 1945–55.

———. "Captured and Abandoned Property During the Civil War." *AHR* 19 (October 1913): 65–79.

———, and Donald, David. *The Civil War and Reconstruction*. 2d ed. Boston: D. C. Heath and Company, 1961.

Reddick, L. D. "The Negro Policy of the United States Army, 1775–1945." *Journal of Negro History* 34 (January 1949): 9–29.

Reid, Whitelaw. *Ohio In the War: Her Statesmen, Her Generals, and Soldiers*. 2 vols. New York: Moore, Wilstach & Baldwin, 1868.

Reynolds, Donald E. *Editors Make War: Southern Newspapers in the Secession Crisis*. Nashville: Vanderbilt University Press, 1966.

Roberts, A. Sellew. "The Federal Government and Confederate Cotton." *AHR* 32 (January 1927): 262–75.

Rose, Willie Lee. *Rehearsal for Reconstruction: The Port Royal Experiment*. Indianapolis: The Bobbs-Merrill Company, Inc., 1964.

Russ, William A., Jr. "Administrative Activities of the Union Army During and After the Civil War." *Mississippi Law Journal* 17 (May 1945): 71–89.

Scott, Mingo, Jr. *The Negro in Tennessee Politics and Governmental Affairs, 1865–1965: "The Hundred Years Story."* Nashville: Rich Printing Company, 1964.

Sefton, James E. *The United States Army and Reconstruction, 1865–1877*. Baton Rouge: Louisiana State University Press, 1967.

Smith, Edward Conrad. *The Borderland in the Civil War*. New York: The Macmillan Company, 1927.

Spain, Rufus B. "R.B.C. Howell: Nashville Baptist Leader in the Civil War Period." *THQ* 14 (December 1955): 323–40.

Stampp, Kenneth M. *And the War Came: The North and the Secession Crisis, 1860–61*. Chicago: University of Chicago Press, 1950.

———. *The Era of Reconstruction, 1865–1877*. New York: Alfred A. Knopf, Inc., 1965.

Stearns, Frank Preston. *The Life and Public Services of George Luther Stearns*. Philadelphia: J. B. Lippincott Company, 1907.

Stryker, Lloyd Paul. *Andrew Johnson, A Study in Courage*. New York: The Macmillan Company, 1929.

Swint, Henry Lee. *The Northern Teacher in the South, 1862–1870*. Nashville: Vanderbilt University Press, 1941.

Taylor, Alrutheus Ambush. *The Negro in Tennessee, 1865–1880*. Washington: The Associated Publishers, Inc., 1941.

Tennesseans in the Civil War, a Military History of Confederate and Union Units with Available Rosters of Personnel. Nashville: Civil War Centennial Commission, 1964–65.

Thomas, David Yancey. *A History of Military Government in Newly Acquired Territory of the United States*. New York: The Columbia University Press, 1904.

Thomas, Emory M. *The Confederate State of Richmond: A Biography of the Capital*. Austin: University of Texas Press, 1971.

Thomas, Wilbur. *General George H. Thomas, The Indomitable Warrior.* New York: Exposition Press, 1964.

Walker, Cam. "Corinth: The Story of a Contraband Camp." *Civil War History* 20 (March 1974): 5–22.

Warden, Robert B. *An Account of the Private Life and Public Services of Salmon Portland Chase.* Cincinnati: Wilstach, Baldwin & Co., 1874.

Warner, Ezra J. *Generals in Blue: Lives of the Union Commanders.* Baton Rouge: Louisiana State University Press, 1964.

Wily, Bell Irvin. *The Life of Billy Yank: The Common Soldier of the Union.* Indianapolis: The Bobbs-Merrill Company, 1951.

Williams, George Washington. *A History of the Negro Troops in the War of the Rebellion, 1861–65, Preceded by a Review of the Military Service of Negroes in Ancient and Modern Times.* New York: Bergman Publishers, 1968.

Williams, T. Harry. *Lincoln and His Generals.* New York: Alfred A. Knopf, Inc., 1952.

Wilson, Joseph T. *The Blank Phalanx.* New York: Arno Press and *New York Times,* 1968.

Windrow, J. E. "Collins D. Elliott and the Nashville Female Academy." *THM,* 2d ser., 3 (January 1935): 74–106.

Winston, Robert W. *Andrew Johnson, Plebian and Patriot.* New York: Henry Holt, 1928.

Wright, General Marcus J. *Tennessee in the War, 1861–1865. Lists of Military Organizations and Officers from Tennessee in both the Confederate and Union Armies . . . .* New York: Ambrose Lee Publishing Company, [1908].

Unpublished Theses and Dissertations

Alderson, William T. "The Influence of Military Rule and the Freedmen's Bureau on Reconstruction in Virginia, 1865–1870." Ph.D. dissertation, Vanderbilt University, 1952.

Bahney, Robert Stanley. "Generals and Negroes: Education of Negroes by the Union Army, 1861–1865." Ph.D. dissertation, University of Michigan, 1965.

England, James Merton. "The Free Negro in Ante-Bellum Tennessee." Ph.D. dissertation, Vanderbilt University, 1941.

Hooper, Ernest Walter. "Memphis, Tennessee: Federal Occupation and Reconstruction, 1862–1870." Ph.D. dissertation, University of North Carolina, 1957.

Kelton, Allen. "The University of Nashville, 1850–75." Ph.D. dissertation, George Peabody College for Teachers, 1969.

Macpherson, Joseph Tant, Jr. "Nashville's German Element—1850–1870." Master's thesis, Vanderbilt University, 1957.

Mooney, Chase Curran. "Slavery in Davidson County, Tennessee." Master's thesis, Vanderbilt University, 1939.

Phillips, Paul David. "A History of the Freedmen's Bureau in Tennessee." Ph.D. dissertation, Vanderbilt University, 1964.

Rose, Stanley Frazer. "Nashville and Its Leadership Elite, 1861–69." Master's thesis, University of Virginia, 1965.

Watson, M. S. "Nashville During the Civil War." Master's thesis, Vanderbilt University, 1926.

Wilson, Spencer. "Experiment in Reunion: The Union Army in Civil War Norfolk and Portsmouth, Virginia." Ph.D. dissertation, University of Maryland, 1973.

INDEX